General Editor
ARNOLD GOLDMAN

AMERICAN LITERATURE IN CONTEXT, II 1830–1865

AMERICAN LITERATURE IN CONTEXT, II
1830-1865

BRIAN HARDING

METHUEN
LONDON AND NEW YORK

First published in 1982 by
Methuen & Co. Ltd
11 New Fetter Lane, London EC4P 4EE
Published in the USA by
Methuen & Co.
in association with Methuen, Inc.
733 Third Avenue, New York, NY 10017

Typeset by Scarborough Typesetting Services
Printed in Great Britain by
Richard Clay (The Chaucer Press) Ltd
Bungay, Suffolk

British Library Cataloguing in Publication Data

Harding, Brian
American literature in context.
2: 1830–1865
1. American literature—History and criticism
I. Title
810.9 PS88

ISBN 0 416 73900 8
ISBN 0 416 73910 5 Pbk

Library of Congress Cataloging in Publication Data (Revised)

Main entry under title:
American literature in context.
Bibliography: v. 4, p.
Includes indexes.
Contents: — 2. 1830–1865/Brian Harding
— — 4. 1900–1930/Ann Massa.
1. American literature—History and criticism—
Addresses, essays, lectures. I. Harding, Brian.
II. Massa, Ann.
PS92.A425 810'.9 81–22302
ISBN 0 416 73920 2 (v. 4) AACR2
ISBN 0 416 73930 X (pbk.: v. 4)

Contents

For My Mother

General Editor's Preface

The object of the *American Literature in Context* series is to offer students of the literature and culture of the United States a coherent, consecutive and comprehensive sequence of interpretations of major American texts – fiction and non-fiction, poetry and drama.

Each chapter is prefaced by an extract from the chosen text which serves as a springboard for wider discussion and analysis. The intention of each analysis is to demonstrate how students can move into and then from the pages of literature in front of them to a consideration of the whole text from which the extract is taken, and thence to an understanding of the author's *oeuvre* and of the cultural moment in which he or she lived and wrote. The extract and its interpretation *ground* the wider interpretation: students need not just take the critic's overall view on trust, but can test it against the extract from the primary text.

The selection of texts is intended to represent the critic's choice from the variety, quality and interest of important American writing in the period. In these essays students can see how a literary and cultural critic responds to the page of writing before him or her, and how sustained critical response to particular passages can be linked to broader analyses of texts, authors, culture and society. With this integrated format, students can better see how background material relates to the text and *vice versa*. While the chapters are not precisely intended as models for students to imitate, those who are learning to write about literature are encouraged to treat extracts of their own choosing in a comparable manner, relating the particular response to wider matters.

Arnold Goldman

Introduction

The context of American literature in the quarter-century that preceded the Civil War is nothing less than the whole life of the nation in those years: the political, economic and social condition of the country, the major events that affected that condition, the attitudes and beliefs that had common currency among the population, and the ideas evolved by the uncommon minds which led the intellectual life of the nation. In the present study there has been no attempt to offer a comprehensive survey of so vast a field; rather the intention has been to relate the literature of the period to its context through detailed examination of a limited number of texts and the works of their authors. In addition to the great literary figures who are given prominence in all histories of American literature in the years of its first flowering, this volume includes analyses of the writings of a minister of the Unitarian Church (William Ellery Channing), an intellectual journalist who wrote on social, political, economic, philosophical and theological issues (Orestes Brownson), two historians (George Bancroft and Francis Parkman), and a professional politician (Abraham Lincoln). Sermons, historical studies and political oratory were all considered 'literature' in an age when that word had not yet been narrowed to apply mainly – or solely – to imaginative or creative writing, and the peculiar strengths of American literature were commonly held to lie in public speaking rather than poetry, drama or fiction.

All the writers included in this study have been selected for the intrinsic quality of their work as well as for their representative significance – there has been no attempt to include examples of merely 'popular literature' – but the method used is obviously open to the objection that other major writers have been omitted whose works would have illuminated the culture of the period. Certainly this volume would have been richer if it had been possible to include chapters on important women writers, particularly Margaret Fuller and Harriet

Beecher Stowe, but limitations of space made additional detailed studies impossible. The hope is that the themes emerging from the detailed analyses that have been made, and – even more – from the interrelationships between those analyses, will suggest perspectives that can usefully be extended to writers not given direct attention.

*

In the years covered here, expansion was one of the salient facts of American life. Between 1835 and 1860 the territory of the United States increased by 1,234,566 square miles. In the same period the population increased from fifteen million to just under thirty-one million. The impact of this vast territorial expansion on the life of the nation was magnified by the effects of the transportation revolution that began in the 1820s with the boom in canal building and continued in the following decades with the development of the railways. By 1836 the railways were already a force; by 1840 they were driving out the canal companies; by 1850 there were 9000 miles of track in the United States; by 1860 a further 20,000 miles of track had been laid.[1] As early as the 1830s, Americans were famous for their restless energy and their love of travel. Foreign observers – among them Charles Dickens – frequently commented on the haste of American life, while one French commentator was so impressed by the American passion for the locomotive engine and steamboat that he thought either would be a suitable emblem for the American people.[2] But if Americans travelled for the sake of travel, they also travelled for the sake of new land. Territorial expansion meant the westward movement of the people, and during this period the geographical centre of population shifted from western Virginia to Ohio.

Most of the vast increase in United States territory took place in the presidency of the Democrat James K. Polk, who took office in 1845, though an earlier form of expansion – Indian Removal – had already made a major impact on the nation while Andrew Jackson was in the White House (1829–37). The policies of both presidents can properly be called expansionist. In the case of Jackson, expansion took place at the expense of the Indian; in Polk's case, at the expense of the Mexicans. The movement that was to result in the acquisition of the future states of New Mexico, Arizona, Utah and California, all of which were the fruits of the war with Mexico that Polk initiated in 1846, can properly be said to have begun ten years earlier with Congressional recognition of the newly independent Republic of Texas that had just renounced allegiance to Mexico. Once Texan independence was recognized, its annexation was a distinct prospect; and once Texas was annexed to the United States, a dispute over the border with Mexico was inevitable. Since Texas came into the Union as a slave state (in 1845), both annexation and the war that followed seemed to many Americans to be part of a movement to extend the area of slavery. Thus territorial expansion intensified sectional rivalry within the Union and contributed to the drift to Civil War. Yet the arguments used to defend that expansion commonly had freedom not slavery as their theme. An explanation of that paradox takes us at once from the facts to the ideology of American life in this period.

By 1845 John L. O'Sullivan, the editor of the *Democratic Review*, a periodical to which Orestes Brownson, Nathaniel Hawthorne, Henry David Thoreau and Walt Whitman all contributed articles at various times, was acting as spokesman for a large section of the Democratic Party when he asserted that the American 'right' to Oregon lay in its 'manifest destiny to overspread and possess the whole continent which Providence has given us'. O'Sullivan's justification of expansionism in terms of his nation's divinely appointed mission was made in his *New York Morning News* On 27 December 1845. A few months earlier, he had contributed an editorial to the same paper stating that the national destiny would be fulfilled only when 'the whole boundless continent is ours'. The title of this frank piece was 'More! More! More!' Not all Democrats, and few Whigs, accepted the doctrine of the nation's 'Manifest Destiny' to encroach on the territory of other nations, yet O'Sullivan's arguments and the words in which he formulated them were exactly right for the dominant mood of the times.[3] In its public voice, at least, that mood was not cynically acquisitive but idealistic, as O'Sullivan's own statements make clear. To absorb the whole continent would be – he claimed – to 'give [it] to man' rather than to steal it from any rightful owner. In this, as in his conception of American destiny, he identified the future progress of the human race with the future of his own country. Beside O'Sullivan's assertions we must place the statements of Stephen A. Douglas, the Democratic Congressman from Illinois who would be Lincoln's rival in the debates over slavery-extension in the 1850s. Speaking on the Oregon issue in Congress on 27 January 1845, Douglas expressed the wish to 'blot out the lines on the map which now marked our national boundaries on this continent, and make the area of liberty as broad as the continent itself'.[4] To believers in 'Manifest Destiny', other national boundaries had to give way to the extension of American 'liberty', but it is worth noting that in 1847 Abraham Lincoln, then a new Whig Congressman from Illinois, challenged the legality of 'Polk's War' precisely on the ground that American troops provoked that war by encroaching on Mexican territory.

To understand the identification of freedom and the progress of mankind with the expansion of the United States, we have to know how Americans regarded their own history. To Americans of the middle period (roughly the period between the Revolutionary and Civil Wars) it seemed, as a modern American historian has put it, that political liberty had been established for the first time in human history on 4 July 1776, with the result that the United States had 'somehow appropriated the progress of liberty to itself'.[5] Since it was also considered axiomatic that human progress was dependent on freedom, the future progress of the whole human race became the 'sacred trust' of the American nation. In Puritan times, the New England colonists had considered themselves chosen by Providence to fulfil a special role in history by setting up a theocracy that would be a model for other nations. In the more secularized America of the early nineteenth century, the special mission had become the fostering of the spirit of liberty. When Alexis de Tocqueville wrote, in the first volume of his *Democracy in America* (1835), that Anglo-American civilization had been given its distinctive character by a combination of the '*spirit of religion*' and the '*spirit of liberty*' (his italics), few Americans would have disagreed with him.

Since the yoke of British rule had been cast off in the Revolution, the cause of freedom within the United States could no longer take the form of resistance to monarchy. By the 1830s it had become the staple of American political rhetoric that the cause of liberty was the progress of 'the people' in their struggle against aristocracy and privilege. Such rhetoric was first given currency by Andrew Jackson, who proclaimed himself the champion of the people and, in his presidential messages to Congress and to the nation, interpreted his own struggle for power as a contest between the interests of the 'real people' and the privileged few who exploited them. Associating republican virtue with occupations that demanded physical labour or immediate involvement with the production of goods, Jackson included mechanics, farmworkers and farmers in the category of 'the people' while the large-scale industrial and commercial capitalists and the financiers whose wealth depended upon speculation were classed with the 'privileged'. The struggle that figured in Jackson's political rhetoric was clearly not a *class* struggle (in the Marxian sense), for Jackson's 'real people' included small-scale land and property owners. Further, against the supposedly corrupting influences of financial speculation Jackson set the virtue of slow and steady effort towards individual self-advancement, not class solidarity.[6] In any case, the realities of politics in the Jacksonian period may have had little to do with party rhetoric, for Jackson appointed rich and successful men to positions of eminence, while the development of the party system of politics effectively distanced the common people from political power just when political rhetoric most flattered them.[7] Moreover, as we shall see when we study Orestes Brownson's essay 'The Laboring Classes', the condition of the workers after the financial Panic of 1837 belied any easy optimism about social progress in the Jackson years. Yet when all the necessary reservations and qualifications have been made, it remains true that the Age of Jackson was the Age of the Common Man in the sense that labour was given a new dignity in the public statements of politicians of both parties. The Whigs won the presidential election of 1840 by stealing the fire of the Democrats and presenting their own candidates as men of the people. From the stump this may have been mere demagoguery, but the new respect for the common people filtered into all aspects of public life and may well have misled even acute observers like de Tocqueville into believing that America was a more egalitarian society than it actually was. Even Herman Melville, whose early fictions testify to his acute sense of social discrimination in America, invoked the Spirit of Equality and named Andrew Jackson as one of the 'selectest champions of the kingly commons' chosen by that spirit when, in Chapter 26 of *Moby-Dick*, he wished to justify his choice of a humble whaling captain as his tragic hero.

To such convinced Democrats as George Bancroft, the 'progress of the people' was an article of faith, and that progress was to be advanced by the party he served. To less politically engaged idealists such as William Ellery Channing, the elevation of the people could not be effected by political action but by moral and spiritual influences. Yet Channing too believed that in America the masses were 'rising from the dust' as nowhere else in the world. Though the visible fact of national prosperity was generally taken to be evidence of the progress in which the age believed, faith in that progress was certainly not confined to men who were materialists.

In 1841 Channing gave a lecture entitled 'The Present Age' in which he defined its most prominent characteristic as 'the tendency in all its movements to expansion, to diffusion, to universality'.[8] In past ages, he argued, the spirit of 'exclusiveness, restriction, narrowness, monopoly' had prevailed, but the age in which he lived tended towards 'expansion' because in it an increasing number of subjects were being opened up to intellectual enquiry. He summed up the difference in a sentence containing a metaphor that was central to his lecture and to his whole system of beliefs: 'Thought frees the old bounds to which men used to confine themselves.' Thought is liberating, Channing believed, when it holds nothing too sacred to be investigated, when it is prepared to examine the foundations of the very things that seemed most settled. When they are free to explore all intellectual realms, he said, 'Men forget the limits of their powers.' Metaphors of bounds, of limits and of escape from them recur throughout Channing's lecture and are applied to various aspects of the life of his nation – to government, to social class, to science, to literature, to religion, to education, to commerce and even to public speaking. In political and social terms, the characteristic expansion of the age showed itself, he said, in the spread of power from the privileged few to the masses. In science, the same tendency led to a diffusion of interest through the whole population and to a bursting of the bounds of knowledge about nature and society. In literature, concern with the aristocratic few was replaced by interest in all mankind and in the features common to all men. In religion, the bounds of traditional authority were broken as men realized that the life of the spirit belonged to them rather than to the churches. Education was spreading among the masses as men came to feel that all had a right to it. No less significant, he believed, was the expansion that was taking place in commerce, for free trade – the levelling of all barriers to free exchange – was the duty of the human race. Even the widespread interest in public speaking in the United States was to Channing a valid example of 'expansion', for it testified to a growing popular enthusiasm for intellectual endeavour.

To the modern reader the most striking characteristic of Channing's lecture is likely to be its sheer daring, its bold readiness to generalize over a range of topics each of which nowadays constitutes a distinct intellectual discipline with its own specialized vocabulary and its own methodology. In fact, in its disregard for intellectual boundaries, the lecture illustrates the very freedom of which it talks. The assurance with which Channing moves from comments on religion to moral observations concerning commerce reveals as much about his outlook and world as any of his specific observations do. In its scope the lecture is representative of its time, for wide-ranging addresses under the heading 'The Age' or 'The Spirit of the Times' were much in vogue in the 1830s and 1840s. In content too the lecture expresses widely held assumptions about the age and about the American nation. For corroboration of Channing's metaphors we have only to turn to the first volume of de Tocqueville's *Democracy in America* to find the most astute foreign observer of the American experiment in democracy writing that Americans were removing, or had removed, the barriers that imprisoned society and were causing old opinions that had controlled the world for centuries to disappear. As a result, he said, 'a course almost without limits, a field without horizon, is revealed: the human spirit rushes forward and traverses it in every direction'.

Tocqueville considered the American experiment in democratic freedom of the greatest consequence for the rest of mankind, not only in terms of political institutions but also in terms of the individual man. In the second part of *Democracy in America* (1840), he used the term 'individualism' to describe the salient American characteristic. The term already had some currency before Tocqueville used it, but it was the Frenchman who gave the word a prominence that it has never lost in subsequent discussions of American thought.[9] To Channing too the age was the age of the individual, for all the varieties of expansion listed in his 1841 lecture were, in his view, manifestations of the one great feature of the age – its development of the 'grand idea of humanity, of the importance of man as man'. Channing was a 'liberal Christian' whose humanitarian idealism conditioned his view of American life. The freedom he prized so highly had value to him because it made possible the cultivation of the self – the development of the individual towards perfection. His beliefs have, obviously, most direct relevance to the writers who clearly shared his values and his optimism, and in particular to the men who, however briefly and tenuously, were associated with the movement known as Transcendentalism: Emerson, Thoreau, Bancroft, Brownson and Whitman. Yet the value of Channing's account of the tendency of the age does not depend upon its usefulness in an approach to the literary expression of New England idealism; rather it lies in the fact that *all* the writers to be discussed in this volume were vitally concerned with limits and bounds of the self, and the possibilities of escape from them. Whether, like Whitman, they exulted in the freedom of the imagination to roam over the vastnesses of the American continent or, like Edgar Allan Poe, they vividly evoked in their most powerful fictions a sense of psychological entrapment or imprisonment, the major writers of the period were urgently engaged with the problem of human freedom and the related problem of human development to full potential.

To some extent, of course, a concern with freedom and limitation is common to all literature in all periods and all cultures, for it is an inevitable part of a serious concern with the human condition. More pertinently for this study, it became a dominant concern in the Romantic period in European literature, for the American writers with whom we are concerned were the heirs of the European Romantics. But ideas and attitudes that were part of the Romantic tradition were given a new and distinctive shape and emphasis by the American experience of expansion and the American conception of liberty. In a lecture series 'The Present Age', given in the winter of 1839–40, Ralph Waldo Emerson acknowledged that the 'Feeling of the Infinite' – the 'love of the Vast' – had been born in Germany, imported into France and had in England given a new spirit to the poetry of the age, before it had reached America. He added, however, that the feeling had found a 'most congenial climate' in American taste. He might have said with equal justification that, when American writers of his age used metaphors of expansion and infinitude for the human spirit, those metaphors seemed to relate closely to the facts of the national life.

Significantly, one type of expansion that was *not* mentioned in Channing's lecture was territorial expansion. In an open letter to Henry Clay written in 1837, Channing had warned against precisely the sort of expansion into Texas that was to occur a few years later, and in doing so Channing had also warned against his nation's restless eagerness to spread itself over a wide space. 'Our people', he had written, 'throw themselves beyond the bounds of civilization . . . under the impulse of wild imagination.'[10] His 1841 lecture returned to this theme and gave it an even more profound application to American life in his time when he acknowledged that there was a relationship between its 'wild lawlessness' and the very freedoms he valued. One of the central themes of the writers to be discussed in this volume will be the 'the wild' and the boundaries between unrestricted liberty and wildness.

Rejecting all limits to human expansion in the cultivation of the self, Channing found a 'perilous tendency' in the intellectual freedom that led men to 'question the infinite, the unsearchable, with an audacious self-reliance' when they were freed from their old bounds. Audacious self-reliance had been demonstrated two months before Channing gave his lecture in the essay on that theme that Emerson had published in his *Essays: First Series*. In the imaginative literature of the following decade, the perils of self-reliance were most vividly evoked in the fictions of Herman Melville, not least in *Moby-Dick*, whose Captain Ahab achieved a tragic grandeur in his quest for truth because he defied all limits to his search and, in perceiving the whole world in terms of the self, became the ultimate lonely man voyaging on the oceans of inner space. Ahab is the archetypal Romantic quester whose search is for metaphysical truths, and yet he is at the same time the archetypal American in an age of expansion.

In America during the period that led to the Civil War, the consequences of territorial expansion and the economic development it brought with it were that traditional American values were sacrificed to capitalistic enterprise.[11] The Jacksonian policies of Indian Removal, of westward expansion, and of the exploitation of the resources of the continent fostered the very spirit of speculation and acquisitiveness that the official morality of the age rejected. As a family-orientated economy gave way to a market economy when the produce of the western territories could reach the markets of the east, the 'esprit of a sacred society, a family brotherhood'[12] struggled to survive in a society dominated more and more by the values of the market. We can trace this shift in the changes in the meaning of the term 'enterprise', one of the hallowed words associated by Americans with the great Puritan endeavour or mission in the New World. In this period 'enterprise' lost its associations with society conceived as an organic whole in the fulfilment of its destiny and became transferred to private enterprise, then to business enterprise.[13] Among the freedoms prized by self-reliant Americans in this age was – as we saw with Channing – the freedom of the market. Economic freedom at its least restrained could involve the exploitation of other human beings, as Stephen Douglas's doctrine of 'popular sovereignty' was to show in the debate over the extension of slavery into Kansas and Nebraska in the 1850s. If the question of slavery had been left to the free will of white American immigrants into those territories, as Douglas advocated, this would indeed have been a form of freedom. It took the moral vision of Abraham Lincoln, himself a believer in individual enterprise and self-advancement, to restrain one conception of American freedom by another and greater. Lincoln's faith was the noblest American faith of the age: faith in the right of all men to develop their humanity to the full.

Notes

1 E. Douglas Branch, *The Sentimental Years, 1830–1860*, New York: Appleton, 1934; repr. New York: Hill & Wang, 1965, pp. 10–13.

2 Michel Chevalier, *Society, Manners and Politics in the United States* (1839), quoted in Fred Somkin, *Unquiet Eagle: Memory and Desire in the Idea of American Freedom, 1815–1860*, Ithaca: Cornell University Press, 1967, p. 84.

3 See Frederick Merk, *Manifest Destiny and Mission in American History, A*

Reinterpretation, New York: Knopf, 1963, 1970, p. 24. The quotations from O'Sullivan are taken from Merk.

4 Quoted in Merk, p. 28.

5 See Rush Welter, *The Mind of America 1820–1860*, New York and London: Columbia University Press, 1975, p. 7.

6 On Jackson's conception of 'the people' see Marvin Meyers, *The Jacksonian Persuasion, Politics and Belief*, Stanford University Press, 1957, 1967, pp. 18–24 and Joseph L. Blau, ed., *Social Theories of Jacksonian Democracy: Representative Writings of the Period 1825–1850*, New York: Hafner, 1947, p. xiv.

7 See Edward Pessen, *Jacksonian America, Society, Personality, and Politics*, Homewood, Ill.: Dorsey Press, 1969, p. 56.

8 William Ellery Channing, 'The Present Age', *Works*, Boston: Munroe, 1841–3, VI.149–83. John Higham gives an illuminating commentary on Channing's lecture, endorsing his interpretation of the spirit of the age and adopting Channing's key metaphor, in his monograph *From Boundlessness to Consolidation: The Transformation of American Culture 1848–1860*, Ann Arbor, Mich.: William L. Clements Library, 1969.

9 See Jehoshua Arieli, *Individualism and Nationalism in American Ideology*, Cambridge, Mass.: Harvard University Press, 1964, p. 194.

10 Channing, *Works*, II. 205.

11 Among the most cogent exponents of this thesis are Somkin, op. cit., and Michael Paul Rogin, *Fathers and Children: Andrew Jackson and the Subjugation of the American Indian*, New York: Knopf, 1975.

12 Rogin, p. 251.

13 Welter, p. 156.

Further reading

Russell B. Nye, *Society and Culture in America: 1830–1860*, New York: Harper & Row, 1974.

G. Harrison Orians, 'The Rise of Romanticism, 1805–1855', in Harry Hayden Clark, ed., *Transitions in American Literary History*, Durham, N. Carolina: Duke University Press, 1954, repr. New York: Octagon Books, 1975.

Larzer Ziff, *Literary Democracy: The Declaration of Cultural Independence in America*, New York: Viking Press, 1981.

I

William Ellery Channing (1780–1842)

That man has a kindred nature with God, and may bear most important and ennobling relations to him, seems to me to be established by a striking proof. This proof you will understand, by considering, for a moment, how we obtain our ideas of God. Whence come the conceptions which we include under that august name? Whence do we derive our knowledge of the attributes and perfections which constitute the Supreme Being? I answer, we derive them from our own souls. The divine attributes are first developed in ourselves, and thence transferred to our Creator. The idea of God, sublime and awful as it is, is the idea of our own spiritual nature, purified and enlarged to infinity. In ourselves are the elements of the Divinity. God, then, does not sustain a figurative resemblance to man. It is the resemblance of a parent to a child, the likeness of a kindred nature.

We call God a Mind. He has revealed himself as a Spirit. But what do we know of mind, but through the unfolding of this principle in our own breasts? That unbounded spiritual energy which we call God, is conceived by us only through consciousness, through the knowledge of ourselves. – We ascribe thought or intelligence to the Deity, as one of his most glorious attributes. And what means this language? These terms we have framed to express operations or faculties of our own souls. The Infinite Light would be for ever hidden from us, did not kindred rays dawn and brighten within us. God is another name for human intelligence raised above all error and imperfection, and extended to all possible truth.

The same is true of God's goodness. How do we understand this, but by the principle of love implanted in the human breast? Whence is it, that this divine attribute is so faintly comprehended, but from the feeble development of it in the multitude of men? Who can understand the strength, purity, fulness, and extent of divine philanthropy, but he in whom selfishness has been swallowed up in love? . . .*

* Unless otherwise stated, ellipses indicate omissions from the original text.

. . . I affirm, and trust that I do not speak too strongly, that there are traces of infinity in the human mind; and that, in this very respect, it bears a likeness to God. The very conception of infinity, is the mark of a nature to which no limit can be prescribed. This thought, indeed, comes to us, not so much from abroad, as from our own souls. We ascribe this attribute to God, because we possess capacities and wants, which only an unbounded being can fill, and because we are conscious of a tendency in spiritual faculties to unlimited expansion. We believe in the Divine infinity, through something congenial with it in our own breasts. I hope I speak clearly, and if not, I would ask those to whom I am obscure, to pause before they condemn. To me it seems, that the soul, in all its higher actions, in original thought, in the creations of genius, in the soarings of imagination, in its love of beauty and grandeur, in its aspirations after a pure and unknown joy, and especially in disinterestedness, in the spirit of self-sacrifice, and in enlightened devotion, has a character of infinity. There is often a depth in human love, which may be strictly called unfathomable. There is sometimes a lofty strength in moral principle, which all the power of the outward universe cannot overcome. There seems a might within, which can more than balance all might without. There is, too, a piety, which swells into a transport too vast for utterance, and into an immeasurable joy. I am speaking, indeed, of what is uncommon, but still of realities. We see, however, the tendency of the soul to the infinite, in more familiar and ordinary forms. Take, for example, the delight which we find in the vast scenes of nature, in prospects which spread around us without limits, in the immensity of the heavens and the ocean, and especially in the rush and roar of mighty winds, waves, and torrents, when, amidst our deep awe, a power within seems to respond to the omnipotence around us. The same principle is seen in the delight ministered to us by works of fiction or of imaginative art, in which our own nature is set before us in more than human beauty and power. In truth, the soul is always bursting its limits. It thirsts continually for wider knowledge. It rushes forward to untried happiness. It has deep wants, which nothing limited can appease. Its true element and end is an unbounded good. Thus, God's infinity has its image in the soul; and through the soul, much more than through the universe, we arrive at this conception of the Deity.

'Likeness to God' (1828), Discourse at the Ordination of the Rev. F. A. Farley, Providence, Rhode Island[1]

* * *

All New Engla
would have kno
New England Pri
was 'To glorify
Channing, who fi
spokesmen for the
orthodox (Congreg
the Puritan past ta
humanity. Summari
collected works (184
'Likeness to God' and
awakening our highes
others the image of God
clearly saw, this was th
inspiring message to his a

In the opening sentence
stated that the 'perfection
should aim is that which m
might seem to imply that th
of the image projected on t
stressed the *activity* of the soul,
men 'more and more partakers
human life as 'a growing liken
introduced his central theme –
that implied his key analogy: an
growth. The 'original and essenti
'lie dormant' and to run the risk
but if they remained free from
'unfold'. The organic metaphors we
Channing stated that men's ability
being showed that they had withi
excellence'. Clearly this organicism r
natural and the good are one. It is an i
doctrine that nature is corrupt as a con

From the beginning of his sermon,
that the soul's growth is natural with a c
ship with God must be understood in term
ships. He used a cluster of expressions to su
God: man feels 'sympathy' with God; he
heart and mind are 'congenial' and 'accordan
ments led to the claim that man feels 'friends

towards the divine. The brief reference to sublimity in the first paragraph of the extract is expanded now as man's 'delight . . . in the vast scenes of nature, in prospects which spread around us without limits, in the immensity of the heavens and the ocean, and especially in the rush and roar of mighty winds, waves and torrents' is understood as a response to divine omnipotence and hence further evidence of 'likeness to God'.

Spatial imagery predominates in this paragraph as the soul's 'deep wants' which 'nothing limited can appease' are shown to be the force that causes it to be 'always bursting its limits'. Starting once more from the assumed contrast between human limits and divine limitlessness, Channing's strategy is to associate these antitheses by means of the 'unfathomable' love and 'immeasurable' joy he attributes to men; since the emotions felt can be beyond measure, they link man with the immeasurable attributes of God. The prose makes up for its lack of subtlety through the force of its incantatory repetitions. The word 'infinity' echoes through the paragraph in apposition to the 'divine' while the 'bursting' of man's imagined limits is suggested in kinetic imagery as the 'tendency' of the soul accelerates into its 'rush' forward and escape from bounds. The vocabularies of the organic and the sublime are fused in the account of that 'piety, which swells into a transport too vast for utterance, and into an immeasurable joy'. In the Calvinist system piety so intense that it could lead to an ecstatic sense of God's presence was possible only for the Elect, for they alone could be redeemed from their natural depravity by God's grace. Channing's definition of human nature makes immediate experience of the divine possible for all men and dignifies humanity by locating God in the self.

Throughout the sermon, the movement of the human spirit towards God has been described as growth and the breaking of bounds, yet Channing has also insisted that the vastness of the natural world corresponds to the interior vastness of the soul. In the last paragraph of the extract, the 'might within' is said to more than balance 'all might without'. Thus all Channing's evocations of the sublimity of the natural world are made to contribute to his account of the immensity of 'the Spirit within'.

*

Perhaps the most interesting testimony to the effect that this sermon had on contemporaries is provided by one of the other writers represented in this volume. When Orestes Brownson came across the sermon 'Likeness to God', he had already become disillusioned with the

Presbyterian and Universalist churches and was searching for spiritual guidance. To him Channing's sermon seemed, as he wrote in his *New Views on Christianity, Society and the Church* (1836), 'the most remarkable since the Sermon on the Mount'. Quoting Channing's words on the likeness of God to man as the resemblance of parent to child, Brownson claimed that in preaching the 'atonement' of Creator and creature, and the 'divinity of humanity', the sermon taught that everything in the world is holy and so made possible a reverence for all men. Even after he renounced this religion of humanity and became a Roman Catholic, Brownson remembered the impact that the sermon had made on him in 'its eloquence, its noble sentiments, and its elevated thoughts'. Looking back, in his autobiographical novel *The Convert* (1857), he recalled that 'Likeness to God' made him see something higher and nobler in man than he had previously acknowledged and made him 'almost a worshipper of man'.

To those who, like Brownson, were looking for help in their spiritual quests, 'Likeness to God' was Channing's most inspiring sermon. Many others of his discourses carry the same theme for, as his nephew W. H. Channing noted, the 'joyful consciousness of the Divine indwelling in humanity' made Channing's spirit 'all aglow with the coming of an age of righteousness and love' that would be 'a Heaven on Earth'.[2] In a related though later sermon, 'The Religious Principle in Human Nature', Channing derives all religious experience from 'the desire to *establish relations* with a BEING more PERFECT than itself' and makes this 'unwillingness to shut itself up within its own limits, this tendency to aspire after intercourse with some Divinity' the essential principle of human nature. As in 'Likeness to God', human delight in the sublime – in the grand and awe-inspiring scenes in nature – and in works of art that lead beyond accepted notions of the human is taken as evidence of man's 'affinity' with the infinite. Here too human reason, conscience and affections are said to be different only in degree from the divine attributes. As a consequence, Channing tells us, 'the world within is our great domain, worth infinitely more than the world without'. In all his major affirmations of the divinity of man, Channing draws the implication that concern with the self is not only legitimate but is also a religious devotion.

In 'God Revealed in the Universe and in Humanity', the main argument is stated with force and clarity. Men carry the image of God within themselves in their moral and intellectual powers. Lacking those powers, men could neither understand nor desire God; with them, they can do both. Here, too, the idea of the 'growing likeness' of man to God is made to promise limitless human progress: 'Human nature . . . has merely begun its development . . . That which man has as yet felt and thought and done is a foretoken only of what he is to feel and think and do.' Human nature is a 'sign' or indication of higher possibilities, just as every particle of the natural world is a symbol of God. As in all Channing's major sermons, the message is an uplifting one of the infinite promise of human life. The great possibilities of which he speaks are to be realized in the world, not in the Kingdom of God after death.

*

Channing's sermons on the theme of human perfectability have an emotional intensity clearly intended to make them appeal to their audience at the deepest levels of experience. Valuing moral fervour above intricate intellectual enquiry, Channing makes simplicity a virtue in his public addresses. In this he is typical of the Unitarian preachers, for although they were highly educated, cultivated men, they wanted to reach the hearts of their congregations. According to one of them, Henry Ware, Jr, it was a cause of satisfaction that the 'rational system' of the Unitarians did not profess to go profoundly into philosophical speculations or to 'perplex the understanding', but was content with the 'few simple principles' that God had revealed to all men.[3] Yet, granted a deliberate simplicity, Channing's sermons are still surprisingly untheological in the sense that they make virtually no reference to almost two thousand years of Christian speculation on the nature of man's knowledge of God's perfection. Channing's exposition of his own conception of man, of God, and of the relationship between them, was founded as we shall see on his rejection of the Calvinist doctrine of the depravity of the natural man. Calvinist belief in the imperfection of unredeemed human nature had its antecedents in the theocentric Christianity of St Augustine,[4] as Channing of course knew. Another tradition of Christian theology, dating back to the fifth-century British monk Pelagius, offered an estimate of human nature that was much closer to Channing's, yet when he formulated his own ideas he made no reference to either tradition, nor did he concern himself with the fine verbal discriminations of Aquinas, who argued that though man can be 'like God', God cannot be 'like' his creatures.[5] Channing's thought can be understood as a consistent exposition of the Christian *via affirmativa*,[6] yet he makes no effort to justify it in these terms. Instead he appeals directly from his own immediate spiritual experience to that of his listeners. Not only is his theology intensely personal, it is also primarily concerned with the ethical implications of his conception of God. In his concern with the moral consequences of man's idea of God, Channing was representative of his age. To understand his Christianity we must study him in the context of that age.

*

Born in 1780 into an eminent New England family, Channing entered Harvard College in 1794, received his approbation to preach from the Cambridge Association of Ministers in 1802, and delivered his first sermon in October of that year. He accepted a call to the Federal Street church in Boston in 1803, the year in which Henry Ware, Sr, became Hollis Professor of Divinity at Harvard and the year in which Ralph Waldo Emerson was born. Ware's appointment marked the beginning of the rule of Unitarian ideas at Harvard. Five years later the orthodox Congregationalists set up their own theological college at Andover to preserve the true faith, relinquishing Harvard to the 'liberal Christians'.

Nineteenth-century Harvard Unitarianism can be seen as the culmination of the Christian Enlightenment in America. The trend in liberal religious thought away from theological dogma and towards ethics that had shown itself in eighteenth-century America achieved its fulfilment in the ideas of Ware, Channing and other cultivated leaders of religious opinion in New England. The Unitarians, as their name suggests, believed in God as *one person*: they considered Christ to be a separate and inferior being, though they did not regard Christ as completely human; instead they considered him to be an archangelic being, intermediate between God and man.[7] Implicit in their attitude to Christ was the essential difference between the Unitarians and the orthodox Congregationalists: their contrasting conceptions of human nature.

Channing's repudiation of the Calvinist tradition was made most clearly and emphatically in an article he published in the *Christian Disciple* in 1820: 'The Moral Argument Against Calvinism'. In it he summed up Calvinism as the belief that, as a consequence of Adam's sin, God brings all his posterity into the world with a wholly corrupt nature, totally incapable of spiritual goodness and completely inclined to evil. Since human nature is thus 'fallen', all men are subject to the wrath of God and condemned to eternal damnation, except for those who are predestined to eternal life, 'elected' by God and saved by Christ. In this religion of terror, as Channing called it, the majority of men are denied redemption and fated to everlasting suffering for the honour of God's justice and power. To the Calvinist – said Channing – the conflict between God's behaviour and human conceptions of justice and mercy was no argument against the truth of this doctrine, for the contradiction revealed the weakness of the human mind – the failure of human reason to comprehend the Divine. Since the conflict between human reason and true religion (as revealed in the Scriptures) merely demonstrated the incapacity of man's rational faculties, those faculties had no place in the Calvinist faith, but to Channing they were of utmost importance, for they were the *godlike* part of man.

Channing gave his own account of Unitarian Christianity in a discourse with that title delivered in 1819. At the centre of his faith he puts the '*moral perfection of God*' (W, III. 82), explaining that the 'justice, goodness, holiness' of God, like his 'kindness' and 'benevolence', must be understood 'in the proper sense of these words', by which he means in a sense appropriate to human behaviour. Here, too, the Calvinist idea that a morally perfect God could 'bring us into life wholly depraved', with a natural propensity to evil, and that only those redeemed by God's grace could escape the general damnation, seems to Channing not only irrational but also cruel and horrible. In contrast, he stresses the 'Parental character' of God in his relationship with man, though the 'likeness' implicit in that relationship is not as vividly evoked as in the later sermon. Between this and the 1828 sermon 'Likeness to God' comes another important statement, Channing's 'Unitarian Christianity Most Favorable to Piety' (1826). In this address he argues that Unitarianism encourages men to piety, defined as 'filial love and reverence' and 'imitation of the ever-active and unbounded benevolence of the Creator', by insisting on the 'absolute and unbounded perfection of God's character'. But at the same time Channing claims that piety is encouraged by making God intelligible to human minds, by presenting him as simple and suited to human apprehension even though he is 'inexpressibly sublime'.

Channing's attitude to Christ is entirely consistent with his emphasis on the moral perfection of God. In 'Likeness to God', he had stated that God's mercy was revealed in Christ (W, III. 232). In an address 'The Character of Christ', he saw the essence of Christ's character as his recognition of a spiritual and immortal nature in man. It was, then, Christ's conviction of the greatness of the human soul that gave Christ his own definition. Christ was the model for human perfection, but he did not isolate himself from men, rather he saw them as capable of ascending to his own height (W, IV. 27). In another sermon, 'Love to Christ', Channing affirmed his belief that Christ was indeed the son of God, but he typically defined that sonship in terms of 'likeness'; Christ was God's son in the sense that he partook of the moral perfection of God (W, IV. 193).

To most modern readers, the debate between the liberal Christians and the orthodox Calvinists is hardly a debate at all, for we are likely to find the Calvinist beliefs repugnant. In this we are the heirs of the human-centred religious spirit that Channing and the liberal Christians of his generation helped to diffuse. They could not comprehend the original Calvinist sense of human life as a 'grand cosmic drama'[8] of man's Fall, his consequent damnation, his ransom by Christ, his rebirth and salvation. Yet by the beginning of the nineteenth century, when Unitarianism presented its challenge, Congregational orthodoxy had itself become a travesty of the original faith of the Calvinists. To the Congregational apologists who defended their faith against Channing, human depravity ('Original Sin') had become identified with moral corruption, while intense piety had been replaced by insistence on conformity to moral laws and belief in a theological scheme supposedly revealed in the Bible. This bibliolatry was a far cry from the faith of the seventeenth-century New England Puritans and from that of the great eighteenth-century theologian Jonathan Edwards, whose god-centred religion interpreted the Fall as man's universal failure to love God and his consequent confinement to the inferior principles of self-love and natural appetite. In his insistence that true piety is love of God, Channing was closer to Edwards than were the orthodox Congregationalists, but in his rejection of the distinction between human and divine love, and in his insistence that the one was continuous with the other, Channing was worlds away from Edwards.

Channing's insistence on the filial relationship of man to God both glorified man and led to the belief that the inner life was of immeasurably greater consequence than man's public life in the world of affairs. Essential to this high valuation of the world within was Channing's conviction that man was spiritually free, that his fate was determined by his own acts of choice. In his sermon 'Spiritual Freedom', given two years after 'Likeness to God', he defined what he meant by that liberty. Most obviously, he meant freedom from social conformity. Freed from the power of the material world and the rule of the senses, the mind could turn from 'the visible, the outward and perishable, to the Unseen, Spiritual, and Eternal'. Typically, Channing describes the freedom of the spirit in terms of space when he claims that man can connect his own mind with the Infinite Mind. Further, he contrasts passive or hereditary faith with true spiritual freedom, using the symbol of 'inner light' that has come to be associated primarily with Emersonian Transcendentalism: the free mind 'opens itself to light whencesoever it may come . . . receives new truth as an angel from heaven [and] whilst consulting others, inquires still more of the oracle within itself, and uses instructions from abroad, not to supersede but to quicken and exalt its own energies' (W, IV. 72).

One consequence of Channing's valuation of the inner life was his belief that the cultivation of the self was a religious duty. In 1838 he gave two lectures under the title 'Self-Culture' in which he made another of his bold declarations of faith: 'every man, in every condition is great. . . . A man is great as a man, be he where or what he may' (W, II. 350). So grand is man's essential nature that 'in the soul, the common is the most precious'. Our common humanity is so grand and precious because 'it is the image of God, the image even of his infinity'. Once again the main ideas of the sermon 'Likeness to God' are present in the statement that when we look within we can see 'in ourselves germs and promises of a growth to which no bounds can be set' and so can 'dart beyond what we have actually gained to the idea of Perfection as the end of our being' (p. 355). The organicism of the earlier discourse leads now to the theory of self-culture as a religion, for the very concept of self-culture depends upon an analogy between human and vegetable growth. 'To cultivate anything, be it a plant, an animal, a mind, is to make it grow', Channing tells us (p. 357). Accordingly, 'in a wise self-culture, all the principles of our nature grow at once by joint, harmonious action, just as all parts of the plant are unfolded together'.

Channing's discourses on self-culture were among his most influential statements, for they spoke directly to the spiritual needs of an age that, in America, wanted to see its new and growing prosperity as a means to human progress rather than the triumph of materialism. Endlessly reprinted and read by vast numbers of his fellow-citizens, Channing's theory of self-culture helped develop the spirit of an age in which, at Harvard, the young Henry Thoreau found himself writing on the assigned theme 'Of keeping a private journal or record of our thoughts, feelings, studies and daily experience'. The undergraduate Thoreau wrote his theme in January 1835, too early to profit directly from the 'Self-Culture' lectures, but by that time Channing's influence was so widely diffused that direct debts to him were unimportant.

The 1838 discourses on self-culture given in Boston were Franklin Lectures, made to an audience chiefly of men 'occupied by manual labor'. Channing therefore began by claiming that he belonged to 'the great fraternity of working men' and that he had already expressed his strong interest in the mass of the people (W, II. 350). In America, he argued, the mass of the people had the means of improvement, or self-culture, that were denied to the working people of other countries. In his address 'Spiritual Freedom', delivered at the time of the 1830 election,

Channing had stressed the connection between an elective government, free institutions and the intellectual freedom of the people. In the 'Self-Culture' lectures, he clearly assumes the dependence of the moral and spiritual progress of the nation on its social justice. Since all real human value is inward, since all true greatness is greatness of character, Channing regards 'the distinctions of society' as superficial and ephemeral. All men have the capacity to develop their humanity to a glorious fulfilment, so that it becomes appropriate for a spiritual leader to 'attach' himself 'to the multitude'. When George Bancroft, another writer to be discussed in this volume, paid tribute to Channing after his death in 1842, he stressed the social implications of the great Unitarian's faith in the moral dignity of man. In all Channing's discourses, according to Bancroft, belief in the divine birth of man implied the great truth of man's equality. Though Channing showed reverence for genius, his view of man as made in the image of God led him to see something divine in every man and thus made the great Unitarian – in Bancroft's view – first and foremost a democrat.

In two lectures he prepared for meetings of 'mechanics' (we would say skilled labourers and craftsmen) in 1840, 'The Elevation of the Laboring Portion of the Community', Channing again expressed his conviction that in America, and particularly in Boston, 'the spirit of improvement' had made more impact on those who 'live by the sweat of the brow' than anywhere else in the world (W, v. 155). Not only had prejudices against labour lost their strength, but labouring men were themselves becoming capable of self-culture. However, in these lectures Channing's innate conservatism shows itself in his determination to keep clear of any political or social radicalism. Believing in the moral value of hard work, he insists that the 'elevation' of the labourer he preaches shall not be construed as raising him 'above the need of labor' and freeing him from his daily work. Effort, defined as 'the striving of the will', is itself virtuous and improving, whereas easy, pleasant work makes men morally slack, so the working man must not expect to rise above his social station; his improvement will have to be internal. In fact, the working man will not even need libraries and the leisure to use them, since, with an ironical twist of Channing's ethics-by-intuition, the worker can make do with those 'glorious, quickening, all-comprehending, eternal' thoughts that are available to him without study. Believing in the efficacy of inner, spiritual reform, Channing took little interest in practical steps to improve the condition of the working classes.

In his literary judgements, Channing certainly attached himself to the masses, for in his essay 'The Present Age' he praised Wordsworth as the poet of humanity who was capable of seeing the beauty of the common and he held up Dickens for admiration as the novelist who celebrated the masses in his fictions. One of the means of developing, or cultivating, the self was to experience the liberating effect of contact with great literature, for Channing valued literary art for its power to dignify human nature. A major event in Channing's life was his visit to Europe in 1822, the high point of which was a meeting with Wordsworth. After that trip, Channing's contributions to the *Christian Examiner*, from 1824 the organ of the Unitarians, began to include articles on literature. Major statements are his essay on Milton in 1826 and his 'Remarks on National Literature' in 1830. In the former, Channing endorses Milton's view that poetical genius is the 'most transcendent' of all God's gifts of intellect, adding that poetry is 'the divinest of all arts . . . the breathing or expression of that principle or sentiment, which is deepest and sublimest in human nature' (W, I. 7). This is that very longing or aspiration for something beyond and greater than the 'earthly prison house' that caused man to grow in 'likeness to God'.

To Channing, poetry was valuable because it expressed the highest human aspirations, but his definition of literature in 'Remarks on National Literature' was broad enough to include 'all the writings of superior minds, be the subjects what they may', so that it was nothing less than 'the expression of a nation's mind in writing' (W, I. 243–4). Works on 'the exact sciences' thus became part of the national literature, since Channing shared the confidence of his age that the laws of physics and the laws of ethics were linked by a system of analogies. The key to Channing's definition is the term 'superior minds', for he is interested in art for morality's sake. Calling for a 'higher literature' than any that has previously existed, he expects that literature to develop out of a 'new action or development of the religious principle' (p. 274). The true life of the intellect develops only when man 'regards himself as the recipient and minister of the Infinite Spirit'. Here the view of man's potential expressed in 'Likeness to God' comes together with Channing's faith in America, for he believes that the true distinction of his country is the high value it places on human nature. Countries burdened with traditions and institutions that embodied class values and privileges lacked the American belief in 'the essential equality of all human beings, founded on the possession of a spiritual, progressive, immortal nature'. To Channing the true distinction of the American mind as expressed in literature should be its moral elevation.

'Likeness to God' would seem to make claims for man that could hardly be exceeded by the most extreme proponent of the greatness of human nature. Yet Channing found that some of the men who admired his sermons most took his ideas further than he wanted them to be taken. In fact he began to suspect that the Transcendentalists were guilty of '*ego-theism*', for he believed that they were obliterating the distinctions that his doctrine of human 'likeness' to God preserved. The issue can be seen at its clearest in a confrontation between Channing and Amos Bronson Alcott, Emerson's most idealistic and least orthodox friend. In 1837, as Alcott recorded in his journal, he attempted to prove to Channing 'the *identity* of the Human Soul in its diviner action, with God'. Far from convincing Channing, Alcott horrified him. Emerson was always a subtler and more complex thinker than Alcott and an immeasurably greater writer, but, also by 1837, Emerson's journal records a sense of having outgrown Channing, though as a young man he had considered the great Unitarian's sermons 'sublime' (L, I. 138).

We can focus the major differences between the two thinkers by comparing their attitudes to Christ and to the Bible. To the end of his life, Channing believed that Christ was the perfect image of God and that the historical life of Christ offered men 'the existence, the realization of perfection'.[9] Believing that Christ's life was the greatest miracle, Channing – like other Unitarians – attributed a special status to the Bible as the record of God's revelation of Himself to man. Emerson, in contrast, had come to believe by the late 1830s that every man could become Christ when illuminated by his own 'Inner Light'. Thus to Emerson the whole of life was potentially a miracle; since God revealed Himself to man in the present, the revelation of God recorded in the Bible gave that book no special elevation. In fact, Emerson decided that the Bible (like all sacred scriptures) was no more than the poem of a past age. Whereas Channing regarded poetry as the expression of the 'deepest and sublimest' elements of human nature, thus giving a religious function to the poet, Emerson identified poetry and religion and claimed that the poet was a God. Yet Emerson's conception of the poet's powers developed out of his faith in the infinitude of the individual man – a faith that Channing had announced to the age.

Notes

1 The text of the extract is taken from *The Works of William E. Channing, D.D.*, 6 vols, Boston: Munroe, 1841–3, III. Parenthetic references to W throughout the chapter are also to this edition of Channing's works.

2 W. H. Channing's comment comes in his introduction to *The Perfect Life* (1873), a collection of twelve of W. E. Channing's sermons that had not been included in his *Works* (1841–3). The next two sermons mentioned in my text, 'The Religious Principle' and 'God Revealed', were published in *The Perfect Life* with no dates given, though the foreword states that all twelve sermons were delivered late in Channing's career.

3 Henry Ware, Jr, 'The Faith Once Delivered', *Works*, Boston: Munroe, 1846–7, II. 232–45.

4 See Herschel Baker, *The Dignity of Man*, Cambridge, Mass.: Harvard University Press, 1947, pp. 159–72.

5 For a summary of Christian ideas of perfection see John. A. Passmore, *The Perfectibility of Man*, London: Duckworth, 1970, ch. IV. On Aquinas, see Robert N. Flew, *The Idea of Perfection in Christian Theology*, Oxford University Press, 1934, 1968, ch. XII.

6 Robert Leet Patterson, *The Philosophy of William Ellery Channing*, New York: Bookman Associates, 1952; repr. 1973, p. 88.

7 See William R. Hutchison, *The Transcendentalist Ministers: Church Reform in the New England Renaissance*, New Haven: Yale University Press, 1959, p. 9.

8 See Joseph Haroutunian, *Piety Versus Moralism: The Passing of New England Theology*, New York: Holt, 1932; repr. New York: Harper & Row, 1970, p. 195. My account of orthodox nineteenth-century Congregationalism is taken from Haroutunian.

9 Channing's statement is taken from letters he wrote on the subject of Christ in 1841. They were later published in Elizabeth Palmer Peabody's *Reminiscences of Rev. Wm. Ellery Channing, D.D.*, Boston: Roberts Brothers, 1880, pp. 423–33.

Further reading

David P. Edgell, *William Ellery Channing: An Intellectual Portrait*, Boston: Beacon Press, 1955.

Daniel W. Howe, *The Unitarian Conscience: Harvard Moral Philosophy, 1805–1861*, Cambridge, Mass., Harvard University Press, 1970.

2

Ralph Waldo Emerson (1803-82)

The magnetism which all original action exerts is explained when we inquire the reason of self-trust. Who is the Trustee? What is the aboriginal Self on which a universal reliance may be grounded? What is the nature and power of that science-baffling star, without parallax, without calculable elements, which shoots a ray of beauty even into trivial and impure actions, if the least mark of independence appear? The inquiry leads us to that source, at once the essence of genius, of virtue, and of life, which we call Spontaneity or Instinct. We denote this primary wisdom as Intuition, whilst all later teachings are tuitions. In that deep force, the last fact behind which analysis cannot go, all things find their common origin. For the sense of being which in calm hours rises, we know not how, in the soul, is not diverse from things, from space, from light, from time, from man, but one with them, and proceeds obviously from the same source whence their life and being also proceed. We first share the life by which things exist, and afterwards see them as appearances in nature, and forget that we have shared their cause. Here is the fountain of action and of thought. Here are the lungs of that inspiration which giveth man wisdom, and which cannot be denied without impiety and atheism. We lie in the lap of immense intelligence, which makes us receivers of its truth and organs of its activity. When we discern justice, when we discern truth, we do nothing of ourselves, but allow a passage to its beams. If we ask whence this comes, if we seek to pry into the soul that causes, all philosophy is at fault. Its presence or its absence is all we can affirm. Every man discriminates between the voluntary acts of his mind, and his involuntary perceptions, and knows that to his involuntary perceptions a perfect faith is due. He may err in the expression of them, but he knows that these things are so, like day and night, not to be disputed. My wilful actions and acquisitions are but roving; – the idlest reverie, the faintest native emotion, command my curiosity and respect. Thoughtless people contradict as readily the statement of perceptions as of opinions, or rather much more readily; for, they do not distinguish between perception and notion. They fancy that I choose to see this or that thing. But perception is not whimsical, but fatal. If I see a trait, my children will see it after me, and in course of time, all mankind, – although it may chance that no one has seen it before me. For my perception of it is as much a fact as the sun.

The relations of the soul to the divine spirit are so pure that it is profane to seek to interpose helps. It must be that when God speaketh, he should communicate not one thing, but all things; should fill the world with his voice; should scatter forth light, nature, time, souls, from the centre of the present thought; and new date and new create the whole. Whenever a mind is simple, and receives a divine wisdom, old things pass away, – means, teachers, texts, temples fall; it lives now and absorbs past and future into the present hour. All things are made sacred by relation to it, – one as much as another. All things are dissolved to their centre by their cause, and in the universal miracle petty and particular miracles disappear. If, therefore, a man claims to know and speak of God, and carries you backward to the phraseology of some old mouldered nation in another country, in another world, believe him not. Is the acorn better than the oak which is its fulness and completion? Is the parent better than the child into whom he has cast his ripened being? Whence then this worship of the past? The centuries are conspirators against the sanity and authority of the soul. Time and space are but physiological colors which the eye makes, but the soul is light; where it is, is day; where it was, is night; and history is an impertinence and an injury, if it be anything more than a cheerful apologue or parable of my being and becoming.

Man is timid and apologetic; he is no longer upright; he dares not say 'I think,' 'I am,' but quotes some saint or sage. He is ashamed before the blade of grass or the blowing rose. These roses under my window make no reference to former roses or to better ones; they are for what they are; they exist with God to-day. There is no time to them. There is simply the rose; it is perfect in every moment of its existence. Before a leaf-bud has burst, its whole life acts; in the full-blown flower, there is no more; in the leafless root, there is no less. Its nature is satisfied, and it satisfies nature, in all moments alike. But man postpones or remembers; he does not live in the present, but with reverted eye laments the past, or, heedless of the riches that surround him, stands on tiptoe to foresee the future. He cannot be happy and strong until he too lives with nature in the present, above time.

This should be plain enough. Yet see what strong intellects dare not yet hear God himself, unless he speak the phraseology of I know not what David, or Jeremiah, or Paul. We shall not always set so great a price on a few texts, on a few lives. We are like children who repeat by rote the sentences of grandames and tutors, and, as they grow older, of the men of talents and character they chance to see, – painfully recollecting the exact words they spoke; afterwards, when they come into the point of view which those had who uttered these sayings, they understand them, and are willing to let the words go; for, at any time, they can use words as good, when occasion comes. If we live truly, we shall see truly. It is as easy for the strong man to be strong, as it is for the weak to be weak. When we have new perception, we shall gladly disburden the memory of its hoarded treasures as old rubbish. When a man lives with God, his voice shall be as sweet as the murmur of the brook and the rustle of the corn.

And now at last the highest truth on this subject remains unsaid; probably, cannot be said; for all that we say is the far off remembering of the intuition. That thought, by what I can now nearest approach to say it, is this. When good is near you, when you have life in yourself, it is not by any known or accustomed way; you shall not discern the footprints of any other; you shall not see the face of man; you shall not hear any name; – the way, the thought, the good shall be wholly strange and new. It shall exclude example and experience. You take the way from man, not to man. All persons that ever existed are its forgotten ministers. Fear and hope are alike beneath it. There is somewhat low even in hope. In the hour of vision, there is nothing that can be called gratitude, nor properly joy. The soul raised over passion beholds identity and eternal causation, perceives the self-existence of Truth and Right, and calms itself with knowing that all things go well. Vast spaces of nature, the Atlantic Ocean, the South Sea, – long intervals of time, years, centuries, – are of no account. This which I think and feel underlay every former state of life and circumstances, as it does underlie my present, and what is called life, and what is called death.

Life only avails, not the having lived. Power ceases in the instant of repose; it resides in the moment of transition from a past to a new state, in the shooting of the gulf, in the darting to an aim. This one fact the world hates, that the soul *becomes*; for, that forever degrades the past, turns all riches to poverty, all reputation to a shame, confounds the saint with the rogue, shoves Jesus and Judas equally aside. Why then do we prate of self-reliance? Inasmuch as the soul is present, there will be power not confident but agent. To talk of reliance, is a poor external way of speaking. Speak rather of that which relies, because it works and is. Who has more obedience than I, masters me, though he should not raise his finger. Round him I must revolve by the gravitation of spirits. We fancy it rhetoric when we speak of eminent virtue. We do not yet see that virtue is Height, and that a man or a company of men plastic and permeable to principles, by the law of nature must overpower and ride all cities, nations, kings, rich men, poets, who are not.

From 'Self-Reliance', *Essays: First Series* (1841)[1]

* * *

Though the theme had concerned him for more than a decade and though his thoughts on the subject had found expression in various sermons and lectures in the 1830s, the essay 'Self-Reliance' gave a new force and prominence to Emerson's belief in the importance of the self. There is an unmistakable line of continuity from Channing's addresses 'Likeness to God', 'Spiritual Freedom' and 'Self-Culture' to Emerson's essay, yet when Orestes Brownson reviewed the *Essays* in his *Boston Quarterly Review*, he decided that 'Self-Reliance' contained *the* lesson for America. Like de Tocqueville, Brownson believed that public opinion could easily exercise a tyrannous rule over the young American democracy, so it is not surprising that he responded with enthusiasm to an essay that stated unequivocally 'Whoso would be a man must be a nonconformist.' In fact, 'Self-Reliance' contains an unambiguous call to spiritual as well as social nonconformity, for among its more resonant and stirring statements is the claim: 'Nothing is at last sacred but the integrity of your own mind.' With breath-taking boldness, Emerson redefines the very idea of the sacred to make it appropriate to his nonconformist vision; it sanctions the deepest impulses of the *self* rather than the tenets of any religion. Similarly, the idea of virtue is appropriated to the Emersonian faith in the self, for to behave virtuously is, he claims, to act from the spontaneous self, not to conform to any pre-established moral code. The only law that is sacred is the law of his own nature, so Emerson says, and if warned that his impulses may come from below, he replies that, if he is the Devil's child, he will live from the Devil. These statements can easily mislead if they are taken out of context. They do quite properly serve to represent their author at his most independent, for – as Stephen Whicher has said – they show Emerson 'stirred with the thought of a radical recovery of natural freedom, a vigor of wild virtue released from the inhibitions of a society entrenched in establishments and forms'.[2] Once we turn from the clarion phrases to the complex texture of the essay, however, we can see how intricate Emerson's ideas are. The essay demands the attention to image and to connotation that we normally give to poetry. It has the inspirational fervour of Channing's most powerful sermons combined with a verbal energy and precision that is not to be found anywhere in the great Unitarian's writings.

The paragraphs selected for analysis are taken from the central and climactic section of the essay. Having argued in his opening pages that trust in the self is inhibited by the desire to conform and by the fear of inconsistency, Emerson goes on to explore the meaning of reliance on the self. In offering to explain the 'magnetism' of original action, he indicates to his reader that the discussion will go beyond conscious motives. (Magnetism and electricity are often used in his writings to suggest psychic forces that cannot be explained rationally.) In fact, the explanation Emerson provides is not a systematic analysis of originality but a series of further metaphors. To describe the 'aboriginal Self' as a star without parallax is to use the language of astronomy to say that its distance from the observer cannot be measured, for if the parallax (the apparent displacement of a star caused by the earth's motion in its orbit round the sun) is not known, the distance cannot be calculated. To call the star 'science baffling' is therefore exact, yet it also introduces a crucial play on the meaning of the word 'science', for though the star defeats scientific enquiry, its rays have a transforming effect that is immediately apparent to the moral vision without any dependence on scientific knowledge. Moving from images to abstractions, Emerson next describes the source of life itself, and hence of genius and virtue, as spontaneity or instinct and the 'primary wisdom' associated with that source as intuition or teaching that comes *from within* the self. At this point, the enquiry into the nature of self-trust seems to be leading towards solipsism – the belief that only the self really exists and that reality is merely subjective – for we seem to be entering a realm in which even the immeasurably distant star is located in interior space, while the self, being ab-original, has existed as long as time. Yet when Emerson says that all *things* have their common origin in the deep force or last fact beyond which analysis cannot go, he is patently not attributing a merely subjective reality to those things; rather he is making them coeval with the self and giving things and self equal status. As explanation, instead of analysis he evokes a 'sense of being' in which the self and things (the me and not-me) are one. This sense of oneness with nature is lost with the dawning of self-consciousness when we become aware of the self as distinct from the natural world. The loss is Emerson's version of the Fall of Man: the lapse into alienated self-awareness. Only in the rare 'calm hours' can the sense of shared life be recovered. Only in these hours can the 'fountain' and the 'lungs' that existed before spirit and matter were felt as separate be once more seen 'here'.

When Emerson tells us that 'we lie in the lap of immense intelligence', his earlier talk of self-reliance seems to be superseded by a suggestion of almost infantile dependence on a power beyond the self. Further, the account of moral knowledge in terms of the passive process of 'discernment' rather than active enquiry seems to reduce the self to the status of a mere recipient of light. Yet the word 'beams' relates to the earlier 'rays' from the aboriginal star of the self, so that the self and the immense intelligence are merged. The controlling metaphor of the paragraph, as of the whole essay, is that of light. In the first paragraph of the essay Emerson called on men to trust the light which flashes across the mind from within rather than any light that originates outside the self, even if it comes from poets and wise men. Now he states that a true perception – rather than a mere notion – 'is as much a fact as the sun' and thus links the mind of the perceiver with the source of all light. The self in which man can place his trust is, then, not dependent on the individual will, nor is it merely personal; it relates him to absolute values, or truths.

The opening sentences of the next paragraph use the traditional language of religion in a way that seems to conflict with the claims made for the self earlier in the essay. When God speaks and the soul receives a 'divine wisdom', there can be no doubt that the 'divine spirit' is greater than the soul. Yet, as in his use of the terms 'sacred' and 'virtue', Emerson here appropriates the language of orthodoxy for his nonconformist purpose. He labels as 'profane' what the orthodox – of whatever creed – would regard as piety: the attempt of any religious authority to mediate between the soul and God. When God speaks, 'teachers, texts, temples' are irrelevant, for the experience of the divine is totally distinct from – and independent of – all past revelations and the religions that are based on them. Churches, including the Unitarian Church, placed immense value on past miracles as God's manifestations of himself in the world, but the self-reliant soul knows that its own experience of God is a 'universal miracle' worth more than any former miracles. Also, the moment of revelation is a new creation; it marks a new 'origin' for the self and for all things. The ambiguity of the pronoun 'it' is central to the meaning here; the 'it' that lives 'now' is both the divine wisdom and the mind that has received it. Returning to his controlling metaphor, Emerson states that whereas time and space are created by and dependent on the eye, the soul is light. He develops this idea in the next paragraph but one (para. 4) when he says that to live truly is to see truly. The life he is attempting to define here is a visionary life. Prophets of former ages had their visions and expressed them in words that became the hallowed scriptures of later generations. The self-reliant soul can treat these treasured words as 'old rubbish'; when it has a new perception, when it lives with God, it can find its own voice. Emerson's words combine the most daring effrontery – a contemptuous dismissal of scriptures – with reverence for the source of all religions: the immediate experience of God in the soul. His reverential attitude does not, however, distinguish the soul from God, for, being 'light', the soul is one with God. Further, since the moment of revelation is always a new creation, Emerson rejects any deference to the great men or events of the past. The *present* moment of the soul's 'being and becoming' is as valuable as any moment in human history.

The words 'being and becoming' at the end of the second paragraph provide the transition to the most vivid – and the most difficult – paragraph in the essay. The roses under the speaker's window clearly represent 'being in the present' and thus contrast with the human failure to *be*. We can readily understand Emerson's point when he tells us that obsession with time (regret for the past and anxiety for the future) prevents men from being 'happy and strong . . . in the present', but though we may well respond to the beautifully controlled rhythms of his prose, we are likely to ask what meaning there can be in the statement that the roses 'exist with God' and what possible relevance their existence can have for man's 'being'. The answer lies in the interrelation between the organicism of this paragraph and the apparently clichéd phrases used, at the end of the next paragraph, for the voice of the man who lives with God. That voice – 'as sweet as the murmur of the brook and the rustle of corn' – contrasts with the hoarded words of past generations of prophets. Taken together, the organic allusions suggest that to live 'with God' and to speak with the voice of a man who lives with God is to be and act with the spontaneity of the natural world. That this is not a primitive retreat from the anguish of consciousness is clear from the fact that the human equivalent of the roses' existence 'with God' is the courage to say 'I think' and 'I am' without citing any religious authority.

The contrast between the timeless perfection of the rose and anxious human obsession with time first occurred to Emerson and was recorded in his journal on 7 July 1839, one week after he had entered in the journal his thoughts on the roses' existence in the present and man's need to quote spiritual authorities. In the lecture 'Religion' that he gave on 22 January 1840, Emerson used his second journal entry on the roses, preserving the phrases from the journal but introducing them with the explanatory words: 'Nature through all her kingdoms admonishes us of our fall, of a broken analogy. Our life of consciousness should be obedient and great and equal as is the existence of her vegetable and animal tribes' (EL, III. 283). When he borrowed from his own lecture for his essay, Emerson dropped the explicit reference to 'obedience', leaving its implication in the words on living with nature in the present, and in his analogies between organic and conscious life. The paragraphs in the essay that precede and follow the one on the roses (paras. 2 and 4) were originally one long entry in his journal for 13 November 1838, when his topic had been the problem of a 'Vocabulary' for the soul's immediate experience of the voice of God. Before this journal passage was used in 'Self-Reliance', it went to form part of a lecture entitled 'Duty' given on 6 February 1839. In combining diverse journal entries that had served different lectures, Emerson was using his 'mosaic' method of composition, which is sometimes thought to have led to logical incoherence,[3] although in the present case at least we can see how thoroughly coherent his method is. The seemingly abrupt change in the sixth paragraph, from talk of self-reliance to that of power that is 'agent', has been prepared by the imagery that has made the voice of the self-reliant visionary perfectly *natural*.

In the fifth and sixth paragraphs we can observe the full range of Emerson's art as an essayist. The visionary experience is presented dramatically, as the reader learns to 'take the way from man, not to man'. Next, the experience is explained in abstract terms, as a vision of identity and eternal causation and a perception of truth and right. In the solemn tone and movement of the sentences which follow, with their balanced repetitions – 'Vast spaces . . . long intervals' – the calm sense of being is evoked with an eloquence that anticipates Whitman's verse rhythms in the climactic sections on 'Song of Myself'. But the calm is not allowed to endure, it is not indulged long enough to become complacency, for Emerson's belief in the need to live in the present is a challenge to the very idea of stasis. With a sudden change of mood and verbal pace, Emerson asserts that the 'being' he has so carefully defined is also 'becoming'. He follows his characteristic images of life as movement with an assertion that must have shocked even his liberal Christian readers: since the soul *becomes*, it must reject Jesus as well as Judas, the saint as well as the rogue. The words reveal the distance between Channing's inspirational sermons and Emerson's inspirational essays.

*

Born in 1803 into a family with a long tradition of service in the New England Church, Emerson entered Harvard as an undergraduate in 1817 and went on to the Divinity School in 1825. He was approbated to preach as a Unitarian minister in the following year and was called to the Second Church of Boston in January 1829. While a student at the Divinity School, Emerson had been inspired by Channing's sermons and addresses, believing Channing's mind to be one of those 'God touches with fire' (L, I. 194). Emerson's own sermons, preached at the Second Church and – after he resigned in October 1832 – when he supplied the pulpits of Unitarian ministers elsewhere, show how close he was to Channing in his conception of religion and of the relationship between man and God.

In Emerson's sermon 'Trust Yourself', preached four times between 1830 and 1837, we can see his idea of self-reliance developing out of Channing's conception of human potentiality. True religion, according to Emerson, teaches man self-respect and gives him confidence in what God has done for the soul. The self-trust advocated here is the 'perfect confidence that there is no defect or inferiority in [man's] nature'. The human soul is an 'infinite spiritual estate' whose worth is established by the fact that it 'contains a divine principle' and is 'a house of God'. The language of Emerson's sermon 'The Choice of Theisms', preached when he supplied the Concord pulpit in 1836, is even closer to that of his former mentor in its assertion that trust in the self is compatible with belief in a God who is infinitely greater than that self. The human need for God is indisputable, he says, because 'the profoundest human need is to discover and admire something beyond the self'. Defining man's religious nature in terms of his 'proneness to admiration', Emerson states that the heart is 'impatient of things finite . . . and loves to lose itself in the contemplation of the vast and unbounded'. The lesson he teaches in these and other sermons (for example, Sermon 155) is the 'infinitude' of the soul that was Channing's central doctrine.

Channing's sermon 'Spiritual Freedom' (1830) seemed to Emerson to be a 'noble discourse'. As we have seen, it anticipated some of the beliefs that we now consider characteristically Emersonian. The confidence that man can join his mind to the Infinite Mind by looking within himself and the doctrine that the 'oracle within' should be trusted more than any external authority in spiritual matters were expressed in Channing's sermon years before they became parts of Emerson's early lectures. To Channing, as later to Emerson, spiritual freedom meant independence – freedom from authority – as well as liberation from the bonds of materialism, yet the older man managed to stay within the bounds of Unitarian orthodoxy, whereas his former disciple felt a growing need to be free from all churches. In October 1832, Emerson entered in his journal a poem containing the following lines: 'I will not see with others' eyes / My good is good, my evil ill / I would be free' (JMN, IV. 47). After further lines on finding God in his own heart and hearing God's voice there, the poet goes on to say that he loses respect for the authorities, whether they are 'books, priests, Worlds' when they tell him that his inner voice is false. Another verse fragment written in the previous year, under the heading 'Know Thyself', states that it is no metaphor but a fact that 'God dwells in thee' and that the soul is 'God himself' (JMN, III. 290–1). In these anticipations of the essay 'Self-Reliance' we can watch Emerson moving beyond the language of 'Likeness to God' and expressing his ideas in those terms that to Channing suggested 'ego theism'.

The journal entries on the God within, the sermons on self-trust and the lectures that culminated in the essay 'Self-Reliance' were clearly not the product of a bland, callow self-assurance, for there is indisputable evidence of doubt and of an anguished struggle for faith in Emerson's writings in the early 1830s. The death of his first wife Ellen, after less than two years of marriage, in February 1831, was a terrible blow to him. His notebook contains a verse fragment asking 'Why should I live[?]' and another lamenting the fact that his lost beloved never comes to him (JMN, III. 230, 285). At the end of 1832, having resigned from the ministry, Emerson travelled to Europe, partly in the hope of recovering his spirits. The months in Europe, his encounters with eminent scientists and men of letters, his friendship with Carlyle and his direct experience of European culture marked the beginning of a new stage in Emerson's career and gave him a new confidence in his powers as a poet, but the self-questioning did not cease, nor did the former minister's temperament become any less volatile. A journal entry for 1834 shows him reflecting on the example of a Quaker woman's faith and adding 'My own bosom will supply, as surely as God liveth, the direction of my course' (JMN, IV. 269). Only a few pages earlier he had written: 'Can you believe, Waldo Emerson, that you may relieve yourself of this perpetual perplexity of choosing? and by putting your ear close to the soul, learn always, the true way?' The answer, plainly, was 'Yes, but not always', for we can find the quintessence of Emerson in a journal entry made three years later: 'in certain moments I have known that I existed directly from God, and am, as it were, his organ. And in my ultimate consciousness Am He. Then . . . the contradictory fact is familiar' (JMN, v. 337). The passage continues with a profound self-questioning: 'Cannot I conceive the Universe without a contradiction[?]' A succinct statement in the same journal entry sums up Emerson's predicament and bears witness to his intellectual honesty: 'A believer in Unity, a seer of Unity, I yet behold two'. The verbal play on 'seer' (prophet) and 'beholder' (viewer) sums up the difficulty faced by a relentlessly honest man who wanted to give to his age a message that would inspire faith.

Emerson's journals, the source-books for his public statements, record his inner life in its various phases and moods, not only in its moments of exhilaration when the inner light revealed what he called (in a letter) the 'strict union of the willing soul to God' (L, I. 432). Since he conceived the role of the lecturer and essayist to be essentially moral, it followed that he tended to select the more uplifting and positive reflections for publication. Thus the lecture 'Ethics' given in 1837 contains a triumphant assertion that, when man suffers, 'it is only the finite' that suffers while 'the infinite lies stretched in smiling repose' (EL, II. 145), whereas the journal passage from which this was drawn is a very complex statement of mood, combining trust with a strong sense of the threat of annihilation to the self posed by the 'Lethean stream' of life (JMN, v. 20). The confident phrases were repeated again in 'Spiritual Laws' in the *Essays* (1841) and thus gained a wider audience, but Emerson the seer was no bland optimist, for some of his most anguished private thoughts were included in his major essays. His journal entry on the struggle against the 'encroaching All' that threatens to engulf the individual (JMN, v. 28) became part of an essay entitled 'The Tragic' that was published in the *Dial* magazine in 1844. Another statement in the journal, on 31 May 1840, honestly recording the infirmity of his own faith (JMN, VII. 362), became a part of 'Circles', a major essay in the 1841 volume: 'Alas for this infirm faith, this will not strenuous, this vast ebb of a vast flow! I am God in nature; I am a weed by the wall.' When Emerson asserts his faith, he asserts it in the face of his own doubt.

On his return from Europe in October 1833, Emerson began a career as a lecturer on the recently instituted 'lyceum circuit'. To Emerson it seemed that the public lecture was 'a new literature' that broke with tradition and offered the speaker a new freedom to range over a variety of topics from philosophy and divinity to poetry and criticism in a variety of moods. In the same lecture he claimed, 'we can laugh and cry, curse and pray, tell stories and crack jokes' (L, II, 460), as well as talk of anything from transcendental theories to rubber boots and railways. He began, in fact, by lecturing on science and the conception of natural science that informs his early lectures helps us to understand his view of the relationship between divinity, ethics and poetry. Common to all is the notion of freedom. As early as 1829 he had come to think that a minister of the Church should 'know science' (JMN, III. 159). In the struggle with his own conscience that led to his resignation from the Unitarian ministry, he found natural science, with its study of material laws, an attractive alternative to what he considered the 'little, positive, formal versions of the moral law' that the Church had to offer.

His first scientific lecture, 'The Uses of Natural History', given in November 1833, states that natural science explains man to himself because the world of nature 'corresponds' to and 'represents' the inner world of thoughts and emotions (EL, I. 24). Since this is remote from what we now mean by natural science, to grasp Emerson's meaning we have to see how he arrived at his belief. The theory that a system of 'correspondences' exists between the spiritual and the natural worlds, so that natural facts can be seen as symbols of spiritual facts, had been formulated in the writings of the eighteenth-century Swedish mystic Emanuel Swedenborg. Emerson encountered Swedenborgian ideas as early as 1826,[4] and though he rejected the fixity of the system of correspondences, considering it another example of the unchanging spiritual vocabulary that confined and falsified the life of the soul, he did find the belief in the symbolic significance of the natural world congenial. In his earliest lectures, he stressed the moral implications of the theory. Intensive reading of scientific works in 1832, followed by attendance at lectures on science in Europe the next year, culminated in an experience in the Jardin des Plantes in Paris on 13 July 1833, when Emerson resolved to become a 'naturalist' as a consequence of an intense feeling that there was an 'occult relation' between man and the world of creatures, including even the scorpion and the worm. In his first lecture he drew closely on his journal record of this momentous experience, with its recognition that all forms of natural life expressed something in the mind of man (JMN, IV. 199–200). Since 'the whole of Nature is a metaphor or image of the human Mind', it follows that 'the laws of moral nature answer to those of matter as face to face in a glass' (EL, I. 24). Ethics, then, had become the province of the naturalist rather than the minister. Moral truth could be found in nature – and found in the present – rather than in any sacred scriptures.

In the last of his lectures on science, 'The Humanity of Science' (December 1836), it is the mutability of forms in nature that provides Emerson with his analogy between the natural and the spiritual: 'All things change; moon and stars stand still never a moment, Heaven, earth, sea, air and man are in a perpetual flux.' Though he sets the changeless law that underlies all change against this metamorphic tendency in nature, Emerson finds in change itself an escape from the materialistic valuation of 'mere' nature. When he observes: 'The same ponderable matter which lay yesterday in a clod of earth today takes the form of a grain of wheat' (EL, II. 30), he is using material change as the promise of 'correspondential' change in the inner world of man.

In the introductory lecture on English literature that Emerson gave in 1835, we can see how his interest in natural science relates to his theory of the human imagination in general and the poetic function in particular. In literature, materialism takes the form of tradition or custom, for that 'presents everything as fixed'. In the intellectual world, habit has the effect that belief in the solidity and stability of matter have in the world of science; all such beliefs inhibit the movement of thought and thus restrict freedom and the life dependent on that freedom. The poet, or the thinker, breaks the chains of custom and frees man from his subjection to the tyranny of established authority because his thought is 'volatile'. Thought is liberating because it is both a sacred fire and a river that runs from the invisible world into the mind of man (EL, I. 228–9). In his journal Emerson noted: 'I never take a step in thought when engaged in conversation without some material symbol of my proposition figuring itself incipiently at the same time' (JMN, V. 77). In the lecture this became the more emphatic statement that 'the moment our discourse . . . is inflamed with passion or exalted by thought, it immediately clothes itself in images' (EL, I. 221). In a lecture on Shakespeare given in December 1835, Emerson returned to this central idea and stated that whenever thought is exalted or passionate the mind clothes itself in natural images; the image is contemporaneous with the thought and acts as a 'garment' for it (EL, I. 290).

The doctrine that images arise spontaneously in the mind that thinks deeply and passionately was, of course, congenial to a man who valued intellectual independence. Direct intuition of truths made traditional authority superfluous, while the image's independence of the will of the inspired thinker seemed, to Emerson, evidence of its validity. Further, that independence meant that the process was not merely subjective: the thought and its image possessed an authority greater than that of any tradition, of any man, and even of the mind that acted as its host. Obviously, then, Emerson's theory of the spontaneous appearance of the image provided him with a 'self-reliant' theory of expression that would be central to his idea of the poet's function.

In 1836 Emerson published *Nature*, as a statement of his 'First Philosophy'. It both recapitulated many of the ideas that he had developed in his early lectures and explored the themes that would later contribute to his essay 'Self-Reliance'. The introduction to *Nature* asserts that the 'retrospective' age in which he lives worships the past and thus devalues life in the present. In the first chapter, Emerson evokes his experience of 'perfect exhilaration' in an apparently inconsequential moment when 'crossing a bare common, in snow puddles, at twilight, under a clouded sky'. His sense of being at one with nature and with God makes all 'mean egotism' vanish as he feels 'the currents of the Universal Being' circulate through him. The elevating experience is also expressed in metaphors of vision: 'I become a transparent eyeball. I am nothing. I see all.' The intensely personal manner of the opening chapter gives way to the expository mode in the four brief chapters on the uses of nature to man that follow. Nature serves man by ministering to his material needs ('Commodity'), to the needs of his soul ('Beauty'), to his intellectual, moral and spiritual needs by providing him with a means of expression ('Language'), and to all these by teaching him practical and ethical lessons ('Discipline'). In the 'language' chapter, drawing on the work of a French Swedenborgian he had recently read,[5] Emerson expounded the theory that every natural fact is a symbol of a spiritual fact and that states of mind can only be expressed by presenting the natural appearance which *corresponds* with the spiritual. In this theory of expression lies the key to the entire 'philosophy' of *Nature*, but its crucial significance is not apparent until we come to the final chapter, 'Prospects'. Here an 'Orphic Poet' speaks for Emerson in a manner that is appropriately oracular: 'A man is a God in ruins'; 'Man is the dwarf of himself.' The poet, however, can recapture the innocent vision of childhood and perceive man to be at one with nature, not alienated from it. When living in the spirit, as the poet lives, man can recognize himself in the world of nature and find all nature expressive of his inner being. But man in time, conscious of the self as separate from nature, can only aspire to discover the meaning of the natural world. He may worship the universe, but he can find only distant connections with it. The relationship of man to nature on which nineteenth-century civilization had based itself is characterized here as materialistic, exploitative, utilitarian and pragmatic. Treating nature as dead matter, modern man was guilty of a failure of vision, whether his vision was scientific or religious, for both the scientist and the dogmatic believer were alienated from the natural world. In contrast, the true or innocent vision saw facts as poetry, the ideal *in* the real. In the final paragraph, an analogy between the sun in the material world and the spirit in the ideal world becomes a metaphor that merges the two realms: the spirit becomes the sun, assuming its light-giving function.

*

The publication of *Nature* in 1836 was an important event for the development of the intellectual movement that came to be known as Transcendentalism, because it provided a summary of Emerson's ideas at this stage of his intellectual career. He made a greater immediate impact on the cultural life of New England with two major addresses to particularly select audiences in the following two years, however: one to the Phi Beta Kappa Society at Harvard in 1837, the other to the Harvard Divinity School in 1838. These addresses can be seen as Emerson's challenge to the academic and the theological establishments of his region, though he seemed surprised at the furore he created. The first of these statements, known as 'The American Scholar', was, in fact, a call to young scholars to trust their own intuitions rather than to defer to the wisdom of authorities who spoke to them of and from the past – to look within the self for the truth instead of seeking it from the mouths of instructors or the books in the college library. In his Divinity School address, Emerson applied the same doctrine of self-trust to theological and moral matters, claiming that moral intuitions, which by definition could not be 'mediated' (could not be experienced at second hand) offered direct insights into the laws of the soul. Here, too, the implication was that the individual's 'inner light' should be given more heed than any authority of church or scripture. In fact, the true church should preach the 'infinite soul of man' and should recognize that 'if a man is at heart just, then in so far is he God; the safety of God, the immortality of God, the majesty of God do enter into that man with justice'. Man becomes 'illimitable' when he recognizes that 'Good is positive. Evil is merely privative, not absolute: it is like cold, which is the privation of heat.' To achieve such awareness is not merely ennobling, it 'is divine and *deifying*' (my emphasis). If this statement were not enough to show that Emerson had moved beyond Channing's 'likeness to God' to an assertion of 'oneness with God', the subsequent statement leaves no room for doubt: God 'incarnates himself' not only in Christ but in any man who thinks as Christ thought when, in a 'jubilee of sublime emotion', he knows that God acts and speaks through him. Emerson summarizes Christ's message thus: 'Would you see God, see me; or see thee, when thou also thinkest as I now think.'

To Andrews Norton, Dexter Professor of Sacred Literature at Harvard from 1819 to 1830 and a pillar of the Unitarian establishment, the address was an 'incoherent rhapsody'. He denied the Emersonian claim that man was capable of 'intuition' or 'direct perception' of the truths of Christianity. Man is weak and ignorant, argued Norton, and therefore depends for his knowledge of God on the revelation recorded in the Scriptures and on the 'exercise of reason'. By 'reason' he meant anything but Emerson's idea of inspired reason, for Norton used a Lockean epistemology to defend his notion of the limits of man's knowledge: all knowledge, except that vouchsafed by the miracles of which the Christian Scriptures were the record, was derived from the senses; the Emersonian inner light was, therefore, mere delusion and his self-trust mere infatuated arrogance. This Unitarian denunciation differed little from the orthodox Congregational attack on 'the first fruits of transcendentalism' in America, delivered by three professors at the Princeton Theological Seminary in 1839. They denounced the 'German insanity' of Emerson's 'empty babble about reason as a faculty of immediate insight of the infinite' and his trust in the inspiration of the individual man rather than the authority of scriptures and church.

Emerson did not publicly accept the term 'Transcendentalism' until December 1841, when he gave a lecture entitled 'The Transcendentalist' to a Boston audience. There he defined it as idealism and derived the term 'transcendental' from Kant's reply to Lockean empiricism. Emerson used his approximate knowledge of Kantian theory to counter a materialism that treated the senses as 'final'; he was patently not interested in the refinements of Kantian metaphysics. The Emersonian idealist 'transfers' the objects of the material world 'into the consciousness' by treating those objects as symbols of mental and spiritual facts. Defining Transcendentalism as 'the Saturnalia or excess of Faith', Emerson claims that the Transcendentalist 'believes in miracle, in the perpetual openness of the human mind to new influx of light and power; he believes in inspiration, and in ecstasy'. But the 'miracle' in which this man of faith believes is not one of the miracles recorded in scripture; rather it is the miracle of his own life in the present.

In 1841, the year of 'The Transcendentalist', Emerson's first volume of essays was published. With a presentation copy he sent to Carlyle's friend John Sterling, Emerson deplored the lack of faith in contemporary literature and clearly implied that his book expressed his belief in what he called the 'pristine sacredness of thought'. In 'Self-Reliance', as we have seen, that 'sacredness' was defined in terms of spontaneity and independence of all human authority. Other essays in the series stress different aspects of Emerson's beliefs, so that to read the whole volume is not to be presented with a system of ideas but to observe thought *in process*. Thus in 'Intellect', while insisting that the spontaneous, instinctive principle is superior to the arithmetical or logical, Emerson attributes more importance to the will than he does in 'Self-Reliance'. Defining the 'intellect constructive' as a marriage of thought with nature, he now argues that man must use his will in order to convert nature into rhetoric. In 'The Over-Soul', the passive implications that we noted in the theory of perception in 'Self-Reliance' are much more fully developed. The self becomes a spectator and adopts an 'attitude of reception' as the 'alien energy' of the divine river flows into it (W, II. 268). Describing this process as 'an influx of the Divine mind into our mind', Emerson uses imagery that he has already employed in his early lectures, but in the essay he gives a new emphasis to the passivity of the self when he writes of the 'tide of being which floats us into the secret of nature'. Similarly, in 'Spiritual Laws' he states that we become divine by 'contenting ourselves with obedience' to the soul at the centre of nature; the stream of power and wisdom 'animates all whom it floats' and 'impells to truth with no effort on the part of the individual'.

*

The message of 'Spiritual Laws' is that we should 'lie low in the Lord's power' and thus 'acquiesce'. Noting the new prominence given to the idea of acquiescence in the 1841 *Essays*, Stephen Whicher argues that the pattern of Emerson's early beliefs underwent modification around the year 1840, when he entered a period of unsettled views.[6] Whicher claims that Emerson was forced to revise his conception of the uses of nature at this stage of his development, for the inspiration he had hitherto derived from nature proved illusory; his sense of the unceasing flow of life became a sense of the ephemerality of all life and, at times, of the mere flux of existence. Though 'Circles' – one of the most important essays in the *First Series* – makes it a cause for rejoicing that 'there are no fixtures in nature', and that 'the universe is fluid and volatile', Whicher finds in Emerson's essay a new respect for the power of time and a new sense of the impermanence of his own thoughts. Following Whicher's lead, recent critics have drawn attention to the contradictory elements within 'Circles' and have shown that in it (as, more generally, in many of Emerson's works) an optimistic and elevating conclusion is wrested from statements of doubt and ambiguity that hardly lead in the direction finally taken. Thus the most resoundingly bold statements in 'Circles' – 'I unsettle all things. No facts are to me sacred; none are profane; I simply experiment, an endless seeker with no Past at my back' – come after the admission that 'our moods do not believe in each other' and the lament for his own weak faith when he feels himself not a God but a 'weed by the wall'. The 'fixture and stability in the soul' that is offered in the essay as a counterweight to the vividly evoked process of endless 'becoming' thus comes to seem something desired rather than attained. Whicher dates Emerson's intense consciousness of the unceasing flow of time from the 1840s, yet the journal passages discussed above illustrate the difficulty of imposing a temporal order on his ideas or his attitudes. When we seek to discover the biography of the inner man, we must stress the shifts of emphasis that give a shape to Emerson's career as a thinker, but since Emerson remained a believer in the inspiration that came extempore, reaffirmations of his early faith in human freedom occur even in a period of his life when, as scholars agree, he became increasingly aware of the limitations imposed on thought – on the freedom of the intellect – by experience.

'Experience', the title of the second essay in *Essays: Second Series*, published in 1844, is the key term in the shift of emphasis. In that essay the personal sadness occasioned by the death of his son Waldo, two years earlier, is most painfully present. Life is described as 'a flitting state, a tent for a night', and souls are said to be separated from the objects they seek by 'an innavigable sea' that 'washes with silent waters between us and the things we aim at and converse with'. The admission that 'it is very unhappy, but too late to be helped, the discovery we have made that we exist' does not lead to a sudden reversal and a final note of optimism in this essay. Instead, the 'world I *think*' is acknowledged to be quite different from the world of actual life and our efforts to realize the world of thought are admitted to be failures (W, III. 75, 84–5).

'Experience' is the second essay in the 1844 collection. The first is 'The Poet', which offers an emphatic restatement of Emerson's theory of the use of nature and a vivid reaffirmation of his faith in the power of the human imagination. Equating the true poet with the prophet, Emerson claims that the poet's birth is a major event in 'sacred history' for his words give meaning to life that had previously been trivial, or mere 'noise'. Throughout the essay the function of the poet is shown to be uplifting in that he gives symbolic meaning to facts, expresses their 'supersensual utility' and thus frees men from their imprisonment in materialistic attitudes. Thus the Emersonian poet of 1844 is still an idealist in the sense defined in *Nature* and in the essay on Transcendentalism; he teaches us that 'we are symbols and inhabit symbols'. The freedom the poet offers to all men is the power to convert 'all the facts of the animal economy, sex, nutriment, gestation, birth, growth' and all scientific facts into symbols of the soul of man. No facts and no aspects of human experience are too humble or lowly to be of use to the poet as vehicles of his thought; even apparently trivial facts can be converted into symbols by the poet's 'superior use of things'.

To the prophet-poet the world is 'a temple whose walls are covered with emblems, pictures and commandments of the Deity'. His poems are the only true scriptures of mankind and the only genuine life in any religion is what it preserves of the inspiration of the poets who wrote its scriptures. Among the poets mentioned in the essay are Plato, Socrates, Orpheus, Proclus, St John the Divine and Swedenborg, as well as Dante, Shakespeare, Chaucer and Homer. Common to all these men of imagination, in Emerson's account of them, is a willingness to 'speak wildly' when inspired, or filled with the 'ethereal tides' that flow into them from the life of the universe. Thus the true poet can express ideas beyond the range of his conscious intellect, in Emerson's view, for inspiration is seen to share with intoxication or inebriation a freedom from the bounds of rational thought. Linked with the notion that poetic vision intoxicates is the belief that the poet 'abandons' himself to a joyous awareness of 'the metamorphosis' when inspired. The wildness implicit in the word combines with the sense that the *self* is abandoned to suggest that the poet also breaks the limits of his ego. Since 'metamorphosis' means the changing of forms, and since the poet is said to respond with joy to that change, and to the implicit ephemerality of all forms subject to change, it is plain that Emerson is offering the poet's imaginative participation in the flux of things as a means of dealing with the sense of human subjection to time and death. The imaginative power that enables man to express the metamorphic process is a fire that transmutes human clay to make it into the very fire – 'the same divinity at two or three removes'. Poetic expression becomes an apotheosis, then, and the poet a 'liberating god'.

Emerson's exalted conception of the role of the prophet-poet led him to regard a concern with the formal aspects of versification or with 'taste' as a sign of the lack of true inspiration. In 'The Poet' he dismisses writers of lyrics whose skill with delicate tunes and rhythms serves no deeper purpose. Such a talented verse-maker is a mere landscape-gardener, while a real poet is a mountain of such size that it reaches from the torrid zone at its base to the clouds at its peak. Whereas, as we shall see, Edgar Allan Poe laid great stress on the musical qualities of verse and argued that taste was the proper realm of poetry, Emerson insisted that moral and spiritual truths were the 'argument' of a poem and that the argument, not the metre, made the poem. To Emerson, Poe was no more than a 'jingle man' in his concern with metrical perfection. Emerson was not indifferent to the music of poetry, but he puts it at the service of the ideas the poem expresses.

'The Poet' offers insights into Emerson's aesthetic in its restatement of his theory of the symbolic function of nature. In 'The American Scholar' Emerson had stated that he 'embraced the common' and explored the familiar and the low rather than the great and romantic. His list of common things had included 'the shop, the plough, and the ledger'. Now he adds factories and railways and so makes his point more immediately relevant to American civilization in the 1840s. Poetry, he argues, should not confine itself to picturesque materials. The true American poet will make his songs from the everyday life of his democratic nation. The American poem – not yet written – will take as its proper subjects 'our log-rolling, our stumps and their politics, our fisheries, our Negroes and Indians, our boats and our repudiations, the wrath of rogues and the pusillanimity of honest men, the northern trade, the southern planting, the western clearing, Oregon and Texas'. America, according to the essay, is 'a poem in our eyes' though it is still 'unsung'.

Emerson's own *Poems*, published in December 1846, included 'Bacchus' – a powerful celebration of the transforming force of poetic ecstasy. But neither 'Bacchus' nor any other of the poems in the volume is the poem of America that Emerson foresaw in his 1844 essay 'The Poet', nor does any 'sing' the typical American activities listed there. The poem of America did not appear until 1855, when Walt Whitman published the first edition of *Leaves of Grass*. Emerson's immediate recognition of Whitman's achievement, in spite of the frank sexuality that he must have found disturbing in 'Song of Myself', proves conclusively that he did not abandon his prospective vision in the 1850s.

*

In his attitude to 'the age', however, Emerson did change after the publication of *Essays: First Series*. In his 1837 lecture 'The Present Age' he had regarded the then-current tendencies towards commercialization and urbanization as pressures for conformity and intellectual timidity. The age valued only facts, he believed, and was therefore hostile to the life of the spirit.

In the same year, in a lecture entitled 'Education', Emerson equated the material prosperity of which his contemporaries were proud with the sleep of the soul. Again, in his 1840 lecture 'Reforms' he asserted that the age was prosaic, that business made it tame and robbed it of the spirit of wildness he associated with nature. But in 'The Young American', a lecture given in 1844, Emerson began to speak of trade in ways that link him with George Bancroft. He began in fact to see trade as a manifestation of the spirit of liberty that had destroyed feudalism and had 'planted America'. The man who had written sympathetically of the young idealists who withdrew from society, rejecting its ideals and its institutions, in 'The Transcendentalist', now found himself re-interpreting and growing reconciled to the dominant spirit of the age and believing in the free market economy as a moral force that would work for the improvement of mankind. With the new attitude to commerce went, naturally, a new attitude to wealth and property. In 'Nominalist and Realist', in *Essays: Second Series*, the realist view that property is morally beneficial in its effects is given a sympathetic statement. In 'Wealth' (W, VI. 83–127) the implications of this conservative strain of Emerson's thought are fully developed.

Emerson's own middle age coincided with that of the century, so it is hardly surprising to find that the dominant note of his writings after *Essays: First Series* is more conservative than it had been in the lectures of the 1830s. From the start, as James Russell Lowell had observed, Emerson combined Yankee shrewdness with the high spirituality, but only a cynical interpretation of his career will deny the genuineness of his idealism. Moreover, the difficulty inherent in giving a chronological ordering to Emerson's beliefs is intensified by the fact that late in his life he reaffirmed some of his most radical and disturbing ideas. In 'Poetry and Imagination' (1872) the power of poetry is likened to a volcanic force that can destroy the stability of the material world and the fixed, confident theories of materialists. Under every man's breakfast table, Emerson states, is the 'gunpowder' of his potential awareness that all forms change when the imagination infuses life with its 'volatility and intoxication'. This is the Emersonian note, first sounded in the lectures of the 1830s, which had made his name synonymous with intellectual independence.

Notes

1 The text of the extract from Emerson's 'Self-Reliance' is taken from *The Collected Works of Ralph Waldo Emerson*, 2 vols to date, Cambridge, Mass.: The Belknap Press of Harvard University Press, 1971–, II, *Essays: First Series*, 1979. Parenthetic references to W throughout the chapter are to the Centenary Edition of *The Complete Works of Ralph Waldo Emerson*, 12 vols, Boston: Houghton Mifflin, 1903–4. References to EL are to the three volumes of *The Early Lectures of Ralph Waldo Emerson*, eds Stephen E. Whicher, Robert E. Spiller *et al.*, Cambridge, Mass.: Harvard University Press, 1959–72. References to JMN are to *The Journals and Miscellaneous Notebooks of Ralph Waldo Emerson*, eds William H. Gilman *et al.*, 14 vols to date, Cambridge, Mass.: Harvard University Press, 1960–. References to L are to *The Letters of Ralph Waldo Emerson*, ed. Ralph L. Rusk, 6 vols, New York: Columbia University Press, 1939.

2 *Stephen E. Whicher, *Freedom and Fate: An Inner Life of Ralph Waldo Emerson*, Philadelphia: University of Pennsylvania Press, 1953; repr. New York: Barnes, 1961, p. 50.

3 The term is Stephen Whicher's in his notes on 'Self-Reliance' in his *Selections from Ralph Waldo Emerson*, Boston: Houghton Mifflin, 1957, 1960, p. 481.

4 In 1826 Emerson read with enthusiasm Sampson Reed's *Growth of the Mind* and as a result became interested in Swedenborgian theories. For a summary of Emerson's interest in Swedenborg, see *Sherman Paul, *Emerson's Angle of Vision. Man and Nature in American Experience*, Cambridge, Mass.: Harvard University Press, 1952, 1969, pp. 66–70.

5 The French Swedenborgian was G. Oegger, whose *Le Vrai Messie* (Paris 1829) Emerson had read in translation in 1835.

6 *Freedom and Fate*, pp. 94–8.

Further reading

Lawrence Buell, *Literary Transcendentalism:. Style and Vision in the American Renaissance*, Ithaca and London: Cornell University Press, 1973.

Joel Porte, *Representative Man. Ralph Waldo Emerson in His Time*, New York: Oxford University Press, 1979.

* Books mentioned in notes and marked with an asterisk are particularly recommended for further reading.

3
Edgar Allan Poe (1809–49)

I shall ever bear about me a memory of the many solemn hours I thus spent alone with the master of the House of Usher. Yet I should fail in any attempt to convey an idea of the exact character of the studies, or of the occupations, in which he involved me, or led me the way. An excited and highly distempered ideality threw a sulphureous lustre over all. His long improvised dirges will ring forever in my ears. Among other things, I hold painfully in mind a certain singular perversion and amplification of the wild air of the last waltz of Von Weber. From the paintings over which his elaborate fancy brooded, and which grew, touch by touch, into vaguenesses at which I shuddered the more thrillingly, because I shuddered knowing not why; – from these paintings (vivid as their images now are before me) I would in vain endeavor to educe more than a small portion which should lie within the compass of merely written words. By the utter simplicity, by the nakedness of his designs, he arrested and overawed attention. If ever mortal painted an idea, that mortal was Roderick Usher. For me at least – in the circumstances then surrounding me – there arose out of the pure abstractions which the hypochondriac contrived to throw upon his canvass, an intensity of intolerable awe, no shadow of which felt I ever yet in the contemplation of the certainly glowing yet too concrete reveries of Fuseli.

One of the phantasmagoric conceptions of my friend, partaking not so rigidly of the spirit of abstraction, may be shadowed forth, although feebly, in words. A small picture presented the interior of an immensely long and rectangular vault or tunnel, with low walls, smooth, white, and without interruption or device. Certain accessory points of the design served well to convey the idea that this excavation lay at an exceeding depth below the surface of the earth. No outlet was observed in any portion of its vast extent, and no torch, or other artificial source of light was discernible; yet a flood of intense rays rolled throughout, and bathed the whole in a ghastly and inappropriate splendor.

I have just spoken of that morbid condition of the auditory nerve which rendered all music intolerable to the sufferer with the exception of certain effects of stringed instruments. It was, perhaps, the narrow limits to which he thus confined himself upon the guitar, which gave birth, in great measure, to the fantastic character of his performances. But the fervid *facility* of his *impromptus* could not be so accounted for. They must have been, and were, in the notes, as well as in the words of his wild fantasias (for he not unfrequently accompanied himself with rhymed verbal improvisations), the result of that intense mental collectedness and concentration to which I have previously alluded as observable only in particular moments of the highest artificial excitement. The words of one of these rhapsodies I have easily remembered. I was, perhaps, the more forcibly impressed with it, as he gave it, because, in the under or mystic current of its meaning, I fancied that I perceived, and for the first time, a full consciousness on the part of Usher, of the tottering of his lofty reason upon her throne. The verses, which were entitled 'The Haunted Palace,' ran very nearly, if not accurately, thus:

I

In the greenest of our valleys,
  By good angels tenanted,
Once a fair and stately palace –
  Radiant palace – reared its head.
In the monarch Thought's dominion –
  It stood there!
Never seraph spread a pinion
  Over fabric half so fair.

II

Banners yellow, glorious, golden,
  On its roof did float and flow;
(This – all this – was in the olden
  Time long ago)
And every gentle air that dallied,
  In that sweet day,
Along the ramparts plumed and pallid,
  A winged odor went away.

III

Wanderers in that happy valley

Through two luminous windows saw
Spirits moving musically
To a lute's well-tunéd law,
Round about a throne, where sitting
(Porphyrogene!)
In state his glory well befitting,
The ruler of the realm was seen.

IV

And all with pearl and ruby glowing
Was the fair palace door,
Through which came flowing, flowing, flowing,
And sparkling evermore,
A troop of Echoes whose sweet duty
Was but to sing,
In voices of surpassing beauty,
The wit and wisdom of their king.

V

But evil things, in robes of sorrow,
Assailed the monarch's high estate;
(Ah, let us mourn, for never morrow
Shall dawn upon him, desolate!)
And, round about his home, the glory
That blushed and bloomed
Is but a dim-remembered story
Of the old time entombed.

VI

And travellers now within that valley,
Through the red-litten windows, see
Vast forms that move fantastically
To a discordant melody;
While, like a rapid ghastly river,
Through the pale door,
A hideous throng rush out forever,
And laugh – but smile no more.

'The Fall of the House of Usher' (1839), *Tales* (1845)[1]

* * *

The narrator is a boyhood friend of Roderick Usher, the master of the House of Usher and sole male heir of an ancient family, who has lived for years in a remotely situated house with no companion but his sister 'the lady Madeline'. A desperate letter from Roderick, admitting his acute mental and bodily disorder, has summoned his friend to the house in the hope that the cheerfulness of that friend's society will alleviate its owner's illness. As this paragraph makes plain, no such alleviation is forthcoming, for the narrator is clearly responding to Roderick's disorder in ways that can only aggravate it. Evidently, he shares the nervous excitement of his hypochondriac friend. In the opening paragraphs of the tale, the most striking characteristic of the prose was its emotional intensity. The narrator approached the House of Usher (so he tells us) alone, at dusk, after travelling through 'a singularly dreary tract of country'. He found his friend's house 'melancholy' and responded to his first sight of it with a 'sense of insufferable gloom' and with 'an utter depression of soul'. *Before* he entered the house and encountered Roderick Usher, whom he had not seen for years, the narrator felt so 'unnerved' by the building and its surroundings that he imagined it to be enveloped by a 'pestilent and mystic vapor' that exhaled from the decayed trees, the tarn, and the grey wall of the house. The narrator's dismissive relegation of his own idea to the status of a dream does not alter the fact that he has anticipated Roderick's own superstitious belief about the house – his fear that it is 'sentient' and will have a fatal influence on his own life. If this narrator is unreliable, as he plainly seems to be, the reader is not going to escape from his haunted consciousness while the tale is being told.

In the passage before us, the narrator says that Roderick's paintings 'overawed' his attention and caused him to feel 'an intensity of intolerable awe' at their abstractions. Both in his references to 'awe' and in his related admission that he cannot find verbal equivalents for his experiences, the narrator may be taken to imply that he has entered the realm of the sublime, though he categorically rejected the term when describing his first mood of utter depression. In his *Philosophical Enquiry into the Origin of Our Ideas of the Sublime and Beautiful* (1757), Edmund Burke had not only argued that terror is the source of sublime emotion but had also insisted that the power of the sublime lay in its effectiveness in robbing the mind of its powers of reasoning. Obscurity and vastness belonged to the Burkean sublime because they contributed to the astonishment, or the mixture of fear and wonder, that he considered characteristic of the experience. Yet the truest test of the sublime, according to Burke, was the 'delightful horror' caused by the concept of infinity, for though we associate power with the idea of infinity we cannot fully grasp the notion – our minds remain overawed, as they do by the idea of eternity. The one pictorial representation of Roderick's ideas that we are allowed to glimpse shows us a long, smooth vault or tunnel with a suggestion of immense depth underground. We already know that Roderick's room is immense, badly lit and has windows placed so high above the floor that it is impossible to see out of them. The tunnel he paints seems, then, to be an intensified version of his own viewless room. His painting suggests his introversion, his self-absorption and his sense of entrapment or premature burial in the depths of his own mind. The lack of any outlet links the vault he has painted with his family name and with his own predicament. 'Usher' is close in sound to 'utter', and in the denouement of the tale it will be the 'superhuman energy of his utterance' that will compell the 'ponderous and ebony jaws' of the door of his room to open and reveal the terrible secret of his sister's living death. Madeline is Roderick's twin. In entombing her alive (albeit unwittingly) Roderick buried a part of himself, though that other self came back from the tomb to carry him to death.

The Usher family has been famous 'time out of mind', the narrator tells us, for its artistic sensibility and particularly for its passionate devotion to the intricacies of musical science, yet Roderick's songs are 'dirges' and the 'last waltz of Von Weber' that provides him with a theme was supposedly written within hours of its composer's death. His obsession with entrapment (entombment) and with death plainly determines his artistic performance. In the poem 'The Haunted Palace', which was first published separately before 'The House of Usher' was in print, music is the central metaphor. The palace, like the House of Usher, is the poet's mind. Before the Fall occasioned by or resulting in the assault of 'evil things, in robes of sorrow' on the rule of Thought, the door of the palace – obviously enough described in terms appropriate to the human mouth – poured forth harmonious sounds that celebrated the glory of the intellect. While Thought ruled in the radiant place, the spirits round the throne moved 'musically / To a lute's well-tunéd law'. After the Fall, in contrast, grotesque forms within the palace of the mind move 'to a discordant melody' and when they do achieve utterance it is as a 'hideous throng' of (madly) laughing creatures. We know, from Poe's introduction to his *Poems* of 1831, that he considered the poet's function to be that of presenting 'perceptible images . . . with *in*definite sensations' and that music was essential to this purpose because 'the comprehension of sweet sound is our most indefinite conception'. In one of his 'Marginalia', published in the *Democratic Review* in 1844, Poe suggested that music gives us a 'suggestive and indefinite glimpse' of the 'supernal ecstacies' denied to us while we are mere mortals. In his theory of the essential music of poetry, Poe was thinking in the tradition of the German romantic E. T. A. Hoffmann, whose seminal essay on Beethoven's instrumental music (published in German in 1813 and thus unavailable as a direct source to Poe, whose German was weak) had declared that music could open to man a new kingdom beyond the range of mere words and having nothing in common with the world of sensuous reality around him. More than most, Roderick Usher needs to escape from the world of sensuous reality for that world is insufferable to his excited nerves, but music offers him no entry into a new kingdom because it too has been affected by the Fall. Instead of redeeming him, Roderick's music only expresses his subjection to the realm of the senses. Dominated by a superstitious dread of the very house in which he lives, Roderick feels that his spirit is subject to the 'mere form and substance of his family mansion'. A fallen artist, Usher's experience of the sublime is limited to terror – he feels nothing of the liberation, of the sense of the kindred infinity of the human soul that, as we have seen, Channing considered to be characteristic of the poet's response to the sublimity of the natural world.

Rockerick's taste in literature is determined by his obsession with the 'sentience' of inorganic matter. The 'mental existence' of the invalid has been formed, we are told, by such works as Emanuel Swedenborg's *Heaven and Hell*, Robert Fludd's *Chiromancy*, and the Inquisitor Nicholas Eymeric of Gironne's *Directorium Inquisitorum*, or instructions for examining heretics. When we learn that Roderick's 'chief delight' was the *Vigiliae Mortuorum secundum Chorum Ecclesiae Maguntinae*, or 'Vigils for the dead according to the use of the second church of Mainz', a book so rare that no copy has been traced in America,[2] we can only suppose that his interest in ancient rites for the dead is the consequence of a preoccupation with death and a premonition concerning his sister's fate. Certainly the narrator thinks of 'the wild ritual of this work' when he hears of the supposed death of the lady Madeline and of Roderick's plan to preserve her corpse in the vaults of the house for a fortnight before burying her. Literature, then, can offer Roderick no more help to transcend his fear and no more opportunity to escape from his mental imprisonment than the other arts can.

At the climax of the tale, the gruesome scene in which Madeline escapes from the vault to return to his room and, in another 'fall', bear her brother to the floor in death-agonies that unite them, the self-fulfilling nature of Roderick's fear is stressed when we are told that he is a 'victim to the terrors he had anticipated'. As we approach that climax, a self-reflexive note enters the fiction as the narrator reads from a book called *The Mad Trist* of Sir Launcelot Canning. This story, told in the unconvincing 'medieval' English of Canning – a name derived from the fraudulently medieval legends of Thomas Chatterton – provides a parallel and parodic fiction within the fiction. The all-too-obtrusive synchronization of the climactic events in the two levels of fiction calls attention to the many-layered world of books in which tales beget tales that haunt the palace of thought.

Poe allows his reader so little information about Madeline that critics have exercised their ingenuity in interpreting her as anything from a vampire to the Apollonian spirit that Roderick, the Dionysian artist, has suppressed in himself. It *is* characteristic of Poe to encode meanings in his fictions, but it is also his firmly stated principle to make every detail of a tale contribute to the 'effect' that the tale was designed to accomplish. In 'The Fall of the House of Usher' the mysterious relationship between Roderick and Madeline is plainly part of the effect. Obviously, the failure of Usher to achieve adequate expression for his anguished thoughts is connected with his inability to accept the knowledge of Madeline's ailment or, possibly, his responsibility for that wasting away of her life. In the apocalyptic conclusion of the story, the destruction of Roderick is followed by the fall of the house as the blood-red moon shines through the fissure that the narrator had barely noticed on his first approach. Falling into fragments, this palace of thought collapses into the deep and silent waters of the tarn. The colour of the moon recalls the 'red-litten windows' of the 'Haunted Palace' and suggests madness, though – just before the end – we have heard Roderick call the narrator '*Madman!*'. The conclusion, like the opening, implicates the narrator in the disorder he represents.

'The Fall of the House of Usher' was first published in *Burton's Gentleman's Magazine* in September 1839 and took its place the following year in Poe's *Tales of the Grotesque and Arabesque*. To read this tale in the context of others with related themes that were included in Poe's first collection of stories is necessarily to notice some clearly marked patterns in his early fiction. 'Berenice', first published in the *Southern Literary Messenger* in 1835, is narrated by its own chief actor, Egaeus. Like Roderick, this scion of an ancient and noble family lives in the gloomy family mansion, but he is even more bookish than Usher, for Egaeus was actually born in the mansion's library, his mother died there, and his earliest memories are of the strange volumes his family has collected. This narrator's entire life has been spent in the monastic seclusion of the library: literally and figuratively he has never left the world of books. The woman in his life is a cousin who has grown up in the family mansion with him but, unlike Egaeus, she is light-hearted and feels at home in the outside world. The beautiful and healthy Berenice begins to succumb to a mysterious malady that works a terrible change on her appearance but – significantly – makes her more interesting to her cousin than she was when in bloom. Egaeus admits that his brain is a 'disordered chamber', for he finds that he has become obsessively concerned with physical objects dissociated from their meanings: with the typography or margin of a page of text rather than its words; with the physical decline of Berenice rather than her moral condition and, ultimately, with her *teeth*, which to him take the place of ideas. (In the versions of this story published before 1845, a 'species of smile' appears on the livid lips of the already putrescent corpse of Berenice.) Poe admitted to the editor of the *Southern Literary Messenger* that the tale was far too horrible, but the gory ending, in which Egaeus wakes from a dream in his library to find that he has robbed Berenice's corpse of its teeth, was unchanged in all versions of the tale.

'Berenice' is obviously not as successful or interesting a tale as the story of Roderick Usher, but its cruder form calls attention to a concatenation of ideas that was also to be present in 'Usher': intensely bookish seclusion and introversion, melancholy and possible madness of the male; mysterious physical decline of the female with whom he is most closely connected; an outrage committed on the woman's body and presumably caused by the man's obsession with the problematic relationship between the spirit and the flesh. In 'Morella', another tale published in the *Southern Literary Messenger* in 1835, a variation on the theme of erudition occurs, for here it is the woman who is profoundly learned, but the theme of forbidden knowledge – of mystical and probably magical writings – is even more clearly announced in this tale than in 'The Fall of the House of Usher'. Morella, predictably, falls into a physical decline that leads ineluctably towards death, but in dying she cries that she will live again and will regain the love of her husband – the narrator of the tale – whose feeling for her has been blighted by his terror of their mutual quest for knowledge. The concluding sections of the story are ritualistic, the language is incantatory. In dying, Morella gives birth to a daughter whose resemblance to her dead mother is such that her father names her Morella and hears a response from beyond the grave. Concern with identity, with the *principium individuationis* (the essence of the self) and the possibility of its survival after death, is explicit in this tale, for the learned allusions are to Pythagorian theories of metempsychosis, to Schelling's theories of identity, to Locke's conceptions of personal identity, and to Fichte's 'wild Pantheism'.

The theme of life after death is also central in 'Ligeia', a tale first published in the Baltimore *American Museum* in September 1838. Ligeia, like Morella, is a prodigy of learning and leads her idolatrous lover into realms of forbidden knowledge. She resists the relentless malady that draws her towards death, for her esoteric studies have convinced her that the human will can triumph over death. She does die, but only after her supernaturally and strangely beautiful eyes have absorbed the soul of the narrator. When he remarries, he takes his new bride to a fantastic bridal chamber whose décor stridently expresses his obsession with death. Ligeia returns, in the narrator's opium-stimulated vision, to take momentary possession of the form of the unloved and ailing second wife. In this tale, as in the two previously discussed, the narrator is the lover whose relationship with the ailing woman is so intense that her death threatens his sanity. 'Ligeia' ranks with Poe's greatest tales in achievement, but its success depends upon the reader's willingness to accept the stylized intensity or extravagance of its plot and its language. Repeated references to opium and the wild visions it engenders, together with the remote, isolated settings and allusions to the 'fantastic display' in the architecture and decoration of the bridal chamber, are clearly intended to avert the bathos that would inevitably result if realistic criteria were brought to bear on this tale. The world of the story is the world of the nameless narrator's nervously over-stimulated imagination. It is a disordered world that at least raises the suspicion of madness.

*

The nervousness of the narrators in each of the four tales discussed would, in twentieth-century terminology, plainly indicate neuroses susceptible of psychoanalytic explanation. A thoroughgoing Freudian interpretation of all Poe's works has, in fact, been offered by Marie Bonaparte in her *Life and Works of Edgar Allan Poe: A Psycho-Analytic Interpretation* (1949) but a less doctrinaire approach to the relationship between the life and the works has to start from the distinction between the narrators and the writer who created them. We may accept Roger Asselineau's useful formulation that Poe was the 'writer of neuroses'[3] without assuming that Poe was himself neurotic. When Poe came to formulate his own theory of the short story, as he did in his review of Hawthorne's *Twice-told Tales* in *Graham's* magazine in 1842, he insisted on aesthetic concerns, on the skilful construction of a tale. In Poe's words, 'having conceived, with deliberate care, a certain unique or single *effect* to be wrought out', the writer 'then invents such incidents – he then combines such events, as may best aid him in establishing this pre-conceived effect'. Every word in the tale should, Poe argued, contribute to the 'one pre-established design'. By stressing the design of the writer and the effect he deliberately and systematically sets out to achieve, Poe is unmistakably arguing that the writer of fiction is a craftsman whose success as an artist depends on his technical skill. Further, the theory of the short story outlined in Poe's article diverts attention from any expressive function it may have for the writer, focusing instead on its manipulative effects on the putative reader. In the extended version of his article on Hawthorne that appeared in *Godey's Lady's Book* in 1847, Poe wrote of the 'idea' of the tale, or its 'thesis', but here too he insisted on the essential subordination of every detail of a tale to its '*single effect*'. When Poe offered illustration of what he meant by the tale of effect, he did so with a shorthand reference to the earlier numbers of *Blackwood's Magazine* in which, he said, many fine examples could be found. Since this allusion to *Blackwood's* follows a list of 'points' that the tale can legitimately treat, and since that list is composed of 'terror, or passion, or horror, or a multitude of such other points', we can legitimately suppose that each of the listed states of feeling constitutes a 'single effect'. Earlier, in his apologetic letter to the editor of the *Southern Literary Messenger*, while admitting that 'Berenice' was too horrible, Poe had claimed that the celebrated magazines – among which he certainly would have ranked *Blackwood's* – owed their fame to articles of a nature similar to his story. In defining the nature of the successful magazine story, Poe went beyond the range of 'Berenice', for he stated that success was produced by 'the ludicrous heightened into the grotesque: the fearful coloured into the horrible: the witty exaggerated into the burlesque: the singular wrought out into the strange and mystical' (L, I. 57–8). Since the purpose of the letter was to persuade the Editor to publish his stories, it is appropriate that Poe extended his account to include comic tales, but the significant pointer to Poe's own methods is the consistent stress on heightening and exaggeration in all modes of successful tale writing.

The consistently anti-didactic emphasis of Poe's literary theories, whether applied to prose (as in his animadversions on the allegoric elements in Hawthorne's tales) or to poetry (as in his lecture 'The Poetic Principle' in 1848–9), makes it clear that his whole conception of literature was remote from Emerson's. Assuming that the true function of literature was a religious function and that its value lay in the expression of moral and spiritual truths, Emerson took no interest in the fiction written by his contemporaries. Poe, on the other hand, explored even his main ideas through the conventions of popular magazine stories. The point is not that Poe was less serious in his literary endeavours than Emerson was in his, but that the seriousness was of a radically different kind.

The tales so far discussed were collected in Poe's first volume of short stories, *Tales of the Grotesque and Arabesque*, in 1840, and like all the other tales in that collection they had first appeared in magazines. Poe was concerned to analyse the nature of the successful magazine story because he depended for his own livelihood on his ability to write tales that would be acceptable to the editors, and to the readers, of such periodicals. Poe was a professional writer in a sense that does not apply to Emerson, for he depended absolutely on the income earned by his pen. He had no private income that could be supplemented by earnings on the lyceum circuit.

Poe is remembered now mainly for his tales of terror and his detective stories or tales of ratiocination, yet, in his contributions to the magazines, comic tales balanced the serious or 'Arabesque' tales in bulk. Among the tales of his 1840 collection belonging to the categories of the 'ludicrous heightened into the grotesque' and the 'witty exaggerated into the burlesque' were 'How to Write a Blackwood Article' and the story within that story called 'A Predicament', originally published as one in the Baltimore *American Museum* in 1838. In Poe's burlesque, an apprentice fiction writer called Signora Psyche Zenobia relates her exquisite feelings while the minute hand of a huge clock severs her trapped neck. While ridiculing the crass sensationalism of the tale of extreme terror, Poe makes allusion to the sort of magazine material that he himself used. Mr Blackwood recommends to Signora Zenobia tales of burial alive, of entrapment (in a boiler and a belfry) that had actually appeared in British magazines after 1820 and had interested Poe sufficiently for him to use variations on these themes. Even the preposterously literal application of the metaphoric 'Scythe of Time' to the neck of Psyche Zenobia can be related to Poe's brilliant use of the same metaphor in 'The Pit and the Pendulum' (1842), where the pendulum used by the Inquisition as an instrument of torture is also an emblem of man's subjection to time. A parodic treatment of a fictional theme did not, for Poe, preclude a serious reworking of theme and effect.

Poe's first published tale, 'Metzengerstein', appeared in the Philadelphia *Saturday Courier* in 1832. Subtitled, at its second publication, 'a tale in imitation of the German' it makes use of the brand of 'terror' that Horace Walpole had made famous in his *Castle of Otranto* (1764) – the first Gothic novel in English – substituting a gigantic horse for the enormous suit of armour that does the work of destruction in Walpole's book. Other conventions with which Poe works in this tale include a remote and ancient castle whose lord is the melancholy heir to an ancient family. In 'Metzengerstein', the Baron who gives the story its title is diabolically evil, but the attribution of vices to him is so casual that the tale resists a solemn reading. In one brief paragraph he is credited with 'shameful debaucheries, flagrant treacheries – unheard of atrocities'; he also has the 'remorseless fangs of a petty Caligula'. In versions of the tale published before 1850, some motivation for all this evil was provided by the early death of the Baron's beautiful mother, but the characterization is so mechanical that the writer seems only partially engaged with his materials. Yet even here, where there are unmistakably parodic intentions, some Poe scholars have argued for a deeply serious moral interpretation of the tale. That they have done so is a tribute to the strengths of Poe's writing in the concluding section of the story, when the fiery character of the demonic horse that embodies the spirit of the Baron's dead rival works the destruction of Metzengerstein. Even in this tale, parody modulates into something more complex when the animal is used to express or suggest passion. The literary convention that Poe adopted in this story of metempsychosis proved congenial in some of its aspects, if unworthy in others.

In his preface to *Tales of the Grotesque and Arabesque* Poe claimed that the terror in his tales was 'not of Germany, but of the soul'. By this he presumably meant that the psychological interest of his fictions was not dependent on the conventions of horror-Gothic (he called it 'pseudo-horror') that had come to be associated with German literature. Yet, since terror was the theme in so many of his tales, subtlety of emotion or action was not likely to be among their characteristics; extravagance in both areas was, in fact, virtually prescribed by the effect they sought. When extreme situations and heighted sensations are the staple of literary art, as in the horror-Gothic of Matthew Lewis or of Charles Robert Maturin, then there is a tendency to self-parody that makes the seriousness of the story problematic. More obviously than in the tales, this is true in Poe's case of his novel *The Narrative of Arthur Gordon Pym* (1838).

Poe's dismissal of the novel as a 'very silly story' cannot be taken to decide the question of its seriousness, and may be obscurantist, but the proliferation of horrors in the story does disconcert most readers, for the mere swift succession of shocking incidents seems guaranteed to weaken the effect of any one of them. The title-page lists mutiny, atrocious butchery, shipwreck, horrible sufferings, massacre and 'incredible adventures and discoveries south of the eighty-fourth parallel' among the attractions within. Having narrowly escaped death by shipwreck, Arthur Gordon Pym and his young friend Augustus go to sea again and narrowly escape death at the hands of mutineers. Surviving the mutiny, they are reduced to cannibalism by the famine that follows the wreck of the second ship. When rescue seems imminent, and the Dutch sailor on the approaching rescue-ship smiles encouragement, Pym gives thanks to God, only to find that the smile is that of a putrescent corpse whose teeth have no flesh around them, whose eyes are gone, and whose flesh is being devoured by a bird. The theme of putrescence, elaborated when Augustus's body rots before the eyes of his friend, follows that of entombment. Pym was entombed in the hold of the ship in which he hoped for adventure. It is as if M. G. Lewis's *The Monk* (1796) had been converted into a sea-story, for with the live burial and the rotting flesh goes an emphatic concern with deceptive appearances that manifests itself in a series of related incidents. First Pym deceives his father and grandfather in order to stow away on the ship and thus deceive Augustus's father, who is the captain. Deception in the boys' world of adventure is followed by adult deception in the murderous form of a mutiny, and this will be followed, when Pym has found a new ship to sail in, by the deceptive friendliness of the natives of Tsalal that preludes their massacre of the white crew.

In the second chapter, Arthur Gordon Pym, whose name plainly echoes Edgar Allan Poe's, and whose grandfather made a fortune in the Edgartown bank, tells us that he is melancholic and that his dreams of travel are visions of 'shipwreck and famine; of death or captivity among barbarian hordes; of a life-time dragged out in sorrow and tears, upon some gray and desolate rock, in an ocean unapproachable and unknown'. These are not just visions, they are also 'desires', for Pym's impulse from the start is self-destructive. But, as in the tales already discussed, the self-destructive impulse of the protagonists or narrators is inseparable from their desire for new knowledge. The quest for knowledge intensifies once Pym is rescued from the wreck of the *Grampus* and aboard the *Jane Guy*, for he urges the reluctant captain of his new ship to press on to the extreme south to solve the mysteries of the Antarctic continent. The voyage ends in disaster for captain and crew, but Pym survives to confront the mysteries of the chasms of the island of Tsalal, and to feel pride in opening the eyes of science to secrets hitherto sealed.

For Pym's new 'knowledge' Poe drew on the theories of John Cleves Symmes, whose notion that the earth is hollow and open at the poles had been given considerable publicity in the United States in the 1820s. Since the Antarctic was still a mysterious and uncharted part of the globe in the 1830s, it was a fitting zone for Pym's quest. The first instalment of the story appeared in the *Southern Literary Messenger* in 1837, together with Poe's review of Washington Irving's *Astoria*, an account of Hunt's expedition from the Missouri to the mouth of the Columbia. Poe found Irving's book more intensely exciting than any other travelogue and wrote admiringly of the 'vast series of adventures encountered' on the expedition. With an even vaster series of adventures, Poe may have intended to make his own travelogue still more exciting, but the effect of his method is to give his story an allegoric force it would lack if it were more plausible. Pym's irresistible desire to know and his self-fulfilling visions of self-destruction have a significance that does not depend on the repeated horrors of the story.

When the novel was published in 1838, the narrative was preceded by a statement in which 'Arthur Gordon Pym' explained that 'Mr Poe' had presented a version of the early adventures of Pym, '*under the garb of fiction*' in the *Southern Literary Messenger* in the previous year. In fact, the *Messenger* had carried only two instalments of the narrative when Poe left the magazine and the serialization stopped. According to 'Pym's' preface to the novel, the readers of the *Messenger* had insisted on treating the 'fictional' version as the truth and had thus encouraged him to publish his story in his own words, knowing that he had 'little to fear on the score of popular incredulity'. This double bluff or variation on the theme of fiction and credulity was developed in an end-note to the narrative in which the 'late sudden and distressing death of Mr Pym' is given as the cause for the loss of the final chapters. Pym survived his plunge into the Symmesian gulf to return to the States and tell his story to 'Mr Poe', but, so the anonymous writer of the note tells us, the 'few remaining chapters' were lost in the accident by which Pym perished. 'Mr Poe' declined the task of completing the story, since he disbelieved the 'entire truth of the latter portions of the narration', according to the writer of the note, who thus shows himself to be more credulous than 'Mr Poe'. More credulous and, by his own account, more perceptive, for he offers an interpretation of the hieroglyphics in the chasms of Tsalal that 'escaped the attention of Mr Poe'. But if the knowledge towards which Pym's quest was directed is provided in an anonymous postscript to the narrative, unauthorized by 'Mr Poe' or Pym, that knowledge itself is hardly conclusive, for it turns out to be no more than a *possible* connection between an Ethiopian verbal root meaning 'to be shady', an Egyptian word meaning 'the region of the south', the 'fact' that the natives of Tsalal knew nothing of the colour white and were terrified of it, and an Arabic verbal root meaning 'to be white'. Thus an end-note to a book in which white treachery and cruelty precede and balance black perfidy and butchery tempts its readers to interpret it as a fable of black insurrection in the Southern States to whose 'peculiar institution' its author – as we know from external evidence – gave his sympathies. Edgar Allan Poe the man approved of slavery and detested Northern abolitionists, but *The Narrative of Arthur Gordon Pym* is a work whose narrative technique makes *definite* interpretation a hoax the reader practises on himself.

If reading Poe's novel is problematic because of the profligacy of its horrors and the sheer quantity of its adventures, his two related sea tales offer superb examples of narrative economy. 'MS Found in a Bottle' is one of Poe's earliest tales – it was first published in 1833 – and one of his best. Here the quest theme is so explicit that the sceptical, unsuperstitious, materialistic narrator finds himself unconsciously daubing the word 'DISCOVERY' on a sail that lies near him on the mystery ship that destroyed the prosaic vessel in which he had sailed. Horror and astonishment give way to feelings for which the narrator admits that he has no name, for we are in the region of the sublime where 'conceptions are indefinite' and where 'a new sense – a new entity' is added to the soul. Combining Symmes's theories of holes at the poles with the legend of the Flying Dutchman, Poe's story takes his narrator out of the world of clock-time by first enveloping him in eternal night and then casting him on a ship that is lost in aeons of time. The immensely aged captain, a hoary and awe-inspiring figure who combines Coleridge's Ancient Mariner with suggestions of Columbus, steers by antique and mouldering scientific instruments, his cabin littered with 'obsolete and long-forgotten charts'. On deck are strewn mathematical instruments that are also obsolete, for all human measurements and all human knowledge have lost their relevance on this quest voyage on the oceans of eternity. As the ship is swept southwards through stupendous ramparts of ice towards a gigantic whirlpool, the narrator's horror is such that no reader can – he presumes – conceive it. But, in this archetypal Poesque narrator, horror yields to a curiosity to 'penetrate the mysteries of these awful regions' even though his knowledge will involve his death. The knowledge to which he feels himself hurrying is 'some exciting knowledge – some never-to-be imparted secret, whose attainment is destruction'. Like all Poe's questing narrators, he welcomes his own annihilation, but the literary record he leaves behind him can take its readers only to the brink of the precipice, the edge of the whirlpool, for beyond that lies the ineffable. The words of the manuscript take us to the limits of language.

There was to be one survivor, however, in 'A Descent into the Maelström' (1841). The inner narrator of this tale is atypical in that he did not seek confrontation with the ultimate mysteries and had no day-dreams of self-destruction. Caught in the maelstrom by a mere mechanical failure in measuring time (his watch stopped), he experiences a crescendo of horrors as he nears the jaws of the gulf. Yet this narrator, too, loses his terror in a positive '*wish* to explore' the depths of the whirlpool once he has renounced all hope of self-preservation, for the vast power of the whirlpool becomes to him a wonderful 'manifestation of God's power' that makes his own life seem trivial. In this tale, release from the desire to save the self becomes the means of saving the self, for the practical reason is freed and can provide an escape by observation. The narrator is saved because he notices that cylindrical objects are most resistant to the pull of the vortex and therefore leaves the apparent safety of his boat for the flimsier protection of a mere cask. Later he learns the 'law' that explains this phenomenon and his escape. Poe helpfully supplies a learned reference to Archimedes' work 'De Incidentibus in Fluido', but the reference is fictional, it does not – as it seems to do – validate the narrator's marvellous escape in terms of an extra-fictional authority. Thus there is an element of hoax in the 'explanation' of the escape. The tale is an unqualified success, its 'effect' is perfectly achieved, but the knowledge brought back by this one narrator who has almost seen God's face and lived is limited by the fact that he descended only half the distance between the surface and the bottom of the gulf. Thus he came close enough to the awful and destructive power he names God for the experience to turn his hair white, but remaining in the realm of reason, and narrative, he could not reach the ineffable depth that is itself an annihilation of language.

In some of his most successful tales of the 1840s Poe returns to the theme of the self-destructive impulse that had sent Arthur Gordon Pym on his travels, but in these later fictions uses the structure of the murder story. In 'The Imp of the Perverse' (1845) a rather perfunctory confession of murder is appended to an essay on the psychological forces that make men seek their own destruction. Delivered as part of the narrator's account of his own experience, this essay on the spirit of perversity acts as a summary of many of Poe's fictional situations, for it vividly portrays the man on the brink of a precipice passing through states of horror to reach a condition in which he acutely desires to plunge to annihilation. Rejecting any attempt to explain such a 'radical, primitive impulse' in terms of the current theories of phrenology or in terms of any rational theory, Poe's narrator uses the analogy of the Arabian Nights genie to suggest the demonic force at work here: the genie is, then, the 'imp'. But to talk of imps or genies is to explain nothing, and the point is made implicitly in the paragraph that rejects any motive. The *imp*ulse that *imp*ells us contains the 'imp' in it! The lexical play contains no rationale; it merely shows that there is a devil in the language.

'The Black Cat' (1843) is one of the rare Poe tales in which the setting is a normal house, inhabited by a once happily married couple, rather than a decaying castle owned by a hypochondriac recluse whose sanity is in doubt. But the normal relationship between narrator and wife ended long before the tale proper begins, for the imp in this tale is the Fiend Intemperance that turned the gentle, affectionate narrator into a cruel, murderous demon. With its spirit of perversity conventionalized as the spirits in the bottle (of gin), this tale is even trite in its motivation until it is redeemed, as 'Metzengerstein' had been, by the totemic force of an animal: here the black cat that gives a vivid embodiment to the narrator's guilt. The murder of his loving wife while he is in a demoniacal rage moves the narrator less than his subjection to a diabolical reincarnation of a cat he has tortured and killed. Both killings, however, plainly serve the need to destroy himself that informs the narrator-murderer's subsequent actions. In Poe the murderer-victim relationship is frequently complicated by suggestions that the murderer identifies with the victim; that the agent projects himself into the situation of his victim and thus inflicts his cruelties on himself. In 'The Tell-Tale Heart', another tale first published in 1843, the murderer's heart and that of his victim beat together in terror – if only in the murderer's imagination – as both listen to the ticking (of the death-watch beetles) in the wall. At once a sensational tale of utmost terror and an allegory of man's subjection to time, this tale illustrates the difficulty of categorizing Poe's fictions.

Cruelty, as we have seen, is an ingredient of some of Poe's humorous tales, even if neutralized by absurdities like those of 'The Scythe of Time'. Even the trivial anecdote 'Why the Little Frenchman Wears His Hand in a Sling' (1837–9) depends for its point on the physical cruelty, as well as the verbal battery, that Sir Pathrick O'Grandison offers to the little Mounseer Frog. Equally crude in its verbal fun and equally dependent on physical cruelty for its anecdotal point is the extravaganza 'Never Bet the Devil Your Head' (1841), but a more interesting tale of physical dismemberment is 'The Man That Was Used Up' (1839), for this grotesque story touches on many of Poe's perennial concerns. Brevet Brigadier General John A. B. C. Smith is a quite remarkably fine-looking man whose magnificent physique and military reputation combine to dazzle the naive narrator of the tale until he visits the General in his dressing-room and finds the real man to be no more than a trunk, whose every limb and organ has had to be artificially supplied to make good the depredations of the Bugaboo and Kickapoo Indians he fought. The point of this unsubtly ironic tale is that, before the revelation, the General has waxed eloquent on the wonders of the age, its railways, steamboats, and other 'truly *useful* mechanical contrivances'. General Smith expressed a confidence and a pride that was shared by millions of Americans when he boasted of the technological wonders of the age. In doing so, he identified 'progress' – one of the sacred words of the period – with material progress. When Poe reduces this fine figure of a man to a mere bundle lying helpless on the floor of its room, he expresses his contempt for what he considers a callow and unworthy conception of human development.

Several of Poe's satirical sketches reveal his alienation from the 'spirit of the age' as that was expressed by faith in progress. 'Some Words with a Mummy' (1845) ridicules American pride in such achievements as the Bowling-Green Fountain in New York and the Capitol at Washington, DC, by contrasting them with the glories of ancient Egypt. Every invention of which the nineteenth century is proud was, so the revivified ancient Egyptian claims, anticipated by his civilization, while the 'Great Movement or Progress' that the Transcendentalist *Dial* magazine supposedly advocates is dismissed by the Egyptian with a reference to the nuisance such movements caused in his day, though they never progressed. American pride in democracy recalls, to the ancient Egyptian, the bragging of thirteen Egyptian provinces that boasted prodigiously of their democratic political system and instituted the intolerable despotism of Mob. Almost the same point is made in 'Mellonta Tauta' (1849), when the wise man of the year 2848 looks back on the absurdities of the ancient 'Amriccan' notions of democratic rule, rating it no higher than a community of prairie dogs.

In 'The Colloquy of Monos and Una' (1841) the tone is solemn, for Monos speaks with the wisdom of one who has passed beyond earthly life, and the verdict on nineteenth-century confidence in the advances of practical science is unambiguous. Looking down and back on the era of belief in the progress of civilization, Monos states that the supposed improvements brought about by science were actually part of a backward movement, a 'retrogradation in the true utility', though only the poets were able to perceive this truth. In those days, when utilitarian philosophy dominated, only the poetic intellect was able to grasp the meaning of the 'mystic parable' of the forbidden fruit of the tree of knowledge and to realize that man's soul was not yet ready for knowledge. The fruits of the forbidden tree are, of course, death. Monos's colloquy tells of the apocalyptic end of the world. In the era of imagined progress, the knowledge on which men prided themselves was their power over nature, yet this produced the hideous ugliness of an industrial civilization and a perversion of the faculty of taste. Taste, as we know from 'The Poetic Principle', was the poetic faculty and concerned itself with the beautiful. In 'The Colloquy', as in his 'Sonnet – To Science', the scientific and the poetic world-views are antipathetic, and to the former belongs the idea of egalitarian democracy as well as confidence in progress.

In a review of poetical works by Joseph Rodman Drake and Fitz-Greene Halleck, written in 1836, Poe stated that poetry had never been defined adequately and perhaps never could be, yet he went on to offer his suggestions for a definition:

> If, indeed, there be any one circle of thought distinctly and palpably marked out from amid the jarring and tumultuous chaos of human intelligence, it is that evergreen and radiant Paradise which the true poet knows, and knows alone, as the limited realm of his authority – as the circumscribed Eden of his dreams.

Earlier, while discussing 'The Fall of the House of Usher', we noted Poe's belief that music gave to mere mortals an indefinite glimpse of supernal ecstasies. Putting these two statements beside Poe's assertion, in 'The Poetic Principle', that poetry and music seek 'the Beauty above' when the artist is inspired 'by an ecstatic prescience of the glories beyond the grave', we can see that he consistently defines the realm of poetry in terms of its distance and difference from the waking world of everyday life. The association of the realm of the poem with the realm of the dream is unmistakable in Poe's thought, from the two poems on dreams in his 1827 volume of verse to the end of his career. In his penetrating essay, 'The House of Poe', Richard Wilbur has argued that the motifs of '*enclosure* or *circumscription*' (Wilbur's italics) that recur in tale after tale suggest the exclusion of the outer or 'real' world and the isolation of the poetic soul in revery, or 'dream-waking' as Poe called it.[4] Taking Poe's fundamental plot to be the effort of the poetic soul to escape from consciousness into the world of dreams and his basic theme to be the conflict between the poetic soul and the earthly self to which it is bound (and, by extension, the actual world in which that self must live), Wilbur considers 'The Fall of the House of Usher' the archetypal Poe story. This is a helpful comment in that it enables us to take the tale very seriously indeed, though we may not want to agree with Wilbur that 'Usher' is not really a horror story but, rather, a triumphant report by the narrator that the poetic soul can shake off the real world and escape to the realm of unfettered vision. Such a reading rewrites the story, changing horror and collapse into putative elevation. Similarly, interpretations of the destruction in Poe's fictions as a stage in the progress from the discordant life of the actual world to an ideal unity that lies beyond the fragmented self, take us beyond the actual fictions. In *Eureka: An Essay on the Material and Spiritual Universe* (1848) Poe announced the great truth that all things and all thoughts of things sprang into being from the 'Original Unity' and that all aspirations towards perfection were 'struggles toward the original Unity', but to read the tales in the retroactive light of his last great prose poem is to distort the fictions. In 'Eureka', the return to absolute unity from which everything was evoked by the will of God is a subsidence into nothingness that will be followed by a swelling into a new existence as the centripetal and centrifugal movements of the 'Heart Divine' prove to be the movements of our own hearts. In the tales, by contrast, Poe's language can only take us through the process, or rather to the edge, of the subsidence into nothingness.

In the 'Idealism' chapter of *Nature*, Emerson quoted lines from *The Tempest* to illustrate the poet's power to work a 'transfiguration' of material objects. The lines selected show Prospero's use of music to cure Alonzo and his companions of their frenzy and restore them to reason. Emerson commented: 'The perception of real affinities between events (that is to say, of *ideal* affinities, for those only are real), enables the poet thus to make free with the most imposing forms and phenomena of the world, and to assert the predominance of the soul.' Prospero, Emerson's archetypal poet here, can control the world of matter through his imaginative power to 'transfigure' the world of phenomena. In one of Poe's most effective tales, 'The Masque of the Red Death' (1842), a prince who is given the name of Prospero encloses himself and a thousand chosen guests in a castellated abbey to keep its inhabitants uncontaminated by the cholera that is raging throughout his kingdom.

Sealing all the gates to prevent any intrusion or any escape, he confines his guests in a world that is entirely dominated by his fancy. Everything in the confined world of the abbey is a product of Prospero's imagination, from the colours of the seven rooms, to the colour of the great clock that, like the most westerly room in which it stands, is deep black. While the pestilence ravages the outside world, the guests dance to music that the prince has provided for a masked ball that he has commanded. They stop only when the clock strikes the hours and momentarily interrupts their frenetic movement. The masked figures, like the people of Merry Mount in Hawthorne's story (to be discussed in Chapter 5), are 'dreams'. They 'writhe' to the prince's music, for they are products of his imagination. But, for all Prospero's despotic power in his micro-kingdom, the plague enters the abbey and appears at the ball in the mask of death. When the enraged prince attacks the intruder in the ultimate, black room, he dies. His death is quickly followed by the death of all his dream-figures. The end of the tale is apocalyptic: 'And Darkness and Decay and the Red Death held illimitable dominion over all'. As Richard Wilbur has argued, this tale can be interpreted as an allegory of the relationship between the circumscribed world of the poet's imaginative control and the pestilential reality beyond it. The contrast between Poe's Prospero and Emerson's reveals more about their conceptions of art than any disagreement concerning the status of metre in poetry.

Notes

1 The text of the extract from 'The Fall of the House of Usher' is taken from *The Collected Works of Edgar Allan Poe*, ed. Thomas Ollive Mabbott, 3 vols to date, Cambridge, Mass.: The Belknap Press of Harvard University Press, 1969–, II, *Tales and Sketches 1831–1842*, 1978. Mabbott takes the version of the tale published in the 1845 *Tales* as his copy-text. It was first published in *Burton's Gentleman's Magazine* in 1839 and subsequently in *Tales of the Grotesque and Arabesque* (1840). There are variations in all of these texts. Parenthetic references to L throughout the chapter are to *The Letters of Edgar Allan Poe*, ed. John Ward Ostrom, 2 vols, Cambridge, Mass.: Harvard University Press, 1948.

2 Poe, *Collected Works*, II, p. 421. See Mabbott's note.

3 Roger Asselineau, *Edgar Allan Poe*, Minneapolis: University of Minnesota Press, 1970, p. 21.

4 Richard Wilbur, 'The House of Poe', in *Poe: A Collection of Critical Essays*, ed. Robert Regan, Englewood Cliffs, NJ: Prentice-Hall, 1967, pp. 98–120.

Further reading

Edward H. Davidson, *Poe: A Critical Study*, Cambridge, Mass.: Harvard University Press, 1957.

4
George Bancroft (1800-91)

JUNE, 1774

On the first day of June, Hutchinson embarked for England; and as the clocks in the Boston belfries finished striking twelve, the blockade of the harbor began. The inhabitants of the town were chiefly traders, shipwrights, and sailors; and since no anchor could be weighed, no sail unfurled, no vessel so much as launched from the stocks, their cheerful industry was at an end. No more are they to lay the keel of the fleet merchantman, or shape the rib symmetrically for its frame, or strengthen the graceful hull by knees of oak, or rig the well proportioned masts, or bend the sails to the yards. The king of that country has changed the busy workshops into scenes of compulsory idleness, and the most skilful naval artisans in the world, with the keenest eye for forms of beauty and speed, are forced by act of parliament to fold their hands. Want scowled on the laborer, as he sat with his wife and children at his board. The sailor roamed the streets listlessly without hope of employment. The law was executed with a rigor that went beyond the intentions of its authors. Not a scow could be manned by oars to bring an ox, or a sheep, or a bundle of hay from the islands. All water carriage from pier to pier, though but of lumber, or bricks, or lime, was strictly forbidden. The boats between Boston and Charlestown could not ferry a parcel of goods across Charles River; the fishermen of Marblehead, when from their hard pursuit, they bestowed quintals of dried fish on the poor of Boston, were obliged to transport their offering in wagons by a circuit of thirty miles. The warehouses of the thrifty merchants were at once made valueless; the costly wharfs, which extended far into the channel, and were so lately covered with the produce of the tropics and with English fabrics, were become solitary places; the harbor, which had resounded incessantly with the cheering voices of prosperous commerce, was now disturbed by no sounds but from British vessels of war.

At Philadelphia, the bells of the churches were muffled and tolled; the ships in port hoisted their colors at half mast; and nine-tenths of the houses, except those of the Friends, were shut during the memorable First of June. In Virginia, the population thronged the churches; Washington attended the service, and strictly kept the fast. No firmer or more touching words were addressed to the sufferers than from Norfolk, which was the largest place of trade in that 'well-watered and extensive dominion,' and which, from its deep channel and nearness to the ocean, lay most exposed to ships of war. 'Our hearts are warmed with affection for you,' such was its message; 'we address the Almighty Ruler to support you in your afflictions. Be assured we consider you as suffering in the common cause, and look upon ourselves as bound by the most sacred ties to support you.'

Jefferson, from the foot of the Blue Ridge of the Alleghanies, condemned the act [of parliament], which in a moment reduced an ancient and wealthy town from opulence to want, and without a hearing and without discrimination, sacrificed property of the value of millions to revenge – not repay – the loss of a few thousands. 'If the pulse of the people beat calmly under such an experiment by the new and till now unheard of executive power of a British parliament,' said the young statesman, 'another and another will be tried, till the measure of despotism be filled up.'

The History of the United States (1858)[1]

* * *

The clocks in the Boston belfries strike twelve as this passage opens, and in doing so they announce more than the beginning of the British blockade of Boston harbour in June 1774. They also mark a stage in the inexorable movement towards American independence that George Bancroft's history dramatizes. Like many of Bancroft's literary devices, the alliteration used to lend a fateful emphasis to the events is too blatant to be completely effective, though it does add a flourish to the opening sentence as it comes to its portentous close: 'the blockade of the harbor began'. Hutchinson, the governor of the Massachusetts Bay Colony, is leaving to carry back to England reports of the colonials' insubordination, so his departure bodes nothing but ill for the people of Massachusetts. They are described as mainly people who make their living from the sea, as sailors, as skilled craftsmen (shipwrights) or as traders. We are thus shown three distinct categories of employment and – by normal reckoning – at least two social classes, but Bancroft's technique here is to stress their common interests and to disregard any potential or actual social divisions among his Bostonians. All share a 'cheerful industry', whether they are engaged in the manual work of weighing anchor, unfurling sails, launching the vessels, or in the provision of capital that makes possible the laying down of ships' keels and the launching of the completed ships. Attention then focuses on the physical activities involved in shipbuilding and in sailing. The sentence that evokes the typical work of the shipwrights and sailors is stylized and rhythmic. Laying the keel, shaping the rib, strengthening the hull, rigging the masts, bending the sails, are of course activities that occur at differing stages of the life of the vessel, so that the sentence takes us on a journey in time through the progress of the work, and the verbs of action combine to give an impression of unceasing effort. But it is not just hard work that is being celebrated here, for the nouns are augmented by adjectives that stress the skill and the expertise of the industrious craftsmen and sailors of Boston: the merchantmen are 'fleet', the rib is shaped 'symetrically', the hull is 'graceful' and the mast is 'well-proportioned'. In this brief passage, then, the industry of the mechanics is more than reported, it is 'sung' in a way that is not dissimilar to that in which Walt Whitman had sung his songs of American occupations in the first edition of *Leaves of Grass* three years before this volume of Bancroft's *History of the United States* was published. The men of Boston, we must suppose, do not labour unwillingly or grudgingly; their 'cheerful industry' is such that the harbour resounds with their 'cheering voices' until they are forced into idleness.

Bancroft takes such trouble to make vivid the happy productivity of the port of Boston before 1 June 1774, because it is essential to his purpose here and throughout his *History* to establish a contrast between the values of the colonists and the values of the British monarchy and parliament. Together the latter have converted busy workshops into scenes of enforced inactivity. In Bancroft's prose the blockaded harbour is an image of idleness and want, with the moral guilt for these evils belonging, not to the American men who are workless, but to their British rulers who have robbed them of their legitimate occupations. The injustice is made more outrageous when we are told, with characteristic Bancroftian superlatives, that the Bostonians are 'the most skilful artisans' with the 'keenest eye' for beauty and speed. The merchants, too, are thrifty, and their commerce is prosperous. To complement the passage on the skills of the craftsmen we have a glowing image of 'costly wharfs . . . covered with the produce of the tropics and with English fabrics' before English tyranny empties them and turns the noisy, bustling, happy commercial activity to silence. British belligerence, given concrete form in the vessels of war that keep the merchantmen idly imprisoned in the port, converts riches into poverty, takes from skilled artisans the opportunity to use their talents, and – to cover the whole social spectrum implied in the passage – adds unnecessarily to the already severe labours of the fishermen of Marblehead by making them bring their fish to Boston by a circuitous land route. Typically, in Bancroft's prose the fishermen do nothing as banal, if worthy, as give away their fish. Instead they 'bestow' on the poor of Boston the 'offerings' wrung from the sea by their efforts. The formality of the language is Bancroft's tribute to the dignity and solemnity of this act of charity and this example of American solidarity.

Having established his contrast between British militarism and Bostonian industriousness, and having dramatized the conflict between cheerful vitality and sombre, potentially deadly tyranny, in the next paragraph Bancroft sets out to establish the idea that the colonies were united in their resistance to British repression. Though Massachusetts was destined to play a leading role in the drama, as all his readers already knew, Bancroft wants to show that the spirit of independence was not limited to the Bay State but was shared by colonies as distant and diverse as Pennsylvania and Virginia. Writing when sectional rivalry and animosity was embittering the national life, the historian plainly intends to show that, at the time of the heroic struggle for independence from England, North and South were united in their opposition to the common enemy. They were united, too, in their piety: the first of June being a Fast Day, in Puritan Massachusetts and episcopalian Virginia the churches are well attended. The message from Norfolk, Virginia, with the reminder that that town, like Boston, is a trading centre and depends for its life on sea-borne commerce, draws the links tighter with its expression of sympathy. The religious language in which that message is phrased, calling on the Almighty for support and referring to 'sacred ties', lets the reader know that the colonists were aware of the Providential nature of American history.

By presenting the message from Norfolk in direct speech, Bancroft gives immediacy to his story and continues the dramatization begun in the first paragraph when the desolation of the harbour was vividly evoked. His purpose, clearly, is to make the events and the men who took part in them come alive in his prose; the scholarship on which the narrative is founded is not allowed to come between the reader and emotional involvement in the story. Thus the Norfolk message is not assigned to a particular source but has to be taken as speaking for the whole town and, indeed, for all the people of the Old Dominion. Next we hear a particular voice – that of Thomas Jefferson, the hero whose name stands at the beginning of the paragraph and picks up the theme announced when George Washington's name was introduced. The great men of the revolutionary period are kept in sight throughout the history. Merely to note that Washington, already a figure of mythic stature in 1858, attended the Fast Day service on the momentous first of June is to remind us that his role in the coming events was to be decisive. Jefferson, only a young statesman in 1774, speaks tellingly on the main theme, which he defines as a struggle between despotism and the spirit of independence.

This passage is taken from the seventh volume (1858) of what was to become a ten-volume history of the United States. In his first volume, which appeared in 1834, Bancroft had introduced and developed the essential themes, one of whose climaxes lies in the story of the blockade of Boston harbour, for the story of Boston is the story of the New England Puritans and had a symbolic value for Bancroft. Before turning back to his account of the seventeenth-century forefathers of the revolutionary generation, we can best explore Bancroft's methods and his meanings by examining the significance he gives to the New England capital in the eighteenth century.

In the sixth volume of the *History*, which was published in 1854, Bancroft had dealt with a crisis that occurred between October and December 1768. In the chapter called 'The King and the British Parliament against the Town of Boston' (ch. 38), vocabulary, style and tone combine to make the issue clear-cut: 'The King set himself, and his Ministry, and Parliament, and all Great Britain, to subdue to his will one stubborn little town on the sterile coast of the Massachusetts Bay. The odds against it were fearful; but it showed a life inextinguishable, and had been chosen to keep guard over the liberties of mankind' (p. 240). The cause for which the town is fighting is dignified and the behaviour of its people made to appear unselfish, disinterested and altruistic when we are told that the liberties of mankind are at stake. But since the 'stubborn little town' has been 'chosen' by what can only be Divine Providence to defend the cause of human freedom and the progress that depends upon that freedom, the contest is not the unequal affair that Bancroft's emotive language at first seems to make it. Boston, representing all New England, is here God's chosen instrument, just as the Bay State had been in the Puritan histories, though when Bancroft details its virtues he selects political, not religious, institutions for praise. In elevated language appropriate to the theme, he tells us that 'the old world had not its parallel' in political equality. The source of all municipal authority was the Town Meeting, attended by 'the great body' of its male inhabitants over the age of twenty, where taxes were voted, affairs discussed and decided, and abstract political principles debated in freedom. Since all the children attended good public schools, this political participation was genuinely open to the people as a whole, for good education was the basis of the political awareness of the people. Summing up, Bancroft claims that the town of Boston came closer to being a 'pure democracy' than any municipality of comparable size ever had.

Bancroft's homage to the citizens of eighteenth-century Boston reveals more about his values than any abstract statement could. He praises them for their intellectual curiosity in the natural sciences as well as in political thought. To avoid any suggestion of anarchic radicalism on their part, they are credited with 'practical judgment' (p. 242). What might have become a realistic admission of their weaknesses is converted by Bancroft's prose into a strength, when the 'calculating shrewdness' and 'fondness for gain' of these Yankees are presented as expressions of their adventurous spirit. Hard bargains must be made at someone's expense, but even when he admits their 'avidity' Bancroft adds that it was 'tempered by a well-considered and continuing liberality'. In fact, Bancroft's Bostonians are his archetypal Americans, for 'nearly every man was struggling to make his own way in the world and his own fortune' (p. 242). But their personal ambition to get ahead is not allowed to make them selfish: 'individually and as a body they were public-spirited'.

In Bancroft's account of Boston society there are three main divisions – ministers, merchants and mechanics – but all are united in their bold speculation on political matters. The evolution of their theory of an independent representative commonwealth is attributed to their powers of analysis and is supposed to have happened spontaneously, without conscious intent. In one of the rhetorical flourishes that shows how close Bancroft's prose style in the *History* could come to the style of public oratory, he concludes: 'While the earth was still wrapt in gloom, they welcomed the daybreak of popular freedom, and like the young eagle in his upward soarings, looked undazzled into the beams of the morning' (p. 243). But if they are heroically turned towards the rising sun of liberty for the people, the Bostonians have been providentially chosen because of their Puritan past.

In 1834, the year in which the first volume of Bancroft's *History* was published, the descendants of the New England Puritans numbered four

million by Bancroft's calculation, so that one third of the white population of the United States could consider the seventeenth-century emigrants their 'parents' (p. 468). Discussing the origins of Puritanism in England, Bancroft identifies that faith with belief in democracy. Under Henry VIII, the issue was, we are told, 'popular sovereignty' (p. 462). The Reformation in England was one manifestation of 'the awakening intelligence of a great nation' that could not be terrified into submission and passivity by the brutal authority of the King. Under Elizabeth, the Puritan clergy became 'tribunes of the people' and their pulpits were used to encourage free discussion (p. 284), so that to them alone can go the credit for tending the flame of liberty. As Bancroft interprets the spirit of the Protestant Reformation, religious and political impulses are fused:

> The enfranchisement of the mind from religious despotism led directly to inquiries into the nature of civil government; and the doctrines of popular liberty, which sheltered their infancy in the wildernesses of the newly-discovered continent, within the short space of two centuries, have infused themselves into the life-blood of every rising state. (p. 267)

Here he is talking specifically of New England's role as the guardian and subsequently the disseminator of the spirit of liberty, but when (in a later volume) he traces the impulse that caused the Reformation back to Augustine, Bancroft defines that impulse as one of independence from all earthly rulers and obedience only to God. The 'truths that would renew humanity' are rescued from an age of collapse and decay by Augustine, and handed down by generations of monks who remain insulated from the corruption of society, until they help to free mankind from the caste system of the Middle Ages by encouraging the spirit of individuality (IV. 151–2). In contradistinction to Channing, Bancroft claims that Calvinism brought with it, as well as intelligence and severity of morals, 'love of freedom' (VI. 192). The Protestant Reformation as a whole was the work of men who 'reverenced and exercised the freedom of the soul', but John Calvin is Bancroft's hero because unlike Martin Luther he can be treated as a social revolutionary.

In making the seventeenth-century New England Puritans champions of popular liberty – political and religious – Bancroft is making them nineteenth-century democrats or, more specifically, Jacksonian Democrats. Those men and women who left England in the 1620s to settle in Massachusetts and subsequently in Connecticut for reasons of conscience did so to escape the intolerable authority of the established church in the home country, but they had no intention of allowing religious freedom in New England. Rather they were determined to establish the rule of the Godly, as *they* understood godliness. By their example they hoped, to be sure, to redeem the corrupted faith of England and of Europe, but tolerance in matters of such vital importance as religious faith was not to them a virtue. When in the first volume of the *History* he deals with the Puritan persecution of the Quakers in the 1650s, Bancroft does not condone their cruelty, for the Quakers expressed the human aspiration for 'a perfect emancipation from the long reign of bigotry and superstition' (p. 451) much more obviously than did their persecutors. Nevertheless, by stressing the suicidal impulse of the Quakers for martyrdom, Bancroft does his utmost to make his readers understand the Puritans' behaviour.

In any event, freedom is not the only American cause that Bancroft traces back to the Puritan 'parents'. Describing the arrival of about a hundred of Endicott's party at Salem in the Great Migration of 1628, he stresses the melancholy scene where nature was completely wild and untamed. He has already detailed the sufferings of the Pilgrims who landed on the inhospitable shores of Cape Cod in November 1620 and faced the first terrible winter at Plymouth, so his readers know what miseries the new arrivals will have to endure, but he adds a key phrase when he says that the 'spirit of enterprise' triumphed over any fears and doubts they may have felt. The 'life-giving spirit' of Puritanism brought with it, so Bancroft argues, as well as courage and intelligence, 'activity' and 'thrift' (I. 462). All these qualities are subsumed under that 'enterprise' exemplified by Endicott's followers.

Though enterprise is consistently associated with the Puritans in the *History*, it does not belong exclusively to them. The opening sentence of the first volume tells us that 'the enterprise of Columbus, the most memorable maritime enterprise in the history of the world, formed between Europe and America the communication which will never cease'. A few pages later, the achievement of Columbus is attributed to 'an enterprise that seemed more divine than human' (p. 8). The first of the great heroes of Bancroft's history is credited with a deep religious enthusiasm and a disinterested magnanimity, and the term 'enterprise' is thus established as the highest accolade.

The term is conspicuously absent in Bancroft's account of the exploits of the chivalrous Spaniards in America. They are credited with great daring and courage, but their motive is ferocious greed. De Soto's expedition to Florida in 1539 is no more than a 'roving expedition of gallant freebooters' in quest of fortune. As Ponce de Leon had been, de Soto and his men are made ferocious by their 'avarice', for even the Spanish religious zeal to convert savages is strangely mixed with 'the passions of avarice' (I. 30). The Spaniards' dream is of gold, of immense riches to be won by robbing and pillaging the indigenous people of the countries they invade; they have no respect for hard and systematic work of the kind that the Puritans were to devote themselves to. Before the Puritans, only Captain John Smith, the hero of the story of Virginia, shows the foresight to realize that the future of the colony lies in 'regular industry' rather than in gold, but we have to wait for the coming of the 'frugal and industrious race' (IV. 149) that peopled Massachusetts before we can observe the true working of the spirit of enterprise.

Returning to the theme of Columbus's great enterprise in the fourth volume of the *History*, Bancroft states that his motive was 'to bring together the ends of the earth, and join all nations in commerce and spiritual life' (p. 8). It was for this purpose that God gave Columbus 'the keys that unlock the barriers of the ocean'. In this last phrase Bancroft is adapting a quotation from a letter written by the explorer himself, but the sentiment is entirely in keeping with the tone in which Bancroft writes of the trade that will develop from the discovery of America. In his belief that commercial activity between nations and the voyaging it entailed not only encouraged friendship but was itself an expression of human brotherhood, Bancroft anticipated Walt Whitman's 'Passage to India' (1871). Assuming the most elevated of his styles, the historian explains the spirit of commerce:

> From the dawn of social being, there has appeared a tendency towards commerce and intercourse between the scattered inhabitants of the earth. That mankind have ever earnestly desired this connection, appears from their willing homage to the adventurers and to every people, who have greatly enlarged the boundaries of the world, as known to civilization. (p. 6)

By reviving the archaic sense of commerce as association or connections between people, Bancroft removes from it any suggestion of rivalry, competition or even profit-making. The prosaic and not necessarily ennobling business of buying and selling is here transformed into an abstract ideal. Appropriately, the passage on Columbus's motives leads to a statement of Bancroft's belief in the law of human progress in which he draws on Immanuel Kant's theory of history: mankind strives for perfection and never reaches the bounds of its capacity for improvement in Bancroft's version of Kant, but it is the 'reason of the whole' rather than the individual soul that makes progress (p. 8), and commerce is a means of its advancement. Here, as elsewhere in Bancroft's works, Channing's perfectionism is combined with a belief in 'the people' or 'the whole' that is much greater than Channing's.

Commerce, of course, means corporations and companies when on a scale that involves the crossing of oceans. In the progress of humanity from medieval oppression to modern freedom, even the privileged corporations are valuable because they are allies of 'the commercial and manufacturing interests' in their struggle against the militaristic aristocracy (II. 261). But Bancroft is against privilege in commerce as in social life, and argues that the true spirit of enterprise was inhibited by the sort of charter granted to John Cabot, with its monopolistic restriction of trade. Only when the principle of the joint-stock company was applied to navigation could that spirit triumph. Valuing trade as a vehicle of progress and regarding freedom as the ultimate good as Bancroft does, it is inevitable that he writes as the champion of free trade. Colonial resistance to British rule was, as he tells the story, occasioned by the British restriction of colonial trade in the Navigation Acts, and in rejecting the British mercantalist policy Bancroft's patriots are portrayed as idealists defending principles of freedom rather than businessmen protecting their profits. Writing of George Grenville's enthusiasm for the Navigation Acts as 'the palladium of his country's greatness', Bancroft steps in to 'correct' the opinion he has recorded and to explain that Britain's greatness as a maritime power was due to its pre-eminence in freedom.

'Freedom and enterprise' together bring temporary greatness to Holland (I. 216), another Protestant nation whose struggle against tyranny earns Bancroft's respect. But though the Dutch are on the side of progress against the retrograde forces of Catholic Spain, their example will have less consequence for the course of world history than that of Bancroft's America. At the end of the sixth volume of the *History*, the 'intrepid, hardy and industrious population' of America is seen moving irresistibly westward through the Allegheny Mountains towards the immensely distant Pacific Ocean. The spirit of that people is made vivid in words culled – as the footnote says – from letters written in February 1774, though no specific source is given. Confident that the progress of their nation in the next hundred years will exceed the utmost stretch of their imagination, the westward-moving people foresee as part of 'the glory of this New World' a vast growth of trade: 'A commerce will and must arise, independent of every thing external, and superior to any thing ever known in Europe, or of which a European can have an adequate idea' (p. 506).

According to Harvey Wish, in concentrating his interest on heroes, political action and the drama of public events, Bancroft neglects economic factors.[2] Certainly Bancroft shows remarkably little awareness of the complexity of economic forces at work within nations, but, as David Levin has pointed out,[3] Bancroft saw something of the connection between Protestantism and capitalism that Weber and Tawney were later to demonstrate. Like his contemporaries W. H. Prescott and J. L. Motley, Bancroft's treatment of that connection served to elevate the economic motive rather than lower the religious one, as Levin helpfully puts it. The 'elevation' is achieved, as we have seen, by subsuming economic and religious motives under the general category of the tendency towards freedom and progress. The process involves a reliance on general concepts or abstract ideas for which Bancroft was indebted to German philosophy, and it is time to turn to the influence of Germany on Bancroft and on his age.

*

Bancroft was born in 1800, into a family less eminent than William Ellery Channing's but one that had a long history in New England. The first Bancroft to come to Massachusetts had arrived in 1632, but most of his descendants had remained humble farmers. George Bancroft's father had worked his way up to become minister of the Old South Church at Worcester, Massachusetts, and had sent his son to Harvard College to train for the ministry. As an unusually promising young student, Bancroft was sent to Germany for advanced study in the classics and in theology after completing his undergraduate study in 1817 and spending one postgraduate year at Harvard. By this time it was already becoming *de rigueur* at Harvard to send outstanding young scholars to Germany; George Ticknor, who was to become the first Professor of Modern Languages, and Edward Everett, future President of Harvard, had preceded Bancroft. The choice of German rather than British universities was both a tribute to the high reputation of German scholarship and an indication of the new American resolve to escape from the traditional dominance of British cultural authority.

Before setting out for Göttingen, Bancroft was warned by his mentors at Harvard against dangerous tendencies towards unorthodoxy in German theological studies, but on his return he was still sufficiently orthodox to prepare himself for the Church and to preach in his father's pulpit. At Göttingen Bancroft heard Eichhorn lecture on theology and from him learned of the new 'scientific' biblical criticism that was bringing linguistic and historical skills to bear on scriptural texts. Moving on to Berlin, Bancroft became a friend of the great theologian Schleiermacher, whose ideas on the relationship between God and man anticipated Channing's and, according to Henry A. Pochmann, influenced the Unitarian.[4] But Bancroft did not only study theology in his German years. Arnold Heeren taught history at Göttingen and taught Bancroft the need for a philosophy of 'universal history', though he failed to impart to his American pupil an adequate understanding of the economic interpretation of history that he was pioneering.[5] In Berlin, Bancroft may have heard Hegel lecture and he would certainly have found the philosopher's ideas on the human aspiration for freedom congenial. Hegel's *Philosophy of History* expounds his theory of a universal history in which the past tells the story of the inevitable progress of the consciousness of freedom. The usefulness of such ideas to Bancroft is obvious, yet in his works he refers not to Hegel but (as we have seen) to Kant, or to Herder, Fichte and Heeren. The most impressive exposition of the belief in the natural (organic) progress of the people (the *Volk*) was to be found in Herder's four-volume *Ideas for the Philosophy of History* (1784–91). There can be no doubt of Bancroft's debt to this philosopher of history, since he wrote on Herder in the years after his return from Germany in 1822. A succession of essays and reviews dealing with German thought in the *North American Review* and the *American Quarterly Review* were Bancroft's contribution to the growth of American interest in German philosophical idealism, though they clearly had less impact than Thomas Carlyle's propagandizing essays on German culture.

Even more obviously than Channing's, Bancroft's career as a writer shows how easily American men of letters in the first half of the nineteenth century moved from one 'discipline', as we would now call it, to another. Before he wrote the first volume of his *History*, he had published a volume of verse (in 1823) and had established a reputation as a critic and scholar with his essays on German literature. Clearly sharing Channing's view that literature was nothing less than 'the expression of a nation's mind in writing', Bancroft recognized no academic boundary-line between philosophy and poetry; he wrote as confidently on Herder as he did on Mrs Felicia Hemans's verse.

Because of his interest in German idealism and his familiarity with Kant's writings, Bancroft is sometimes associated with the Transcendental movement in New England.[6] Without doubt, Bancroft anticipated Emerson in his interest in German Romantic philosophy, in his belief in the divine potentiality of human nature, and in his belief in moral laws that could be intuitively perceived. Indisputable, too, is Bancroft's personal sympathy with many of the American writers and thinkers who were to be – however variously – linked with the New Light philosophy in New England: George Ripley, James Freeman Clarke, John Sullivan Dwight and Margaret Fuller. However, Bancroft is to be distinguished from all of these by his active and continuous engagement in American political life after 1834, and particularly by his close involvement with Democratic Party politics.

According to Arthur Schlesinger, Jr, it was the writing of the *History* that released Bancroft's sympathies with Jacksonian democracy.[7] By 1836 Bancroft was an important figure in Massachusetts Democratic politics; in 1838 he was given a political appointment as Collector for Boston, losing that position when the Whig victory of 1840 ousted his party; in the 1844 Democratic convention he helped to swing the vote to Polk and for the next year and a half became Secretary of the Navy in Polk's presidential administration, before becoming acting Secretary of War in 1846 and subsequently Minister to England until 1849. Under President Andrew Johnson, Bancroft was appointed Minister to Prussia in 1866 as a reward for his services and remained in Berlin to 1874. Thus Bancroft was at the centre of Democratic Party politics in the expansionist years and intimately involved with the war with Mexico that was to disgust the more delicate conscience of the more genuinely Transcendentalist Henry David Thoreau (see below).

Bancroft's 'Spread-Eagleism' involved him in no hypocrisy because his belief in human progress was inseparable from his belief in 'the People': a faith that, with him, took a less complex form than it had in the theory of his German mentor, Arnold Heeren. In his 1835 oration 'The Office of the People', Bancroft clearly had Channing's famous sermon in mind when he wrote: 'If it be the duty of the individual to strive after perfection like the perfection of God, *how much more ought a nation to be the image of Deity*' (my emphasis). In speaking for the 'spirit in man' rather than in 'the privileged few', Bancroft is faithful to the sense of Channing's sermon as that was to be developed in the later lectures on self-culture, but in his assertion that the 'collective mind' rather than the cultivated individual is the best judge of taste, he was adapting the notion of culture to fit his populist leanings. When he goes on to say that 'individuals are but shadows . . . the race is immortal', Bancroft has moved very far indeed from Channing and from anything resembling Transcendentalism. The belief that 'the movement of the species is upward irresistibly' is combined in Bancroft's address with a readiness to accept the loss of the individual that would have seriously disturbed Emerson.

Almost twenty years later, in an oration entitled 'The Progress of Mankind' (1854), Bancroft again borrowed from Channing in formulating his central idea that man is capable of progress because he 'cannot separate himself from his inward experience and his yearning after the infinite', but here too the insistence that individuals, families, peoples, and the whole human race 'march in accord' tends to devalue the individual soul even though the tune all march to is the 'Divine will'.

Bancroft's contemporaries – in particular the perceptive Orestes Brownson – saw his *History* as a vote for Jackson. Schlesinger – a recent apologist for Jacksonian Democracy – takes Bancroft's theme to have been the struggle between capital and labour and sees the historian as the champion of the working man.[8] But, as we have seen, Bancroft's commitment to commercial development and the capitalist system on which his ideal 'free trade' depended led him to blur any incipient class divisions in his conception of the American *Volk*. Brownson, as we shall see, had a much clearer vision of the divisive effects of the expanding factory-based economy of the 1830s and 1840s.

Bancroft's reputation as the father of American historians rests on the immense amount of original research he undertook in the course of his busy life, his prodigious labour in archives, his indefatigable work with source materials. His immense popularity with the reading public (his first volume had reached its fifteenth edition by 1852) was due to his ability to infuse life into the historical characters he portrayed and to dramatize vividly the struggle that was his theme. That popularity derived, too, from the rhetorical style that is likely to alienate modern readers, for the declamatory mode was one with which American readers were familiar from their well-loved orators. One of those orators, Edward Everett, had pointed out to Bancroft that the spine of his first edition, with its American eagle surrounded by a circle of thirteen stars, carried a misquotation ('Westward the star of empire takes its way'), a corruption of Bishop Berkeley's line on the '*course* of empire'. Yet the fifteenth American edition of Volume I still bore the eagle on its cover and the misquotation with it, as did the first edition of Volume X in 1874. (English editions tactfully had neither eagle nor slogan on the spine.) The introduction to Volume I both celebrates American achievements – justice, inventiveness, prosperity shared by all classes – and projects a vision of the glorious American future as the course of progress continues: 'New states are forming in the wilderness; canals, intersecting our plains and crossing our highlands, open numerous channels to internal commerce; manufactures prosper along our watercourses; the use of steam on our rivers and rail-roads annihilates distance by the acceleration of speed.' Repeatedly, in the *History*, Bancroft contrasts the 'melancholy grandeur' of the unimproved American wilderness with the harmonious beauty of the scene when 'improved' by the abstract force of American 'enterprise'. Other writers – among them the historian Francis Parkman – were soon to express a clearer vision of the material particularities of that enterprise and industry, and a more ambivalent response to the progress of the civilization that depended on it.

Notes

1 The text of the extract is taken from Bancroft's *History of the United States from the Discovery of the American Continent*, 10 vols, Boston: Little, Brown, 1834–74, VII (1858). Parenthetic references to Bancroft's *History* throughout the chapter are also to this edition.

2 Harvey Wish, *The American Historian: A Social-Intellectual History of the Writing of the American Past*, New York: Oxford University Press, 1960, p. 86.

3 *David Levin, *History as Romantic Art: Bancroft, Prescott, Motley and Parkman*, Stanford University Press, 1959; repr. New York: Harcourt, Brace & World, 1963, p. 41.

4 Henry A. Pochmann, *German Culture in America 1600–1900*, Madison: University of Wisconsin Press, 1957, p. 110.

5 Wish, p. 74.

6 *Russell B. Nye, *George Bancroft, Brahmin Rebel*, New York: Knopf, 1944, p. 126.

7 Arthur M. Schlesinger, Jr, *The Age of Jackson*, Boston: Little, Brown, 1945, p. 161.

8 Schlesinger, p. 162.

5
Nathaniel Hawthorne (1804-64)

There is an admirable foundation for a philosophic romance, in the curious history of the early settlement of Mount Wollaston, or Merry Mount. In the slight sketch here attempted, the facts, recorded on the grave pages of our New England annalists, have wrought themselves, almost spontaneously, into a sort of allegory. The masques, mummeries, and festive customs, described in the text, are in accordance with the manners of the age. Authority on these points may be found in Strutt's Book of English Sports and Pastimes.

Bright were the days at Merry Mount, when the May-Pole was the banner-staff of that gay colony! They who reared it, should their banner be triumphant, were to pour sunshine over New England's rugged hills, and scatter flower-seeds throughout the soil. Jollity and gloom were contending for an empire. Midsummer eve had come, bringing deep verdure to the forest, and roses in her lap, of a more vivid hue than the tender buds of Spring. But May, or her mirthful spirit, dwelt all the year round at Merry Mount, sporting with the Summer months, and revelling with Autumn, and basking in the glow of Winter's fireside. Through a world of toil and care, she flitted with a dreamlike smile, and came hither to find a home among the lightsome hearts of Merry Mount.

Never had the May-Pole been so gaily decked as at sunset on midsummer eve. This venerated emblem was a pine tree, which had preserved the slender grace of youth, while it equalled the loftiest height of the old wood monarchs. From its top streamed a silken banner, colored like the rainbow. Down nearly to the ground, the pole was dressed with birchen boughs, and others of the liveliest green, and some with silvery leaves, fastened by ribbons that fluttered in fantastic knots of twenty different colors, but no sad ones. Garden flowers, and blossoms of the wilderness, laughed gladly forth amid the verdure, so fresh and dewy, that they must have grown by magic on that happy pine tree. Where this green and flowery splendor terminated, the shaft of the May-Pole was stained with the seven brilliant hues of the banner at its top. On the lowest green bough hung an abundant wreath of roses, some that had been gathered in the sunniest spots of the forest, and others, of still richer blush, which the colonists had reared from English seed. Oh, people of the Golden Age, the chief of your husbandry, was to raise flowers!

But what was the wild throng that stood hand in hand about the May-Pole? It could not be, that the Fauns and Nymphs, when driven from their classic groves and homes of ancient fable, had sought refuge, as all the persecuted did, in the fresh woods of the West. These were Gothic monsters, though perhaps of Grecian ancestry. On the shoulders of a comely youth, uprose the head and branching antlers of a stag; a second, human in all other points, had the grim visage of a wolf; a third, still with the trunk and limbs of a mortal man, showed the beard and horns of a venerable he-goat. There was the likeness of a bear erect, brute in all but his hind legs, which were adorned with pink silk stockings. And here again, almost as wondrous, stood a real bear of the dark forest, lending each of his fore paws to the grasp of a human hand, and as ready for the dance as any in that circle. His inferior nature rose half-way, to meet his companions as they stooped. Other faces wore the similitude of man or woman, but distorted or extravagant, with red noses pendulous before their mouths, which seemed of awful depth, and stretched from ear to ear in an eternal fit of laughter. Here might be seen the Salvage Man, well known in heraldry, hairy as a baboon, and girdled with green leaves. By his side, a nobler figure, but still a counterfeit, appeared an Indian hunter, with feathery crest and wampum belt. Many of this strange company wore fools-caps, and had little bells appended to their garments, tinkling with a silvery sound, responsive to the inaudible music of their gleesome spirits. Some youths and maidens were of soberer garb, yet well maintained their places in the irregular throng, by the expression of wild revelry upon their features. Such were the colonists of Merry Mount, as they stood in the broad smile of sunset, round their venerated May-Pole.

Had a wanderer, bewildered in the melancholy forest, heard their mirth, and stolen a half-affrighted glance, he might have fancied them the crew of Comus, some already transformed to brutes, some midway between man and beast, and the others rioting in the flow of tipsey jollity that foreran the change. But a band of Puritans, who watched the scene, invisible themselves, compared the masques to those devils and ruined souls, with whom their superstition peopled the black wilderness.

Within the ring of monsters, appeared the two airiest forms, that had ever trodden on any more solid footing than a purple and golden cloud. One was a youth, in glistening apparel with a scarf of the rainbow pattern crosswise on his breast. His right hand held a gilded staff, the ensign of high dignity among the revellers, and his left grasped the slender fingers of a fair maiden, not less gaily decorated than himself. Bright roses glowed in contrast with the dark and glossy curls of each, and were scattered round their feet, or had sprung up spontaneously there. Behind this lightsome couple, so close to the May-Pole that its boughs shaded his jovial face, stood the figure of an English priest, canonically dressed, yet decked with flowers, in heathen fashion, and wearing a chaplet of the native vine leaves. By the riot of his rolling eye, and the pagan decorations of his holy garb, he seemed the wildest monster there, and the very Comus of the crew.

'The May-Pole of Merry Mount', *The Token and Atlantic Souvenir* (1836) and *Twice-told Tales* (1837, 1842)[1]

* * *

Having alerted his readers to the allegorical significance of his tale in his introductory note, Hawthorne sets two abstractions – jollity and gloom – in opposition to each other, telling us that these forces or principles were contending for rule in New England when the colony of Merry Mount existed. In metaphoric terms, sunshine and flower-seeds represent jollity, while gloom is embodied in the rugged hills of New England. The emblem of the 'mirthful spirit' of May is, of course, the maypole of the gay Merry Mounters. For the opposing emblem we have to wait until the Puritans appear. Then we learn that they danced only round the whipping-post, for that was their totem. In the first part of the tale, attention is focused on the merriment of the colonists at Mount Wollaston. In their devotion to the spirit of May they are linked with the fertility of the natural world, represented by the green of the forest and the midsummer roses. Yet the positive associations of natural growth and joy are qualified by a false, or forced, note: the mirthful spirit of May 'dwelt' all the year round at Merry Mount, we are told. The pun on the word 'dwelt' makes Hawthorne's point succinctly and unobtrusively. For May to dwell (live) with its devotees is natural, but for May to remain or linger on Mount Wollaston, prolonging its stay and its spirit through summer, autumn and even winter, is unnatural, even perverse. Mirth that goes on sporting, revelling through the seasons until it basks before the warmth of winter fires, is unseasonable mirth and wilful in its disregard of change.

In the second paragraph we focus on the maypole itself. We see it on midsummer eve, long after any May Day celebrations, and we notice that the emblematic tree has the characteristics of youth and age: the slender grace of the one and the lofty height of the other. It is, of course, fitting that the tree should be decorated only with gay colours and with both wild and cultivated flowers, but the metaphor that makes the flowers 'laugh' amid the green of the pine tree, though it here seems an apt and decorative literary phrase, will become disturbing when the implications of the spirit of mirth are developed. Similarly, the pine tree is, like its devotees, 'happy'. The wild roses that hang from the lowest bough of the pine bring with them a suggestion of the sunshine in which they grew, while the cultivated roses are associated with the Old England that, before the rule of the Puritans, was itself merry. At the end of the paragraph, the Merry Mount colonists are, it seems, given their most positive association: they are linked through their cultivation of flowers with the innocent, Edenic condition of man before the Fall brought the curse of hard toil on him. To the Puritans, the Original Sin that led to the expulsion from Eden had so corrupted human nature that, in post-lapsarian man, the natural was synonymous with the sinful; unless redeemed by God's grace, man was doomed to eternal damnation. If the Merry Mount people are indeed living in the Golden Age, before the Fall of Man, they are 'innocent' and may well venerate an emblem of the natural order, but the hint of unnaturalness in the opening paragraph is developed in the words 'fantastic' and 'grown by magic' in the paragraph that follows. The implication – though slight – that there might be something forced, or even sinister, in the ornamentation of the pine tree picks up a suggestion of unreality that lurked among the positive associations at the end of the first paragraph. The spirit of May, we were told, 'flitted with a dreamlike smile' through the world of toil and care in order to reach Merry Mount. If the world of toil and care is the real world, then the spirit of May, when extended through the year, is 'dreamlike' in its merriment. Further, the worship of that spirit is possible only to those who live in a world of fantasy and whose actions are fantastic.

When we look closely at the people of the Mount Wollaston community, we see that they are 'wild' in the sense that they belong to the wilderness – to the untamed, uncivilized world beyond the extent of moral laws. Associating the masquers with the fauns and nymphs of classical legend, driven out of Europe by the spread of Christianity, Hawthorne wittily links them with all exiles from Europe who sought freedom in the New World, including the Puritans. But the classical association is quickly displaced by that of the Gothic, for the costumes worn by the masquers are grotesque, even monstrous. The mixture of human and animal forms indicates that the Merry Mounters are intimate with nature in a way that the Puritans are not, but the union of man and beast is not harmonious: it works to the detriment of the human, making it necessary for the man to 'stoop' in order to meet the bear. The colonists are pictured in sunlight, but even here the language used has insidious connotations for the 'broad smile' of the sunlight links with the mouths 'stretched from ear to ear in an eternal fit of laughter'. The vocabulary of merriment used to convey the spirit of Merry Mount has already extended from gaiety and jollity to mirth, sport, revelry, in the first paragraph. Now the 'gleesome spirits' of the masqueraders are linked with the tinkling bells of the fool's-caps, with the result that even the laughter of the flowers and the smile of the sun are implicated in the suggestion of fatuity. The costumes of the Merry Mounters are as fantastic as the ornaments of the maypole. The shapes that appear in the masque are 'counterfeit', not real, but mere figments of the imagination. They belong, with the 'dreamlike' smile of May, to the world of illusion.

At this point in the tale the Puritans enter the narrative, though only the outer scene, for they are not yet visible to the masquers. With them they bring moral judgement on the equivocally natural world of Merry Mount, for to the Puritan imagination the masques are diabolic, while the woods are the home of devils. The Puritan sees the wilderness as 'black', the Devil's colour, for there is no place in his system of belief for the green – innocent – natural world. Since the Fall, any identification of the natural with the good must, in the Puritan view, be illusory, part of a fantasy. The narrator of the tale distances himself from the Puritans, describing their belief in devils as itself a superstition, but by imagining a bewildered wanderer's feelings in the 'melancholy' forest the narrator has, for the moment, adopted the Puritan view. The identification of the Merry Mounters with Comus's wild rabble is offered as no more than a possible 'fancy' of a lost and puzzled traveller – the narrator does not lend his authority to the idea – but the mere suggestion of a link with the corrupting and debased figure created in Milton's *Comus; A Masque* is enough to counter the earlier connotations of natural innocence at Merry Mount. Milton's Comus is the enemy of chastity; his spell has the power to bestialize human beings.

The narrator's judgements and evaluations in this tale are elusive. Associations that at first appear positive are transformed into their opposites by the magic of the prose. The voice that speaks to the reader is, we might say, that of a weaver of powerful spells who seems to let us wander, bewildered, in a forest of suggestions. But a pattern begins to emerge clearly when the insinuations of the early paragraphs harden into explicit moral judgements. The pagan dress and the riotous eye of the priest who officiates at the heathen marriage ceremony associate him with Comus, while his advice to the young lovers is patently frivolous. The narrator comments, describing the continual carnival of Merry Mount as one of 'jest and delusion, trick and fantasy'. When the young woman about to be married startles her lover with a look that is 'pensive' in spite of all the jollity, the moral is drawn clearly: 'No sooner had their hearts glowed with real passion, than they were sensible of something vague and unsubstantial in their former pleasures, and felt a dreary presentiment of inevitable change.' To love truly, the narrator adds, is to subject oneself to 'earth's doom of care, and sorrow, and troubled joy' and to feel that Merry Mount is no real home. The bland vocabulary of pleasure is now replaced by that of complex emotion. From jollity and merriment we have moved to the oxymoron 'troubled joy'.

Turning from his tableau to provide some historical information about the Mount Wollaston colony, the narrator explains that these refugees from Puritan austerity preserved the ancient ceremonies and customs of Old England. From Hawthorne's account of them, these rites were plainly pagan. His reading in Joseph Strutt's *The Sports and Pastimes of the People of England*, mentioned in the introductory note, had taught Hawthorne that the maypole ceremonies had been occasions for sexual licence,[2] but though he borrowed details of the decoration of the sacred tree from Strutt's book, he left it to his readers to draw their own conclusions about the moral effects of an obviously phallic cult. The sexual freedom of Merry Mount receives no explicit comment, but the deliberate frivolity of the elders of the colony does. Any dignity that might accrue to their natural religion is undermined by the verdict pronounced on their wilful devotion to a counterfeit happiness. The aged members of the colony 'play the fool' instead of acquiring wisdom.

The Puritans, when we meet them, are stern and grim. Their cult of the whipping-post plainly expresses their repression of all natural impulses, including the sexual. With their piety goes cruelty and aggressiveness; they carry armour with them and use it in their wars of extermination against the Indian. These 'men of iron' reject the natural life. Endicott, the Puritan of Puritans, seems made of iron himself and 'assaults' the maypole with his sword, destroying its leaves and rosebuds. Representatives of the 'gloom' that was opposed to 'jollity' in the first paragraph of the tale, the Puritans reject the fanciful as well as the natural, and personify the 'sternest cares of life'. The triumph of the Puritans in the conflict with the people of Merry Mount meant, the narrator has told us, the banishment of sunshine and flowers from New England, and the reign of hard toil in a land of 'clouded visages', sermons and psalms.

Until the entrance of Endicott on the scene, the narrative interest of the tale has been concentrated in the evaluation of clusters of opposed ideas. Instead of dramatic action, we have witnessed the interaction of sets of values, so that the story has been static or essayistic. With the destruction of the maypole, the oft-told tale of Puritan victory has been told again, and the interest must lie in the fate of the Lord and Lady of the May, the young lovers who have been cast down from the gaiety of their pagan marriage ceremony. Though Endicott orders that the young man's love-knot be severed, the man of iron is sufficiently softened by the sight of true love to spare further punishment. What is more, he actually garlands the lovers with their emblematic roses. Their future must lie in the Puritan fold, for their wild home has been made desolate, yet though they are to be subject to the forces of 'gloom', the narrator concludes his tale with a moral judgement that apparently commits him to the Puritan side in the conflict of values. His earlier apparent neutrality seems superseded when he tells us that the lovers 'never wasted one regretful thought on the vanities of Merry Mount' as they 'went heavenward, supporting each other along the difficult path which it was their lot to tread'. We cannot really suppose that the narrator has aligned himself with the Puritans, for his earlier images of their severity and grimness remain with us, but we must recognize that the deceptively simple antithesis with which the story started has now been replaced by the concept of 'troubled joy' and by the association of 'real passion' with the clouded, thoughtful brow of the Puritan rather than the broad, sunshiny smiles of the masquers of Merry Mount.

'The May-Pole of Merry Mount' is a relatively early Hawthorne story – it was published first in *The Token*, in 1836, and then included in the 1837 collection *Twice-told Tales* – yet it introduces many of the themes that were to interest Hawthorne throughout his writing career. The contrast between the wild freedom of the forest and the repressive code of Puritan law plays a crucial part in *The Scarlet Letter* (1850). The theory that the innocence of the natural man, though it gives him the youthful spontaneity of the animal, may be incompatible with the full development of his human nature, is a central concern of *The Marble Faun* (1860). Almost all Hawthorne's fictions deal to some extent with the relationship of fancy or imagination, and reality, and many of them use the Puritans to stand for the reality principle. Hawthorne's perennial theme is the necessity, and the sadness, of human love. Though his later versions of the theme are more extended in their treatment, involving fictional characters of far greater complexity than the Lord and Lady of the May, Hawthorne's early tale illuminates his major novels.

Between 1830 and 1837 he published nine tales based on the history of his region in the seventeenth century,[3] though by the latter year he seems to have felt that his art should relate more obviously to the contemporary world. Writing to Henry Wadsworth Longfellow in that year, Hawthorne complained of his lack of literary materials. 'I have seen so little of the world', he wrote, 'that I have nothing but thin air to concoct my stories of, and it is not easy to give a lifelike semblance to such shadowy stuff.' This damaging association of his own imaginative world with thin air and shadows, and a sense of isolation from the 'real world', was not confined to the letter to Longfellow. As we shall see, it recurs in many of Hawthorne's explicit comments on his art and in many of his fictional accounts of the artist. In 'The May-Pole of Merry Mount' the narrator clearly associated the fantasy world of Mount Wollaston with the realm of art, for he pointed out that many of the refugees from the severity of Puritan rule in England were entertainers, including minstrels and actors. In 'The Custom House' section of *The Scarlet Letter*, Hawthorne imagines the horror his Puritan ancestors would have felt had they known that their family tree would one day produce an 'idler', a mere 'writer of story books'. To such men, there was little to choose between being a story-writer and being a fiddler, Hawthorne admits, but he also adds that, however much they would have despised him, strong traits of their nature have intertwined themselves with his own. In his sometimes disparaging comments on his own art, it is as if Hawthorne temporarily allowed the Puritan in himself to speak, making use of that voice to carry on a debate within the self.

If the Puritans rejected the arts and destroyed the realms of fancy and dream so closely associated with the imagination, how, then, could the young lovers of 'The May-Pole' find a more fitting home with them than with the masquers? To love truly is to subject oneself to care and sorrow, we were told, but – as another tale on a related theme makes clear – care and sorrow without love give the bleakest of all possible worlds. In 'The Canterbury Pilgrims' (1833), the Shakers replace the Puritans as the representatives of a piety that rejects sexual love. The young lovers of this tale are not placed between the forces of mirth and gloom, but they must choose between the safety of the cold, loveless Shaker community and the dangers of the world outside it. They choose the world where human love includes sexuality, and in doing so they choose the possibility of passion and the likelihood of suffering. All the evidence they have warns them that even their love may not survive the frustrations of life in the world of toil and sadness, yet only there can the love they feel flourish. As in 'The May-Pole of Merry Mount', the only soil where true passion can grow is that of the 'real' world of human anguish. 'The Canterbury Pilgrims' was not published with *Twice-told Tales*, but another tale with a related theme, 'The Shaker Bridal' (1838), was collected in the second and enlarged edition of those tales in 1842. In it we are present at another moment of choice, and here the decision must be made by former lovers who have long since entered a Shaker community, largely because the man has been so disappointed with life that he has lost all hope and all capacity to love. If they accept the offer made to them and take over the leadership of the Shaker settlement at Goshen, Adam and Martha, like all eminent Shakers, will have 'overcome their natural sympathy with human frailties and affections', for the Shakers permit no 'closer tie than the cold fraternal one of the sect'. Adam, whose severe aspect and corpse-like rigidity is stressed throughout the sketch, is ready to sacrifice any possibility of renewed love with Martha, but she still has the capacity to feel, for she has 'a woman's heart' that is appalled at his cold resolution. The title of the sketch is heavily ironic, for Martha's bridegroom is death, while the piety and moral determination of the Shaker sect is consistently associated with the coldness of the tomb.

In both sketches, the icy coldness of the Shakers is attributed to their renunciation of the joys as well as the sorrows of earthly life. They are Merry Mounters in reverse, but no more admirable or attractive. Endicott, the iron Puritan of Puritans, seems almost warm-hearted in comparison to the Shakers, yet – as some of Hawthorne's best tales illustrate – the Puritan sense of sin could be totally destructive of human love. Young Goodman Brown, in the tale that takes his name as its title, becomes so obsessed with the sin he senses all around him, even in the Puritan village of Salem, that he wanders in the dark forest of his dreams until, aided by the diabolical guide his fancy offers him, he discovers the forms of all the virtuous members of the village community participating in a witches' Sabbath. Taught by the Devil that all whom he had thought holy were implicated in the dark mysteries of sin, Young Goodman Brown sees his wife Faith at the evil altar and thus loses his 'Faith' and his love at once. Throughout the description of Brown's forest journey, the language of the tale leaves the status of the events in doubt. Everything 'seems' or 'appears' to the young man, nothing unequivocally *is*. Though the status of the figures that haunt the forest is in doubt, the effect of his vision on the young man is not. From the night of his dream he becomes 'a stern, a sad, a darkly meditative, a distrustful, if not a desperate man' whose love for his wife has turned to distrust and even repugnance. This young Puritan has espoused the cause of 'gloom', the word on which his story ends.

'Young Goodman Brown' was first published in the *New-England Magazine* in 1835, though it was not included in *Twice-told Tales* but had to wait until *Mosses from an Old Manse* (1846) to take its place in a collection of Hawthorne's works. A tale with a closely related theme that did find its way into the earlier collection was 'The Minister's Black Veil', subtitled by Hawthorne 'A Parable'. The veil of black crêpe with which the Reverend Hooper covers his eyes until his dying day is an emblem, the narrator tells us, that probably did not interfere with his sight 'farther than to give a darkened aspect to all living and inanimate things'. When challenged by Elizabeth, his betrothed, Hooper will only say that the veil is a 'type and a symbol'; he refuses to be specific about what the veil signifies, though the first sermon he preached after adopting the veil was on the secret sin that would like to hide itself from God. The effect of that sermon was to make his congregation feel guilty, and the effect of his veil is to make him feared or hated. His presence at a marriage ceremony makes it funereal, though at funerals his appearance is fitting enough. Typically, in this tale Hawthorne is concerned with the effect of the emblem that 'shadows forth horrors' and particularly with the effect on the woman who loves Hooper. In separating the minister from the world, as he says it must, the veil cuts him off from woman's love, for he refuses to allow Elizabeth to see his face. Though she remains devoted to him till his death, we are told that he had no 'natural connections' when he came to die, for the veil had isolated him from the human race. In the death-bed scene, the irony that has accompanied every reference to the veil achieves a new prominence: though Hooper's donning of the veil has been justified, in his terms, by the belief that 'any mortal' has secret sin enough to make the symbolic gesture appropriate, when about to die he speaks of the Black Veil he sees on every human face. Sense of one's own sin, for this minister as for Goodman Brown, means obsession with the imagined pollution of the entire race.

One further tale develops the theme in a direction that makes it central in Hawthorne's works. In 'The Man of Adamant' (1837), Richard Digby's intolerable awareness of human sinfulness has as its corollary a heightened form of the Puritans' sense that salvation is possible only for the chosen few: Digby believes that he alone is to be saved. Physically removing himself from 'communion' with his fellow men out of fear of moral contagion, he retires to a cave in the forest. But the cave is a 'tomb-like den' and Digby's severance of human ties is a choice of death rather than love. The emblematic nature of the cave is not left in doubt, for just as its moisture petrifies the leaves, foliage and shrubs within it, Digby suffers from a disease that is likely to 'change his fleshly heart to stone'. To complete the picture of the moral bigot, we see that he rejects the vision of a woman 'angelic' in her pity and love for him, fending it off with a reading of the Bible that converts its message into vengeance instead of mercy. As the allegory takes its course, Digby's moral and emotional petrification is signified, on the literal level, by the conversion of flesh to stone; he becomes a 'man of adamant'. In the concluding moral, Digby's horribly lonely sepulchre is said to be inimical not only to human but also to 'celestial' sympathies. To break communion with one's fellow men is to turn one's higher faculties to stone: 'Friendship, and Love, and Piety' are equally petrified in the isolated human heart. Digby, like the Reverend Hooper, lacks charity. In both cases, the lack of charity blinds the 'pious' man to the true meaning of Christ.

In 'The Canterbury Pilgrims', the young man leaving the Shakers to live and to love in the world outside the commune explains that Father Job, the Shaker elder, has little charity for what he calls the 'iniquities of the flesh' and is therefore an awe-inspiring man. In Hawthorne's fictions, *caritas* and *eros* seldom if ever exist apart. Those who react with horror to human sexuality, or who are obsessed with guilt at their own sexual impulses, are invariably lacking in charity, and are often capable of great cruelty, even to the extent of having a deadly effect on those who can and do love. But if Hawthorne's positives are as uncontentious as love and human warmth, and if his ideal is the 'mutual bond' of the domestic fire, whose warmth and beauty he celebrates with great tact and self-deprecatory wit in 'Fire-Worship' (1843), they do not make him a sentimentalist, nor does it mean that he has nothing to offer as a thinker. The avowedly unheroic use to which Hawthorne puts the Promethean gift draws its psychological significance from the most sustained theme in all his writings: that of the difficulty with which human warmth is created and preserved in a world where all life leads to death. The corollary of this theme is a haunting sense of the ease with which the reflective man or the artist feels cut off from humanity: incapable of sharing love and experiencing its warmth.

'The Christmas Banquet' (1844) was included in *Mosses from an Old Manse* with a note describing it as one of an unpublished series of 'Allegories of the Heart'. This allegory tells of Gervayse Hastings, whose outward life has been perfectly successful, and whose family life has been blessed with a beautiful and affectionate wife and promising children. Yet Hastings is the most wretched of mortals because he is unable to respond to love. His 'cold abstraction' chills all who come into contact with him. In a final *cri de cœur*, Hastings explains his own misery as 'a chillness – a want of earnestness – a feeling as if what should be my heart were a thing of vapor – a haunting perception of unreality!' Since he cannot feel, he cannot possess either joy or grief, and all the human beings who should have been taken into his heart have been mere shadows to him. Hastings is no Puritan or Shaker bigot whose isolation results from a sense of human sinfulness. He can offer no motive for his coldness, nor any cause for it. In this he is like the title character in 'Wakefield' (1835), who for no clear reason casts himself out of the human race by simply leaving his wife and his home after ten years of placid marriage, and plays the voyeur on his wife's loneliness for twenty further years. Though we are told that Wakefield retained his original share of human sympathies through his long, self-imposed exile and was still involved in human interests, the sketch creates a haunting sense of his lasting loneliness in his role of 'Outcast of the Universe'. That Hawthorne was fascinated by the 'lonesome heart' of the man who can feel nothing acutely is clear from 'The Old Apple-Dealer' (1843), a sketch of an old man whose whole aspect suggests 'a moral frost'. No dark secret is revealed in this ruminative essay on a figure observed only from the outside, but the sketch is a study in 'the soundless depths of the human soul'.

The 'student of human life' who examines the Old Apple Dealer's soul looks on him, he tells us, with 'a stranger's eye'. The voice that speaks in a very early sketch, 'Sights from a Steeple' (1831), speaks from a great height above the tumult of human life and states that 'the most desirable mode of existence might be that of a spiritualized Paul Pry, hovering invisible round man and woman, witnessing their deeds, searching into their hearts, borrowing brightness from their felicity, and shade from their sorrow, and retaining no emotion peculiar to himself'. In this sketch the mood of the artist-voyeur is exultant, but in the later 'Fragments from the Journal of a Solitary Man' (1837), the artist Oberon feels that he has merely skimmed the surface of life, for the meditative man who devotes his talents to writing takes no part in 'the serious business of life'. Oberon feels doomed to eternal loneliness and feels his life to have been a mere shadow because he has not married. Wisdom, he now feels, consists in following the common path and accepting domestic responsibilities. In a nightmare vision he sees himself wandering through the busy, life-filled Broadway but not belonging to it; to the horror of the crowd, he is walking there in his shroud. Another Oberon sketch, 'The Devil in Manuscript' (1835), expresses the nausea of the writer who feels that his tales have displaced the real world for him, that his writing has been a dream-activity, and that the shadowy world he has created in his fictions has led him into a terrible solitude.

In the letter to Longfellow written in 1837, Hawthorne wrote 'for the last ten years I have not lived, but only dreamed about living'. The ten years were those after Hawthorne had left Bowdoin College, in 1825, and during which he had lived at home in Salem, with no occupation except that of writing. To Longfellow he wrote that he felt as if he had been carried apart from the main current of life and that he felt it impossible to get back again. In the preface to *The Snow-Image* (1851), which took the form of a letter addressed to his friend Horatio Bridge, Hawthorne used strikingly similar phrases to refer to his years of seclusion before *Twice-told Tales* brought him some fame in 1837: 'I sat down by the wayside of life, like a man under enchantment', Hawthorne wrote, adding that Bridge's confidence in his work had alone enabled him to break out of 'the entangling depths of my obscurity'. In the same year (1851) the preface to a new edition of *Twice-told Tales* referred to the 'pale tint' of these literary flowers whose blossoming had taken place in 'too retired a shade'. With typical self-deprecation, Hawthorne accuses his fictions of lack of passion and admits that 'even in what purports to be pictures of actual life, we have allegory, not always so warmly dressed in its habiliments of flesh and blood, as to be taken into the reader's mind without a shiver'. In conceding that allegory was 'colder' than realistic fiction, Hawthorne was consistent with those statements in which he expressed admiration for the realistic novel and seemed to prefer it to his own 'romances'. We know, for example, that he considered Anthony Trollope's novels solid and substantial in a way that his own were not and that he pronounced their earthiness exactly to his taste. Even in the 'Custom-House' section of *The Scarlet Letter*, Hawthorne accuses himself of folly in choosing to 'create the semblance of a world out of airy matter' when he could have used his thought and imagination to discover the deeper significance of the daily life that seemed so dull and commonplace to him. Yet in the same place he states emphatically that the atmosphere of the Custom-House was so inimical to his imagination that he could create nothing while he actually worked there. The ideal setting for creative imagination, he argues, is the family parlour, when, late at night, it is deserted by all but the writer. The mixture of firelight (emblem of domestic warmth) and moonlight (emblem of the fancy) makes this 'a neutral territory, somewhere between the real world and fairy-land, where the Actual and the Imaginary may meet, and each imbue itself with the nature of the other'. Hawthorne's fictional artists seldom manage to combine the warmer light of the domestic fire with the 'cold spirituality of the moonbeams'.

Hawthorne's most complex study of the connection between artistic detachment and emotional coldness is Miles Coverdale, the narrator of *The Blithedale Romance* (1852). Coverdale once had sufficient moral enthusiasm to commit himself to joining the idealistic, experimental community at Blithedale, but when he tells his tale he is already a 'frosty bachelor' and the perfectionist scheme that caused him to quit his bachelor fireside to share in its Paradisiac vision is long since exploded. When he joined the commune, Coverdale hoped that its influence would inspire him to create true, strong and natural poetry, but he is never able to acknowledge the impulses of his own heart sufficiently to produce inspired art. Obviously attracted to the beautiful Zenobia, this unreliable narrator never admits the force of his interest in her and deliberately misleads his readers by confessing to a love for the less sexually attractive Priscilla. Coverdale is drawn to Zenobia because to him it is clear that she is a sexually experienced woman: her presence makes the idyllic experiment of Blithedale seem like 'an illusion, a masquerade, a pastoral, a counterfeit Arcadia'. Blithedale, then, in Coverdale's account of it, has some features in common with Merry Mount, though the Blithedalers like to think that they have taken up the 'high enterprise' of the Pilgrims and are going on to loftier ideals than their forefathers dreamed of. Yet even while they are building their homes, Coverdale remarks that the soil beneath their feet was 'fathom deep with the dust of deluded generations' on whose virginal innocence the world had imposed experience. His thoughts turn half-humorously, but portentously as it turns out, to the need for a cemetery in Arcadia, for Coverdale is always aware of the cold climate of this New England idyll.

The artist who lacks emotional conviction is the artist who observes the lives of others from his steeple. Coverdale admits to a 'cold tendency, between instinct and intellect' that made him 'pry with a speculative interest into people's passions and impulses' and he is aware that his heart has lost much of its humanity as a result. But he cannot resist the impulse to pry, and he even justifies it to himself, claiming a generous sympathy with those in whose lives he lives vicariously and whose secrets he endeavours to learn. Zenobia, the passionate and proud woman, is destroyed by Hollingsworth, the bigoted reformer, rather than by Coverdale the minor or failed poet, but there can be no doubt that Coverdale fails Zenobia through his faint-heartedness. Coverdale was no Transcendentalist – in fact he describes himself as a realist; Hawthorne, as he wrote in his introduction to 'Rappaccini's Daughter', published in the *Democratic Review* in 1844, occupied the middle ground between the Transcendentalists and the general public. In 'The Old Manse' introduction to *Mosses from an Old Manse* (1846) he wrote with great respect of Emerson as an original thinker, and with affection of Thoreau and Ellery Channing the poet; yet in this sketch he is severe in his judgement of the lunatic fringe of Transcendentalism – the wild reformers who seem to him stupid. In 'The Old Manse', as in 'Fire Worship', the positive is the 'hearth of a household fire'; against that sacred symbol he sets a comic, but typical, allusion to Eden in the rain. In *Blithedale* the idea recurs in the coldness of a New England Arcadia in early spring. In both, idealistic fancy seems like fantasy when it is set in a bleak natural environment.

If Coverdale is a portrait of the artist with a cold heart, in the same romance Hollingsworth is a portrait of the nineteenth-century man of iron: the inheritor of the bigotry of Puritan idealism. He is, appropriately, described as a polar bear on his first appearance at Blithedale, so cold is he within and without. To Coverdale, Hollingsworth seems not altogether human, because he has given himself up to a dominant purpose. Ironically, that purpose is philanthropic, but – as Coverdale forcefully puts it – a man who is prepared to sacrifice individual human beings to an overriding scheme or purpose, even if that is nominally a philanthropic programme, is a 'steel engine of the Devil's contrivance'. Not only does Hollingsworth have 'iron features', he has a brow on which a frown forms an 'adamantine wrinkle'. Since his great scheme is to build a reform-house for criminals, and since this project proceeds from his dark vision of human depravity, he is fittingly associated, through Coverdale's imagery, with Hawthorne's 'Man of Adamant' as well as with his Reverend Hooper. He is also linked with Roderick Elliston, the man who, in one of Hawthorne's 'Allegories of the Heart', is gnawed by 'Egotism; or the Bosom-Serpent'; but Hollingsworth does not realize, as Elliston did, that he has become a prey to the monster of his own creation. Nor is his bosom-serpent banished by a woman's love, for he exploits all who love him. Hollingsworth, as a character in a romance, is more individualized than either Elliston in the allegorical sketch referred to or Ethan Brand in the tale named after him, yet the moral pattern informing his behaviour is exactly that which determines the form of the two related allegorical sketches. The difference is that, in *The Blithedale Romance*, Hawthorne has given the abstract principle of egotism a concrete manifestation in terms relevant to the cultural situation of the 1840s. Reformist zeal was a reality in Hawthorne's New England. He understood it – typically – by exploring its relation to the Puritan past.

In *The House of the Seven Gables* (1851), Hawthorne had already to some extent tackled contemporary issues in his art, though in his preface he had argued that as a romancer he was free from the obligation to be faithful to the probable and ordinary course of experience. There was, obviously, enough of 'the Marvellous' in this romance to justify Hawthorne's apologia in his preface, but in the character of Holgrave, the young man who at the age of twenty-two has already changed jobs half a dozen times and is as unsettled in his convictions as in his career, we are dealing with a plausible representative of the culture of 'expansionist' America. Holgrave is a Northern radical; to him the past is the corpse of an old giant that must be thrust out of the way if the present generation is to be able to live. Rejecting the rule of dead generations in the system of laws and the inheritance of property, he wants to start life anew, for he has the spirit of hope. To Holgrave, all ancient houses – both the buildings and the families – inhibit the possibilities of life for the new generation. All moss-covered buildings represent to him the great burden of the past on all new life, for they are emblematic of time-honoured institutions, but he has particular reason to regard the Pyncheon house as a symbol of a corrupt past, since it was cursed by his ancestor whose life was sacrificed to the greed of a Pyncheon.

The founding father of the House of Pyncheon was an iron-hearted Puritan whose family mansion was built on corruption and enshrined class distinction. The nineteenth-century descendants of the Puritan line are Judge Jaffrey, the inheritor of the Pyncheon greed and materialism, whose smiling surface conceals the rock of his true nature, and Clifford, his victim, who has in excess the sensibility that the iron men of the family have repressed for generations. For Clifford is another failed artist: he is an aesthete and a man of active fancy, but he lacks all strength of will or sense of purpose. Remaining in a state of arrested development as an artist as well as a man, Clifford's *heart* lacks warmth. A lover of the beautiful, Clifford has 'never quaffed the cup of passionate love' and has consequently remained a child. When restored to the House of the Seven Gables from the prison in which he has unfairly spent the best years of his life, Clifford hates the house as an impediment to human happiness and improvement. Pathetically, he exults in the symbols of nineteenth-century progress, the railroad and electricity, though he needs the shelter of a home more than any other outcast.

The attitude to the past expressed through Holgrave's radicalism in *The House of the Seven Gables* reminds us that, in 'Main Street' (1849), Hawthorne depicted the Quakers in Emersonian terms as the inspired idealists whose life of the spirit was a threat to the civic and religious institutions of New England. In language that seems to echo Emerson's essays, Hawthorne contrasts the rigidity of traditional ways, descended from the first – Puritan – settlers with the fervour of the Quakers who threaten to topple the spire of the meeting-house. Speaking through the 'showman' who interprets the Main Street scene, Hawthorne seems to share the conviction that the forces of tradition and conservatism are destructive of both heart and intellect, but even here a balance is maintained as the value of continuity and the gradual accumulation of human associations is also acknowledged. The apparent volte-face at the end of *The House of the Seven Gables*, when Holgrave renounces his earlier radicalism and under the influence of Phoebe Pyncheon – the spirit of sunshine and human warmth – decides to establish his own family house, was predictable in the light of Hawthorne's consistent commitment to the ideal of domestic love. The Pyncheon house has become a symbol of the human heart as the romance has evolved, and though Holgrave will not live in so guilt-laden a mansion, his acknowledgement that he must have a house is, at one level, only realism. The message of 'Earth's Holocaust', one of Hawthorne's finest sketches, is that the human heart will remain unchanged in its depths in spite of all reforms and all idealistic schemes for change. Nevertheless, we may still feel some unease at Holgrave's readiness to become the conservative with a house of stone. When we first met him, Holgrave was introduced to us as the 'artist'; we see him at the last as an *arriviste*.

Hawthorne's ambivalent attitude to the artist informs 'The Prophetic Pictures' (1837) and 'Fancy's Show Box' (1837), both of which explore the possibility that the artist should feel guilt for his treatment of the human heart. In the former tale, the coldness of the artist is once more the theme, for his dedication to his art kills his natural human response to the subjects he uses; he sees the inmost soul of man, but his lack of feeling makes him, in the mechanism of the tale, a possible agent of evil, since – godlike – he foresees all. The second sketch draws analogies between plotting a tale and plotting a crime; both involve dreaming, or exercising the fancy. Even the triumph of the artist over the sceptic and materialist in 'The Artist of the Beautiful' (1844) is qualified by the 'moral cold' and emotional isolation of Owen Warland, the devotee of 'the spirit of beauty'. Only in 'Drowne's Wooden Image' (1846) does the warmth of human passion convert the merely 'wooden' work of the wood-carver Drowne into great art. When that happens, the art-work itself becomes an expression of human love.

Opposed to the Puritan men of iron in *The Scarlet Letter* stands Hawthorne's most passionate artist, Hester Prynne.[4] Her art is needlework, the only art a woman was permitted to engage in in seventeenth-century Massachusetts, and her only theme is the scarlet 'A' she wears on the breast of her gown. Pearl's clothes, on which she also employs her artistry, are an extension of the 'A', for Pearl is the 'living hieroglyphic' in which the secret she and Dimmesdale sought to hide is set before the world. Hester has embroidered the scarlet letter 'so artistically . . . and with so much fertility and gorgeous luxuriance of fancy' that her work seems to announce not shame but the belief she later makes explicit: that her act of love with Dimmesdale 'had a consecration of its own'. Her skill in embroidering the letter is 'delicate and imaginative', and expresses her taste for the 'gorgeously beautiful'. Yet Hester is not just a lover of the beautiful: she is a passionate and independent woman who threatens the Puritan system of authority as well as its severe moral code. The glancing reference to Anne Hutchinson in the first chapter of the romance associates Hester's transgression against the moral law with Anne Hutchinson's Antinomian challenge to the spiritual authority of the New England ministers of the Church. The wildness of Hester's nature was such, the narrator tells us, that it might have assimilated itself to the forest dwellers to whom Puritan law was alien – the Indians. In the forest with Dimmesdale, Hester feels the wild, free atmosphere of the lawless and unchristianized region so 'exhilarating' that she believes she can throw off the past with the scarlet symbol. In doing this, she escapes from what the narrator calls the 'dungeon' of her own heart, and as a consequence her youth and her rich beauty return to her. The nature of the forest sympathizes with Hester and with Dimmesdale, for it is heathen nature, unsubdued by law. Forest and ocean are appropriate regions for the rejection of the symbol of her shame, for both are beyond the control of human law, but if Hester could ever be associated with the ethos of Merry Mount, her experience in the forest makes it clear that she could not be implicated in the frivolity and foolishness of the masquers.

Hester's freedom from the symbolic 'A' is brief because Pearl, who is herself as wild as the sea-breeze, a law unto herself, a child of the forest, an elf, a fairy rather than a human being, insists that her mother continue to wear the emblematic letter. Psychologically this is plausible, for Pearl cannot recognize her mother without the ornament she has always worn in the child's memories of her. Morally this is appropriate, for since Pearl is the scarlet letter endowed with life – the fruit of the deed signified by the 'A' – Hester cannot both reject the symbol and keep Pearl. Though she is the 'pearl of great price' for which her mother has sold all that she had, Pearl is not fully human until she has been recognized by her father and until she has experienced sorrow. When Dimmesdale acknowledges his child, Pearl can love him and share his grief. She at once learns something that the inhabitants of Merry Mount could never learn: the experience of human love involves knowledge of human death. At Merry Mount, funerals were conducted with the jollity that characterized all life there. For that reason, in 'The May-Pole of Merry Mount' the world of art was the world of the dream and was itself chimerical. In *The Scarlet Letter* the artist survives in a world of 'care, and sorrow, and troubled joy', and makes art out of sadness.

Notes

1 The text of the extract from 'The May-Pole of Merry Mount' is that of *Twice-told Tales*, Centenary Edition of *The Works of Nathaniel Hawthorne*, 14 vols to date, Columbus: Ohio State University Press, 1960– , x (1974).

2 For useful information on Hawthorne's use of Strutt's *Sports and Pastimes*, see Neal Frank Doubleday, *Hawthorne's Early Tales, A Critical Study*, Durham, N. Carolina: Duke University Press, 1972.

3 For Hawthorne's interest in New England history, and for the vogue of Scott, see Doubleday, pp. 13–49. Also Michael Davitt Bell, *Hawthorne and the Historical Romance of New England*, Princeton University Press, 1971.

4 *Nina Baym, *The Shape of Hawthorne's Career*, Ithaca: Cornell University Press, 1976, pp. 124–48, argues that, in his treatment of Hester Prynne, Hawthorne represents the conflict between passionate creativity and repressive society. Baym also takes 'Drowne's Wooden Image' to be the first Hawthorne tale in which passion is the source of art.

Further reading

Richard H. Brodhead, *Hawthorne, Melville and the Novel*, University of Chicago Press, 1976.

6

Orestes A. Brownson (1803–76)

No one can observe the signs of the times with much care, without perceiving that a crisis as to the relation of wealth and labor is approaching. It is useless to shut our eyes to the fact, and like the ostrich fancy ourselves secure because we have so concealed our heads that we see not the danger. We or our children will have to meet this crisis. The old war between the King and the Barons is well nigh ended, and so is that between the Barons and the Merchants and Manufacturers, – landed capital and commercial capital. The business man has become the peer of my Lord. And now commences the new struggle between the operative and his employer, between wealth and labor. Every day does this struggle extend further and wax stronger and fiercer; what or when the end will be God only knows.

In this coming contest there is a deeper question at issue than is commonly imagined; a question which is but remotely touched in your controversies about United States Banks and Sub Treasuries, chartered Banking and free Banking, free trade and corporations, although these controversies may be paving the way for it to come up. We have discovered no presentiment of it in any king's or queen's speech, nor in any president's message. It is embraced in no popular political creed of the day, whether christened Whig or Tory, *Juste-milieu* or Democratic. No popular senator, or deputy, or peer seems to have any glimpse of it; but it is working in the hearts of the million, is struggling to shape itself, and one day it will be uttered, and in thunder tones. Well will it be for him, who, on that day, shall be found ready to answer it.

What we would ask is, throughout the Christian world, the actual condition of the laboring classes, viewed simply and exclusively in their capacity of laborers? They constitute at least a moiety of the human race. We exclude the nobility, we exclude also the middle class, and include only actual laborers, who are laborers and not proprietors, owners of none of the funds of production, neither houses, shops, nor lands, nor implements of labor, being therefore solely dependent on their hands. We have no means of ascertaining their precise proportion to the whole number of the race; but we think we may estimate them at one half. In any contest they will be as two to one, because the large class of proprietors who are not employers, but laborers on their own lands or in their own shops will make common cause with them.

Now we will not so belie our acquaintance with political economy, as to allege that these alone perform all that is necessary to the production of wealth. We are not ignorant of the fact, that the merchant, who is literally the common carrier and exchange dealer, performs a useful service, and is therefore entitled to a portion of the proceeds of labor. But make all necessary deductions on his account, and then ask what portion of the remainder is retained, either in kind or in its equivalent, in the hands of the original producer, the workingman? All over the world this fact stares us in the face, the workingman is poor and depressed, while a large portion of the non-workingmen, in the sense we now use the term, are wealthy. It may be laid down as a general rule, with but few exceptions, that men are rewarded in an inverse ratio to the amount of actual service they perform. Under every government on earth the largest salaries are annexed to those offices, which demand of their incumbents the least amount of actual labor either mental or manual. And this is in perfect harmony with the whole system of repartition of the fruits of industry, which obtains in every department of society. Now here is the system which prevails, and here is its result. The whole class of simple laborers are poor, and in general unable to procure anything beyond the bare necessaries of life.

In regard to labor two systems obtain; one that of slave labor, the other that of free labor. Of the two, the first is, in our judgment, except so far as the feelings are concerned, decidedly the least oppressive. If the slave has never been a free man, we think, as a general rule, his sufferings are less than those of the free laborer at wages. As to actual freedom one has just about as much as the other. The laborer at wages has all the disadvantages of freedom and none of its blessings, while the slave, if denied the blessings, is freed from the disadvantages. We are no advocates of slavery, we are as heartily opposed to it as any modern abolitionist can be; but we say frankly that, if there must always be a laboring population distinct from proprietors and employers, we regard the slave system as decidedly preferable to the system at wages. It is no pleasant thing to go days without food, to lie idle for weeks, seeking work and finding none, to rise in the morning with a wife and children you love, and know not where to procure them a breakfast, and to see constantly before you no brighter prospect than the almshouse. Yet these are no unfrequent incidents in the lives of our laboring population. Even in seasons of general prosperity, when there was only the ordinary cry of 'hard times,' we have seen hundreds of people in a no [*sic*] very populous village, in a wealthy portion of our common country, suffering for the want of the necessaries of life, willing to work, and yet finding no work to do. Many and many is the application of a poor man for work, merely for his food, we have seen rejected. These things are little thought of, for the applicants are poor; they fill no conspicuous place in society, and they have no biographers. But their wrongs are chronicled in heaven. It is said there is no want in this country. There may be less than in some other countries. But death by actual starvation in this country is, we apprehend, no uncommon occurrence. The sufferings of a quiet, unassuming but useful class of females in our cities, in general sempstresses, too proud to beg or to apply to the alms-house, are not easily told. They are industrious; they do all that they can find to do; but yet the little there is for them to do, and the miserable pittance they receive for it, is hardly sufficient to keep soul and body together. And yet there is a man who employs them to make shirts, trousers, &c., and grows rich on their labors. He is one of our respectable citizens, perhaps is praised in the newspapers for his liberal donations to some charitable institution. He passes among us as a pattern of morality, and is honored as a worthy Christian. And why should he not be, since our *Christian* community is made up of such as he, and since our clergy would not dare question his piety, lest they should incur the reproach of infidelity, and lose their standing, and their salaries? Nay, since our clergy are raised up, educated, fashioned, and sustained by such as he? Not a few of our churches rest on Mammon for their foundation. The basement is a trader's shop.

'The Laboring Classes' (1840)[1]

* * *

In the first sentence of the extract, Brownson asserts that to 'observe the signs of the times' carefully is to perceive that a crisis in the relations between the classes is approaching. The prose does more than convey the writer's opinion here: it also enforces his theory by means of its lexical strategy. To see the signs is necessarily to accept the writer's interpretation of them, for they exist as signs only if they signify what he claims they do. But if to see the signs is to accept Brownson's interpretation of their significance, not to see them is merely to prove oneself (in the logic of the sentence) unobservant, for the words are telling us that the signs in question are *the* signs of the times. To read the sentence is thus to enter an enclosed system of thought that is structured by the peremptory judgements of the writer, yet the following sentence asserts that the approaching crisis is a fact; not to see it is to be worse than unobservant, for it is deliberately to bury one's head, ostrich-fashion. The series of related words used to express the meaning of the crisis moves from danger, to war, and on to struggle. In doing so it associates the hypothetical class conflict with the historical strife between royalty and nobility. In an earlier part of his article, which begins as a review of Carlyle's *Chartism*, Brownson had already asserted that war was the only means by which a fairer distribution of wealth could be achieved in England. Now he extends the prophecy to American society. The implication of the final sentence is that the struggle is growing wider and fiercer even as one reads. So grave is the situation that the writer cannot predict its final outcome. Since 'God only knows' how or when the inevitable struggle will end, we may be sure that it will be great and terrible.

Brownson's strategy in the second paragraph is a development of that adopted in the first. The party-political issues of the day are alluded to and dismissed as trivial when compared to the profounder concerns that make the 'coming contest' inevitable. 1840, the year in which Brownson's two-part article 'The Laboring Classes' appeared in his *Boston Quarterly Review*, was the year of a presidential election that seemed to him crucial for the future of American democracy. After years of holding aloof from both major parties, Brownson had decided that the Democrats were at last becoming truly the party of liberty and humanity. He had allowed George Bancroft, a leading member of the Massachusetts Democratic Party, to enlist his services in the campaign to get Van Buren re-elected as president. Once convinced that the party was no longer corrupt, Brownson was able to support its cause with enthusiasm, for his belief that the banks were allied with the business classes against the working people coincided with Democratic Party policy. Brownson had attacked the banks in an article, 'The Sub-Treasury Bill', in 1838, but he now appeals over the heads of all politicians of whatever party or persuasion to 'the hearts of the million'. At the end of the second paragraph there is a shift of register as Brownson assumes the role of the Old Testament prophet. The promise that the social question will be asked 'in thunder tones' is followed by the biblical echoes of the words 'Well will it be for him who, on that day, shall be found ready to answer it.' The day is the Day of Doom; Brownson's vision is apocalyptic.

With another sudden shift of tone and style, Brownson drops his thundering prophecy to ask a direct question in plain language. He enquires into the 'actual condition' of the working classes in the Christian world. Before attempting to answer his own question, he offers an analysis of the structure of society that seems logical and unimpassioned. Defining the labouring classes as those who have no property or capital and must therefore depend for their livelihood on the wages they receive, Brownson argues that the labourer is the 'original producer' of the 'proceeds' of industry, even though he makes use of his employer's capital and property. In formulating his general rule that rewards are distributed in inverse ratio to the amount of actual service performed, Brownson adopts the language and the stance of the political economist who examines economic facts with detachment. By admitting that merchants perform a service and so deserve a portion of the proceeds, and by including the mental with the manual in his category of 'actual labor', Brownson clearly intends to be rational and fair, but the paragraph ends with a severe indictment of the system that leaves 'the whole class of simple laborers' so poor that they must live at subsistence level.

The next paragraph illustrates Brownson's propensity to follow his logic wherever it will lead him, without regard to his readers' sense of propriety. When he argues that the system of free labour is more oppressive than that of slave labour, he adduces the favourite argument of Southern apologists for slavery. As late as 1856, Abraham Lincoln found himself obliged to refute similar arguments in favour of the extension of slavery (see p. 235). In 1840 Brownson obviously knew that Northern readers of the *Boston Quarterly Review* who opposed slavery would be shocked by his argument, but the key to his strategy lies in the phrase 'actual freedom', which relates to his announced intention of enquiring into the 'actual condition' of the labouring classes. By asserting that the labourer for wages has all the *disadvantages* of freedom from which the slave is protected, Brownson challenges the unreflecting use of the word 'freedom' as a slogan. Justifiable pride in America's progress towards political freedom could go with complacency about social injustice and economic servitude, so he believed. Freedom is Brownson's major theme in this essay, as in all his writings up to 1844, but where George Bancroft had seen the triumph of the mercantile classes as a stage in the great march towards liberty, Brownson sees the middle classes, not the aristocractic, as the enemies of the proletariat.

When he writes of the actual condition of the workers, Brownson constructs a sentence on a series of infinitives: 'to go days without food, to lie idle for weeks . . . to rise in the morning with a wife and children you love, and know not where to procure them a breakfast'. The grammatical form bypasses the question of evidence, for the proposition we are asked to accept is self-evident: we cannot disagree that it is 'no pleasant thing' to experience the deprivations listed. But if the judgement seems mild, the rhetorical strategy is forceful, for the actuality of the labouring man's frustration and suffering is assumed in the syntax. To be sure, the general propositions are followed by personal witness when Brownson assumes the role of historian of the lives of men too poor and humble to find a place in the official histories, but if the chronicle of their wrongs is kept in heaven, in writing his articles he is acting as God's agent. Though 'The Laboring Classes' contains a bitter attack on the organized priesthood – the hireling clergy – as an ally of the rich in their enslavement of the poor, the rejection of all institutionalized religion goes with a high regard for the value of immediate religious experience. Accepting no religious authority, every man should 'speak out of his own full heart'. Here Brownson is speaking out of his full heart and preaching a lay sermon. A Universalist minister himself from 1826 to 1830, Brownson had joined the Unitarian Church in 1832 and had been invited to come to Boston as an independent preacher because his earlier association with the Working Men's Party suggested that he would preach effectively to the labouring classes. In his 1840 articles, however, he preached to the *middle* class and shocked some of its members, among them Channing, who believed that Brownson greatly exaggerated the sufferings of the workers.[2]

Though Brownson admits that conditions in America are less severe than they are in many European countries, he does assert that death by starvation is 'no uncommon occurrence' in his own land. The Panic of 1837, in which hundreds of banks had failed and factories closed, had in fact brought misery to precisely the wage-dependent class with which the article is concerned, and had visibly affected the deserving poor who sought work. The rhetoric used to rouse our sympathy for the industrious poor is conventional enough, with its 'miserable pittance' that is 'hardly sufficient to keep soul and body together', but once launched on his most subversive theme, the complicity of Christian society in social injustice, Brownson's indignation produces language that is not hackneyed. His method is dramatic and his style denunciatory: there *is* a man who *grows* rich while the poor starve to increase his wealth. The present tense and the verbs in the singular make vivid the presence of exploiting hypocrisy among the respectable class of readers. In extending his attack to the clergy, Brownson introduces a theme that will be developed at length later in his article. Here he is content with a brief but bitter comment on the triumph of material over spiritual values. To accuse the rich employer would be to risk the charge of infidelity because the faith has become worship of mammon. If the priest loses his standing he will assuredly lose his salary, for he is himself an employee of the rich man.

In the paragraph that follows the extract, Brownson takes his readers on a journey through the manufacturing villages of New England and takes Lowell as an example of the wage slavery that he considers no better than the chattel slavery of the South. By making Lowell his example of Northern industrial slavery, Brownson was deliberately challenging the pieties of Whig industrial paternalism, for Lowell had been planned as a showpiece of enlightened management.[3] By the standards of the day, Lowell offered its employees something of the care that was lacking in the factory system as a whole. Housing, a hospital, a school, subsidized churches and even a literary periodical, the *Lowell Offering*, were provided by the Lowell company, but in providing a total environment the mill-owners exercised complete control over the lives of their workers. With dividends at an average 12 per cent, investors did much better than employees, for by hiring women the company was able to pay lower wages than were paid to men by British employers at this time. The limits of paternalistic benevolence were plainly revealed in the employers' resistance to demands for a ten-hour day and in the occasional enforcement of increased working rates. In treating the Lowell 'model' as an example of wage-slavery, Brownson was insisting that any system based on the separation of labour from property was a form of wage-slavery.

In attacking the Lowell system, Brownson incidentally offended the mill-hands, for his words on the factory girls seemed to suggest that they were morally degenerate. Rebuked in the pages of the *Lowell Offering*, Brownson replied with a letter to the factory girls in the pages of his own *Boston Quarterly Review*, assuring them that he had intended no defamation of their morals. His anger, he said, had been directed at the injustices they suffered (BQR, IV. 261). The misunderstanding in itself is instructive, for it indicates the weakness of Brownson's rhetoric when he indulged his righteous indignation. But if the offence caused to the workers was the effect of a lack of control in Brownson's prose, the outrages offered to the bourgeoisie in other parts of his article were anything but inadvertent. A reference early in the essay to the French Revolution as 'a glorious uprising of the people in behalf of their imprescriptible, and inalienable rights' was calculated to offend all but the most radical American readers. It earned Brownson the title of the American Robespierre and led John Quincy Adams, the former president, to class him with the 'Marat-Democrats'. Yet this was a mild assault on middle-class sensibility compared to the one prepared in the closing section, where Brownson argued that abolition of hereditary monarchy and nobility must be followed by abolition of hereditary property if social justice were ever to be achieved. The only effective way of raising the labouring classes, Brownson asserted, was to remove the economic privilege enshrined in the right to bequeath and inherit wealth. As long as there were gross inequalities in men's fortunes when they began life, political equality would be meaningless. Moreover, since the rich would never consent to this disinheritance, force would have to be used. In his final paragraph, Brownson anticipated 'contumely and abuse' for daring to broach such a subject and offered himself as a willing martyr, ready to die on the scaffold, for the cause of God and man. In his view, God's cause was the cause of social justice.

An article that began as a literary book review thus developed into a prophecy of doom, a socio-economic analysis of contemporary American society, an impassioned denunciation of the priesthood and all institutionalized churches as allies of the rich and exploitative classes, a challenge to the sacred institution of hereditary property, and a heroic assumption of the martyr's role. Without impugning Brownson's sincerity, we have to respond to his article as a literary performance in which the writer has adopted a variety of roles and styles in order to have the maximum effect on his readers. Arthur Schlesinger, Jr, the most appreciative critic of the article, not only argues that it is probably the best study of society written by an American before the Civil War, but also claims a high place for it in revolutionary literature whether as analysis or polemic.[4] Since the two modes would normally be considered incompatible, Schlesinger's appraisal is a tribute to Brownson's skill in the use of his literary *personae*. In part, Brownson was following the example of the man whose book he was reviewing, for Carlyle himself adopted the roles of analyst, prophet and sage, but it is also true that for Brownson the review article was a form as free as the lyceum lecture was for Emerson. In the pages of the *Boston Quarterly Review*, Brownson discussed politics, philosophy, theology, literature and the relations of all these to man in society. In so doing, he conducted his own education in public, explored his own idea of America and wrote a sort of autobiography. If the judgements in 'The Laboring Classes' sound peremptory, that is evidence of Brownson's logical absolutism – his thoroughgoing trust in the processes of logical thought – but his motive for founding his own review was, as he was later to write in *The Convert* (1857), not propaganda but enquiry. According to this later testimony, when he edited and wrote most of the articles for the *Boston Quarterly Review* he had no set views to promulgate. He plainly *did* have an intense need to explore ideas.

The circulation of the *Boston Quarterly Review* was never large. In the four years of its existence its subscribers probably never numbered more than a thousand, but its influence was enough to cause the Democratic Party embarrassment in states as far away as Virginia. So unhelpful were Brownson's radical reviews in 'The Laboring Classes' to the campaign to re-elect Van Buren that George Bancroft felt the need to disown his friend's opinions and stated in private that the Democrats were no more responsible for Brownson's notions than the Whigs were for Mormonism.[5] In fact, 'The Laboring Classes' was more radical than almost anything else that Brownson wrote, but more important than any particular article was the mere existence of his review, for the *Boston Quarterly* was in itself a very interesting sign of the times. Brownson's friend George Ripley, a Boston Unitarian Minister before he initiated the communitarian experiment at Brook Farm, wrote in the Transcendentalist magazine *Dial* to say that the *Boston Quarterly* was 'the best indication of the culture of philosophy' in America.[6] On reading the first number of the review, Henry David Thoreau wrote to tell Brownson that he was glad to find '*American* thoughts' expressed in it. He also made a comment that more than any other indicates the significance of Brownson's review and of its editor's career: 'I like the spirit of independence which distinguishes it.'[7]

In the course of his attack on the priesthood in 'The Laboring Classes', Brownson defined the true mission of Christ on earth as 'a solemn summons . . . of the human race to freedom' (BQR, III. 384). His main charge against the clergy was collusion with the rich, but he saw this as just one aspect of their enslavement of the 'free soul' of man and their attempt to smother his 'etherial fire'. As we have seen, when Brownson came to review Emerson's *Essays* in 1841, he picked out 'Self-Reliance' as the one that offered the most important lesson for Americans (BQR, IV. 305). This is hardly surprising, for freedom of thought was the cause to which he devoted himself with most energy in the years before his conversion to Roman Catholicism in 1844. All the particular ideas that Brownson endorsed in those years related to, or were posited on, his belief in intellectual self-reliance. As far back as 1828, when the radical Fanny Wright began to print some of Brownson's articles in her *Free Enquirer*, it was his rejection of dogma and his uninhibited pursuit of free intellectual enquiry that earned him the respect of the celebrated champion of free thought.[8] Just over ten years later, in a personal statement at the end of the second volume of the *Boston Quarterly Review* (1839), Brownson interpreted his whole life to that date in terms of liberty: 'I sucked in democracy with my mother's milk; I imbibed a feeling and a love of independence as I roamed over the Green Hills' (of Vermont). Since those childhood years, he added, he had 'always been found on the side of freedom in its widest signification' (BQR, II. 516).

Brownson's defence of freedom of thought was not conducted only in the pages of his review. In May 1836 he preached at the Lyceum Hall, Boston, a sermon entitled 'The Wants of the Times', and so impressed the English reformer Harriet Martineau that she published his address as an appendix to her *Society in America* (1837). In the sermon Brownson argued that to question, to reason, to think for oneself was to be a true Christian, not an infidel, and he claimed that the spirit of freedom was the very spirit of the Gospels. As the first article of his own creed Brownson put 'free, unlimited inquiry, perfect liberty to enjoy and express one's own honest convictions'. In the New Church of which he dreamed, 'unlimited freedom of the mind' would be acknowledged; there would be no interdict on thought.

1836 was the year in which Emerson made his contribution to 'the Newness' with the publication of *Nature*. Brownson's declaration of intellectual independence came in his *New Views of Christianity, Society, and the Church*, which also appeared in that year. He had just founded the Society for Christian Union and Progress in Boston and regarded his book as an explanation of the principles of the society. In it he argued that all modern philosophy was founded upon 'the absolute freedom and independence of the individual reason', for the tendency of history since Luther's time had been toward 'the most unlimited freedom of thought and conscience' (W, IV. 20). Inseparable from Brownson's concern with freedom was his belief that humanity is engaged in an endless career of progress toward perfection. The doctrine, stated as a law of human nature in Brownson's book, plainly indicates the influence of William Ellery Channing, whom Brownson took to exemplify a distinctively American combination of intellectual freedom and faith in ideas (p. 45).

The mission of the age, as Brownson saw it, was the reconciliation of spirit and matter, God and man; this could only be achieved when the Augustinian tradition that, according to Brownson, demeaned human nature had been replaced by one that dignified man. Channing had offered an alternative to the doctrine of human depravity. From Channing, Brownson took over the doctrine of the 'at-onement' of God and man, making it the essence of true Christianity. Six years after the publication of *New Views*, he published an article, 'The Church of the Future', in which he re-examined his first book and reaffirmed his belief in the potentiality of human nature. The incarnation of Christ still seemed to the Brownson of this 1842 article to proclaim the divinity of man, for in Christ God had become a real man, born of woman, and had thus become 'concreted in his works, a living God'. Thus, though God was distinguishable from man, he was not separable from him (W, IV. 62).

Brownson's belief in human progress was an expression of the spirit of the age that linked him with both Channing and Bancroft. The idea that 'humanity eternally aspires. It ever sees before it new heights to be scaled', and can never remain satisfied with what it has achieved because the ideal always hovers before it, was a Romantic commonplace by the time that Brownson expressed it in 'The Church of the Future' in the *Boston Quarterly Review*. In one of the few articles contributed to the *Review* by writers other than its editor, 'On the Progress of Civilization', George Bancroft proclaimed his belief in the irresistible tendency of the human race to advancement (BQR, I. 406). Yet where Bancroft was satisfied to let the Democratic Party carry on the great cause of progress, Brownson believed that the best hope for reform was to convert the clergy to the cause of the common people. His anger with the hireling priests in 'The Laboring Classes' was the reverse side of his hope for social reform through a clergy devoted to social justice. In his article 'The Education of the People' in the Unitarian *Christian Examiner* in 1836, Brownson argued that the priests had too long neglected the social mission of Christianity and had thus failed to play their part in the progress of the people (vol. XX. 153–69). In *Charles Elwood, or The Infidel Converted*, an autobiographical novel published in 1840, Brownson's central character makes a religion of social reform when he sees the plight of the poor. Developing the same trend of thought in 'The Laboring Classes', Brownson defined genuine Christianity as the religion that seeks to establish the kingdom of God *on the earth* instead of awaiting its fulfilment in heaven. Where Channing remained content with a somewhat imprecise belief that a higher form of Christianity would come 'in a socialist direction',[9] Brownson, in a second article on the labouring classes published in the *Boston Quarterly Review* in October 1840, left no doubt that it was the Christian's *duty* to work for reform. The 'at-onement' of God and man, the development of man's divine potentiality that Channing hoped to realize through the spread of self-culture, was simply not to be achieved without social progress. As Brownson put it in his first 'Laboring Classes' article, 'Self-culture is a good thing, but it cannot abolish inequality . . . as constituting in itself a remedy for the vices of the social state, we have no faith in it' (BQR, III. 375).

By 1842 Brownson had a new enthusiasm and a new means of conceiving the union of God and man. In July of that year he reviewed Pierre Leroux's *De l'Humanité* (1840) and once more triumphantly identified Christianity as the religion of humanity. Taking over Leroux's doctrine that God and man were united in the life of Christ, Brownson combined a recognition of Christ's 'mediatorial life' with a claim that the truest interpreter of Christ's message in the nineteenth century was the French socialist Saint-Simon, whose theories he had used in his 'Laboring Classes' analysis of society. Saint-Simon and his followers had understood better than any other Christians the *social* character of the new covenant God had made with man through Christ and had, in Brownson's view, rightly made social progress their ideal. There is, however, an insistence on the role of religion in this review of 'Leroux's Humanity' that was obscured by the denunciation of the priesthood in 'The Laboring Classes'. By 1842 Brownson was ready to admit the hopelessness of all efforts at reform that were not sustained by religion. Humanity, he now argued, could not be satisfied with intellectual speculation: it demanded a practical philosophy, and that meant a religion.

In an open letter to Channing, 'The Mediatorial Life of Christ', published in June 1842, Brownson fully explored the implications of Leroux's ideas and went on to look closely at Channing's conception of 'likeness' as a familial relationship of child to father. Though he was careful to exonerate Channing from any responsibility for the extravagancies of ego-theism that had shown themselves in Transcendentalism, Brownson now firmly denied that man was *naturally* divine. The divinity of man was, he asserted, not natural but 'superinduced upon his nature' (W, IV. 151); consequently, the child–father 'likeness' posited in Channing's sermon could be misleading. Indeed, Brownson now argued that human nature was depraved before the divine was 'superinduced' upon it, for experience plainly showed that man was by nature sinful. If this seemed closer to Calvinism than to the liberal Unitarianism of Channing, Brownson also announced his new belief that the life of Christ offered a 'mediation' between man and God that was profoundly unlike the Calvinist notion of divine grace. Following

Leroux, Brownson now claimed that man could achieve communion with God through Christ, for the *life* of Christ had given man access to God. The significant difference from Channing's conception of human nature lay in Brownson's acknowledgement that man could have *no* communion with God except through Christ, for the finite could not communicate directly with the infinite.

Brownson's theological ideas were not separable from his social and political theories. The implications of his new conception of man's relationship to God and his new awareness of human sinfulness were soon making themselves clear in his essays on the state of the nation. The defeat of the Democrats in the 1840 election meant that Brownson could no longer afford to maintain the *Boston Quarterly Review*, for he lost the political appointment as steward of the Chelsea Marine Hospital that Bancroft had found for him in 1838, and with it went the income that had supported him. Accepting an offer from John L. O'Sullivan, Brownson next began to write as a contributing editor of the *Democratic Review*, and almost immediately began to shock and offend O'Sullivan's readers. An article entitled 'Democracy and Liberty' in the April 1843 issue of the *Democratic Review* caused O'Sullivan such embarrassment that he was obliged to add an editorial disclaimer to it. The Whig victory in the election had occasioned a revolution in Brownson's views, it appeared, for he led off his article with the announcement that, since the election, he had lost all confidence in the 'intelligence of the people'. A people so gullible that they could be swayed by the demagogic devices of the Whigs deserved only contempt, in Brownson's opinion, and although he still claimed to be the champion of their cause, he announced that the doctrine of the virtue and intelligence of the people was mere humbug. The people, he went on, were not competent to govern themselves. Though the great goal was still freedom, an irrational enthusiasm for liberty was the great danger to liberty itself. Brownson's new slogan was 'LIBERTY ONLY IN AND THROUGH ORDER', for it now seemed to him that 'Liberty without the guaranties of authority, would be the worst of tyrannies' (W, xv. 281).

The authority in which Brownson was now ready to put his trust was that of a 'constitutional party' rather than a revolutionary party, as he made clear in a follow-up article, 'Popular Government', in the May 1843 issue of the *Democratic Review*. The danger from the mob, stirred up by demagogues, was so great that a constitution was no defence against tyranny unless there were some power to guarantee the constitution. Brownson's solution was one he found in the theories of John C. Calhoun, a Southern champion of states rights, for in the system of 'concurring majorities' there seemed to be the only safeguard against the tyranny of popular rule. In fact, while writing for the *Democratic Review*, Brownson was secretly campaigning to get Calhoun the Democratic nomination in 1844.

Brownson's volte-face on the subject of authority did not mean that he had thrown in his lot with the privileged classes, at least in his view of it. His articles for O'Sullivan's *Review* continued to denounce the 'American system' of protective tariffs as a means of enslaving the workers. Defending himself against the charge of apostasy, Brownson maintained that he no more trusted the virtue and intelligence of the mercantile and manufacturing employers than he did that of the proletarians. In an article entitled 'The Present State of Society' published in July 1843, he reminded the readers of the *Democratic Review* of the starvation wages paid to labourers in America and of the need for bread and soup societies in Boston. He also reiterated his charge that the 'vicious' injustice in distribution of the products of labour was the cause of surpluses and the unemployment they brought with them. Yet even here he stated plainly that Americans 'must be conservative, and study to preserve the order established by the wisdom of [their] fathers' (W, IV. 432). In countries where there was no hope of social progress through the machinery of government, violent revolution was inevitable, but it was not the best way of achieving the advancement of humanity, and in America it was not necessary. Renouncing all specific reforms, Brownson was now ready to substitute for them a vague call to the leaders of industry and finance to act altruistically.

In the summer of 1843 Brownson prepared a series of articles under the title 'The Origin and Ground of Government' for the *Democratic Review*. They were to prove more than O'Sullivan's magazine could bear, for subscriptions were being cancelled as a direct result of Brownson's articles. In the course of these long, rambling essays Brownson totally renounced any faith in popular sovereignty, arguing that the good man, and hence the good citizen, needed a 'sense of a power above him that he is bound to obey'. Such a sense of a power higher and greater than that of the self was the origin of man's feeling of LOYALTY – he gave the word capitals – and loyalty was 'the sum and substance of all virtue' (W, XV. 308). Brownson's devotion to the principle of intellectual and political independence here underwent a notable metamorphosis, for he defined civil and political liberty as 'freedom from all obligation to obey any commands but those of the legitimate sovereign' (p. 309). Struggling to reach an adequate idea of true sovereignty, Brownson was clear enough about his rejection of self-reliance. Freedom from all but self-imposed restraints now seemed to him mere licence. Earlier in this same year, in his 'Democracy and Liberty', Brownson had described the conduct of the individual who goes to jail rather than pay his taxes as merely anarchic (W, xv. 276). Three years later, his earlier admirer, Henry David Thoreau, would do exactly what Brownson now deplored. In 1843 the exemplary refusal to pay taxes was that of Amos Bronson Alcott, no less a champion of intellectual independence than Thoreau, if considerably less tough-minded. Brownson's political theorizing now put him worlds away from any of the Concord Transcendentalists. His reiterated conviction that some higher power, some greater authority, than the individual conscience was needed is in itself testimony to the strain imposed by the attempt to lead a life of intellectual self-reliance.

To O'Sullivan's relief, Brownson's association with the *Democratic Review* came to an end with the publication of his articles on the theory of government. In January 1844 Brownson launched a new magazine with the title *Brownson's Quarterly Review* and quickly set about reversing most of the theories he had expressed in the *Boston Quarterly Review*. In April 1844 he gave up his Society for Christian Union and Progress. In May he left the Unitarian Church and began to receive instruction in the Roman Catholic faith. On 19 October 1844 Brownson was received into the Church of Rome. An article in the April 1844 issue of his new *Review* carried the title 'No Church, No Reform' and stated plainly that the 'fundamental vice of all modern schemes of reform' is the false assumption that man 'is sufficient for his own redemption'. With his new sense of man's limitations went a revised conception of man's capacity for progress. It now seemed to Brownson that man was progressive only '*by virtue of a wisdom and a power not his own*'. Talk of the divinity of man was, by the same token, mere prattle or Babel language, for man is divine 'only by the inflowings of divine efficacy *ab extra*' (W, IV. 507–9). The insistence on a spiritual power beyond and above man parallels Brownson's growing conviction that the individual must submit to a higher authority than his own conscience in the political realm. The two strands of his thinking come together in an article entitled 'Come-outerism: or the Radical Tendency of the Day' in the July 1844 issue of his *Review*. Designating the revolutionary spirit 'satanic', Brownson consigns Socialists and Associationists (Robert Owen, Fourier, Saint-Simon) and literary Romantics (Byron, Shelley, Hugo, George Sand, Carlyle and even Balzac) to the realms of the damned. The satanic spirit of 'come-outerism' reveals itself, according to this article, in its assumption that 'the individual is his own judge'.

In America it is the result of the belief that government derives its power from the consent of the governed, for when such a belief is added to the Quaker doctrine of the Inner Light, the individual is credited with an authority that is mistakenly taken to be divine (W, IV. 547–57). While the watchword of the young radical is 'Liberty', when he becomes the mature conservative his slogan will be 'Order', in Brownson's opinion. He speaks in general terms here, but the case is obviously his own.

In 'Come-outerism', Brownson's views are consistent with his 'Laboring Classes' article in one respect: he treats the triumph of business interests under the Whig administration as part of the gradual but relentless subjection of the mass of the workers. In 1844 Brownson still considered reform to be the duty of all true Christians, though he was careful to add that reform must be achieved by conservative, not revolutionary, methods. Just two years later, in the article 'Schiller's Aesthetic Theory', Brownson follows the implications of his new view of man further. Making a categorical distinction between man's 'real good' and his 'external condition', he renounces all interest in reforms that aim to improve man's condition in the world. The mistake of all socialists, he asserts, is to believe that man's true good can be realized here on earth. To do so is to substitute love of man for love of God; it is part of the 'modern idolatry' that worships man rather than God (W, XIX. 127).

To treat Brownson as a radical democrat until 1844, and to argue that his conversion to Roman Catholicism marks a complete break with his earlier intellectual life, is to simplify. In his *Contradiction and Dilemma: Orestes Brownson and the American Idea*, Leonard Gilhooley offers the most thorough study of Brownson's writings up to 1859 and argues persuasively that there were conservative 'secondary emphases' in Brownson's thought as it was expressed in some of his earliest articles for the *Boston Quarterly Review*. In the first number of that *Review* (January 1838), and in the first article, 'Democracy', Brownson warned against the dangers of seeking progress by means of revolution and argued in favour of reform from within the established political system. The American people, he asserted, were not revolutionists but conservatives; in America, to be a conservative was to be a democrat. Summing up his own position, he wrote: 'We would think with the radical, but often act with the conservative' (W, XV. 33). In this article, too, he rejected the doctrine of the sovereignty of the people because he saw in it the danger of tyranny. Absolute rule of the majority led to demagoguery and corruption, he argued, and this was *before* the fateful

Whig victory in the 1840 election. But while acknowledging this important qualification of Brownson's earlier enthusiasm for social change, we must also take note of the fact that his fear of absolute majority rule is occasioned by his jealous concern with individual liberty. In 1838 what he feared most was the disenfranchisement of the individual, and it must surely have been this element of Brownson's thought that made Thoreau respond so warmly to the first issue of the *Boston Quarterly Review*.

In Leonard Gilhooley's apt formulation, 'the problem of tension between order and liberty would plague [Brownson] all his life'.[10] This was not merely Brownson's problem, but the problem of his generation of American intellectuals. The very issue of his *Review* that carried his thoughts on democracy contained an article entitled 'The Philosophy of Common Sense' in which Brownson rejected Lockean epistemology and claimed that 'Reason is the true light, and it enlighteneth every man who cometh into the world.' Spontaneous reason, he argued, was natural to all men; consequently the true philosopher reverenced human nature and found in all men the elements of truth and virtue that were part of his own conscience (W, I. 10–18). Dressing the theory of the Scottish Common Sense philosophers in the language of Coleridgean Reason, Brownson was here coming close to the New England Transcendentalists. In January 1839 Brownson reviewed Andrews Norton's *Evidence of the Genuineness of the Four Gospels* (1838), and gave his verdict on the doctrine that all God's revelations to man had been made in the miracles recorded in the Bible, i.e. that God spoke to man only through certain authorized messengers. Such a doctrine, said Brownson, denied man all inherent power of attaining to truth and consequently destroyed 'all free action of the mind, all independent thought, all progress, and all living faith'. In denying the divinity in man that could respond to and vouch for the divinity of God, Norton's doctrine was also politically unsound, for in rejecting the 'inner light' in all men, Norton was undermining democratic faith in the ability of all men to act as their reason dictated, and thus to seek truth.

In 1842, when he reviewed his own *Charles Elwood*, Brownson took the word 'intuition' – the key term in the Transcendentalists' rejection of Lockean empiricism – and gave it a significant new interpretation. He defined it as looking *on* to ideas that were 'objects or realities' rather than looking *in*, or looking within the self for truths. Absolute ideas are 'objective to the *whole me*' and are therefore '*not me*, existing out of the *me*, and independent of it', he now argued (W, IV. 336–46). Nothing could reveal more clearly his essential predicament. Wanting –

needing – to maintain the independence of the self, he at the same time felt the necessity of looking beyond the self for an authority to which he could submit. The article 'Schmucker's Psychology' in the *Democratic Review* in this same year states that religion is 'always authoritative, always legislative; it imposes the law' (W, I. 21). By 1849, in the article 'Authority and Liberty', he defined Christianity as an authoritative religion, an external revelation from God, given by the Supreme Law-giver, and binding upon all men (*Essays and Reviews*, p. 276). By this time, the Church that represented the divine authority was, of course, the Roman Catholic Church; the Reformation now seemed to Brownson to have meant the substitution of human sovereignty for the divine. In the preface to *The Convert* (1857), he wrote: 'I . . . consider submission to the teaching of the church the noblest exercise I can make of my reason and free will' (W, V. 2).

The Convert, as its title suggests, tells the story of Brownson's intellectual career from his youthful dismay at the God of terror preached by the Methodists to his glad acceptance of the doctrines of the Roman Catholic Church. A complementary way of reviewing his career as a thinker is to glance at his changing attitudes to George Bancroft's *History of the United States*. When he reviewed the early volumes in his *Boston Quarterly* in 1841, Brownson thought the *History* a 'marvellous production' because it expressed a profound belief in human progress and was given unity by Bancroft's recognition that the idea of America was the idea of liberty, and the mission of America was the realization of that idea. At this stage, Brownson's only reservation was a feeling that Bancroft's trust in the collective will of the people made him careless of the dangers to individual liberty. Eleven years later, reviewing Bancroft's *History* up to volume four (1852), Brownson rejected the view of the American past it embodied as totally false, claiming that Bancroft's theological, ethical and political theories had corrupted every aspect of his narrative. Bancroft's great heresy, according to the Brownson of 1852, was his belief that the people were the infallible Church and that humanity was God; that God 'speaks only in and through popular instincts and tendencies' (W, XIX. 388). In this worship of humanity, Bancroft revealed his allegiance to 'the dominant idolatry or superstition of the age' (p. 411). The story does not end here, for the Civil War stirred Brownson to a passionate intellectual defence of the Union and a rejection of his own earlier belief in states rights. Dedicating his *The American Republic* (1865) to Bancroft, 'as a sort of public atonement', Brownson now defined the mission of America as that of realizing the 'dialectic of authority and liberty'.

While still maintaining that loyalty is the highest of human emotions, Brownson here resolves his own difficulties concerning the nature of authority by arguing that civil rulers hold their authority 'from God' yet 'through the people' (W, XVIII. 68). Though he did not waver in his faith as a Catholic, Brownson's dedication to the idea of America led him to believe that sovereignty is 'under God, in the nation' (p. 107). Thus the man who had excoriated the Whig Party as the party of privilege in the 1840 election, when Abraham Lincoln had campaigned wholeheartedly for the Whigs and for Harrison, found in the Union a fusion of the secular and the sacred that Lincoln himself, for all his totally contrasting intellectual background, had discovered in the years leading to the Civil War.

Notes

1 The text of the extract from 'The Laboring Classes' is taken from the *Boston Quarterly Review*, 5 vols, Boston: Greene, 1838–42, III (1840). Parenthetic references to BQR throughout the chapter are also to the *Review*. References to W are to *The Works of Orestes A. Brownson*, collected and arranged by Henry F. Brownson, 20 vols, Detroit: T. Nourse, 1884–1902; repr. New York: AMS Press, 1966. References to *Essays and Reviews* are to *Orestes A. Brownson, Essays and Reviews, Chiefly on Theology, Politics, and Socialism*, New York: D. & J. Sadlier, 1852; repr. New York: Arno Press, 1972.

2 *Arthur M. Schlesinger, Jr, *A Pilgrim's Progress: Orestes A. Brownson*, Boston: Little, Brown, 1966, p. 102. Originally published as *Orestes A. Brownson: A Pilgrim's Progress*, Boston: Little, Brown, 1939.

3 Daniel Walker, Howe, *The Political Culture of the American Whigs*, University of Chicago Press, 1979, p. 102.

4 Schlesinger, p. 95.

5 Schlesinger, p. 195.

6 Schlesinger, p. 48.

7 Theodore Maynard, *Orestes Brownson: Yankee, Radical, Catholic*, New York: Macmillan, 1943, p. 83.

8 Maynard, pp. 32–3.

9 Brownson provides this information in *The Convert*, *Works*, v. 78.

10 *Leonard Gilhooley, *Contradiction and Dilemma: Orestes Brownson and the American Idea*, New York: Fordham University Press, 1972, p. 44.

7
Francis Parkman (1823-93)

Meanwhile, Bouquet's little army crept on its slow way along the Cumberland valley. Passing here and there a few scattered cabins, deserted or burnt to the ground, they reached the hamlet of Shippensburg, somewhat more than twenty miles from their point of departure. Here, as at Carlisle, was gathered a starving multitude, who had fled from the knife and the tomahawk. Beyond lay a solitude whence every settler had fled. They reached Fort Loudon, on the declivity of Cove Mountain, and climbed the wood-encumbered defiles beyond. Far on their right stretched the green ridges of the Tuscarora; and, in front, mountain beyond mountain was piled against the sky. Over rocky heights and through deep valleys, they reached at length Fort Littleton, a provincial post, in which, with incredible perversity, the government of Pennsylvania had refused to place a garrison. Not far distant was the feeble little post of the Juniata, empty like the other; for the two or three men who held it had been withdrawn by Ourry. On the twenty-fifth of July, they reached Bedford, hemmed in by encircling mountains. It was the frontier village and the centre of a scattered border population, the whole of which was now clustered in terror in and around the fort; for the neighboring woods were full of prowling savages. Ourry reported that for several weeks nothing had been heard from the westward, every messenger having been killed and the communication completely cut off. By the last intelligence Fort Pitt had been surrounded by Indians, and daily threatened with a general attack.

At Bedford, Bouquet had the good fortune to engage thirty backwoodsmen to accompany him. He lay encamped three days to rest men and animals, and then, leaving his invalids to garrison the fort, put out again into the sea of savage verdure that stretched beyond. The troops and convoy defiled along the road made by General Forbes in 1758, if the name of road can be given to a rugged track, hewn out by axemen through forests and swamps and up the steep acclivities of rugged mountains; shut in between impervious walls of trunks, boughs, and matted thickets, and overarched by a canopy of restless leaves. With difficulty and toil, the wagons dragged slowly on, by hill and hollow, through brook and quagmire, over roots, rocks, and stumps. Nature had formed the country for a war of ambuscades and surprises, and no pains were spared to guard against them. A band of backwoodsmen led the way, followed closely by the pioneers; the wagons and the cattle were in the centre, guarded by the regulars; and a rear guard of backwoodsmen closed the line of march. Frontier riflemen scoured the woods far in front and on either flank, and made surprise impossible. Thus they toiled heavily on till the main ridge of the Alleghanies, a mighty wall of green, rose up before them; and they began their zigzag progress up the woody heights amid the sweltering heats of July. The tongues of the panting oxen hung lolling from their jaws; while the pine-trees, scorching in the hot sun, diffused their resinous odors through the sultry air. At length from the windy summit the Highland soldiers could gaze around upon a boundless panorama of forest-covered mountains, wilder than their own native hills. Descending from the Alleghanies, they entered upon a country less rugged and formidable in itself, but beset with constantly increasing dangers. On the second of August, they reached Fort Ligonier, about fifty miles from Bedford, and a hundred and fifty from Carlisle. The Indians who were about the place vanished at their approach; but the garrison could furnish no intelligence of the motions and designs of the enemy, having been completely blockaded for weeks. . . .

On the morning of the fifth, the tents were struck at an early hour, and the troops began their march through a country broken with hills and deep hollows, covered with the tall, dense forest, which spread for countless leagues around. By one o'clock, they had advanced seventeen miles; and the guides assured them that they were within half a mile of Bushy Run, their proposed resting-place. The tired soldiers were pressing forward with renewed alacrity, when suddenly the report of rifles from the front sent a thrill along the ranks; and, as they listened, the firing thickened into a fierce, sharp rattle; while shouts and whoops, deadened by the intervening forest, showed that the advance guard was hotly engaged. The two foremost companies were at once ordered forward to support it; but, far from abating, the fire grew so rapid and furious as to argue the presence of an enemy at once numerous and resolute. At this, the convoy was halted, the troops formed into line, and a general charge ordered. Bearing down through the forest with fixed bayonets, they drove the yelping assailants before them, and swept the ground clear. But at the very moment of success, a fresh burst of whoops and firing was heard from either flank; while a confused noise from the rear showed that the convoy was attacked.

The Conspiracy of Pontiac (1851; rev. 1870)[1]

* * *

Colonel Bouquet's 'little army' is moving along the Cumberland Valley in July 1763 to repulse the hitherto victorious Indians who, under their bold leader Pontiac, have attacked and besieged the lonely English outpost of Fort Pitt, two hundred miles west of the main line of settlements, have captured most of the forts beyond that line and killed their garrisons, and have terrorized the frontiers of Pennsylvania, Maryland and Virginia. The panic-stricken frontiersmen have poured into the town of Carlisle, leaving behind them their burned farms and crops with, in many cases, the bodies of relatives slaughtered by Indian raiding parties. Bouquet's force, consisting of less than five hundred men, is marching into a vast wilderness inhabited now only by their savage enemies.

The immense mountain ranges that confront the advancing troops and hem in the outlying settlement of Bedford seem in this extract to offer resistance to the westward movement of the white men and to threaten those whites who dare to enter their precincts. The forests not only shelter and conceal the savage enemy, they 'encumber' the defiles through which the army must pick its laborious way as it struggles 'over rocky heights and through deep valleys'. The woods, like the mountains, seem almost to be malevolent in their resistance. With the settlers turned into terrified refugees, and the messengers of the English all intercepted by the Indians and killed, the wilderness is mysterious and full of danger. White expansion on the western frontiers has been checked; the mountains and forests have been returned to the red men.

In the second paragraph, the phrase 'sea of savage verdure' develops the implication that the forest and the Indian are one in their resistance to the troops. The word 'savage' derives, as Francis Parkman and Henry David Thoreau both knew, from the Latin *silva* ('woods'); it contains in its etymology a key to the significance of the American Indian for both writers. In the earliest version of this passage, published in the first edition of *The Conspiracy of Pontiac* in 1851, Parkman had written that 'the whole country lay buried in foliage' and that 'the unbroken forest, like a vast garment, invested the whole'. In the revisions for the text of the 1870 edition quoted here, Parkman has not merely replaced some clichéd phrases, he has expressed a deeper awareness of his own theme. The fact that the road on which the army travelled in 1763 had been 'hewn out by axemen' of General Forbes's expedition five years earlier is not mentioned in the first version of this passage. Its inclusion accentuates the violent effort needed to make even a 'rugged track' through the forests, whose tree-trunks, boughs and matted thickets continue to resist the progress of the forces of civilization. Three pairs of nouns, one abstract ('difficulty and toil') and two concrete ('hill and hollow . . . brook and quagmire'), represent the accumulating obstacles and lead to the triple resistance of 'roots, rocks, and stumps'. Consonants cluster and impede forward movement of the prose as the unyielding terrain opposes the convoy. When we are told: 'Nature had formed the country for a war of ambuscades and surprises' (for Indian warfare, in fact), we are ready to take the implication that nature is as purposively malevolent as the Indian. The 'mighty wall of green' formed by the main ridge of the Alleghenies opposes the westward advance of Bouquet's army just as it has resisted the westward migration of English settlers for over a century. This 'green' is no emblem of pastoral innocence, for we already know that the woods are full of 'prowling savages' – men who are as predatory, in the mind of the English, as the wild beasts who hunt in the wilderness.

Bouquet's march was an historical fact, not a literary invention. Parkman is drawing on source materials for his information, but his conception of the historian's role, like Bancroft's, involved breathing life into his materials, so the vivid sensory details he provides in the lolling tongues of the oxen and the strong resinous smell of the pine trees in the intense heat are, in his view, legitimate means of recreating the past. Here, as throughout *The Conspiracy of Pontiac*, Parkman's endeavour is to make his readers feel what his historical characters felt, to make them experience the moments of drama. In that endeavour, Parkman was able to employ what his best critic has aptly called his 'uncanny sympathy with all forms of physical movement',[2] for his theme is always violent action, the expression of national and racial conflict. The actual Highland soldiers of the 42nd Regiment who marched with Bouquet can hardly be supposed to have thought of 'boundless panoramas', but we can feel with them the relief of the 'windy summit' after the suffocatingly 'sultry air' of the forest.

As the troops march through 'the tall dense forest, which spread for countless leagues around', they are attacked by the Indians who have been lying in ambush close to a small stream called Bushy Run. In his account of the battle that follows, according to Parkman one of the most fiercely fought encounters ever to take place between Indians and white men, we are to some extent detached observers, watching the English regulars charge with the bayonet to drive the Indians from the concealed positions from which they have been harassing the regulars with accurate rifle-fire; but we are taken closer to the wounded soldiers in the surrounded camp, as they lie on the ground 'enduring agonies of thirst' and anticipating a horrible fate if their comrades are defeated. On the second day of the battle, as the British defensive perimeter is weakening and the troops, 'maddened by the torments of thirst', know themselves in danger of being overrun and annihilated, the full terror of the predicament is brought home by a description, not of the soldiers' feelings, but of the frantic behaviour of the horses in the camp, maddened by the bullets and the war-whoops of the Indians. The day is saved and the Indians routed only by the skill of Colonel Bouquet, who feigns a retreat, lures the Indians to the attack and, with a cunning that rivals that of his enemy, launches a countercharge by men hidden on the Indians' flank. The men who charge are the Highlanders, who fall on their enemy with the bayonet and with yells 'as wild as their [the Indians'] own'. Earlier in the volume, in an account of the British attack on Ticonderoga in 1758, Parkman wrote of the Highlanders 'screaming with rage' as they hewed at the branches of trees impeding their charge, and 'struggling to get at the enemy' (I. 123). To Parkman, the Highlanders' blood-lust is one of many indications that the line between savagery and civilization is a shifting one. In the battle of Bushy Run, the British win by excelling the Indians in both cunning and ferocity.

*

When he began to work on the book that became *The Conspiracy of Pontiac*, Parkman's intention was, as he wrote in a letter to a friend in 1845, to make 'something like a biography' of the 'famous Ottawa chief' (L, I. 31). He was interested, he said, in every aspect of the Indian War of 1763–4, but especially in Pontiac. However, finding that little information about the chief's life was available, Parkman decided to give a detailed account of the causes, progress and results of the war 'chiefly with the view of exhibiting the traits of the Indian character'. Four years later, Parkman wrote to another friend to say that he had been interested for some time in writing a general history of the Indians, but for the time being was limiting his researches to the uprising of the northern tribes against the English after the collapse of the French in

Canada. Here, too, he states that the events of the war 'afford an admirable opportunity of representing Indian manners and character' (L, I. 62).

The book Parkman actually wrote is less about the Indian character than about Indian violence and treachery, as the white man saw them. In fact, the violence in *The Conspiracy* is not limited to the pitched battles between Indians and English and the devastating Indian raids on forts and settlements, for in an early chapter, 'The Collision of the Rival Colonies, 1700–55', Parkman anticipates some of his later works on the conflict between France and England in the New World, and tells the gory tale of General Braddock's disastrous defeat by French and Indian forces at Fort du Quesne in 1755, the fierce fighting at Lake George, at Ticonderoga, and the great battle of Quebec in 1759. In terms of the Indian conspiracy, a peak is reached in the account of the massacre of the British garrison of Michillimackinac in June 1763, for this episode demonstrates both Indian guile (the troops are massacred as they watch a supposedly friendly game of lacrosse) and Indian brutality (most of the garrison are butchered and scalped, and the warriors drink the blood of their victims). But this climax occurs at the end of the first volume of the two-volume edition; in the second volume the violence is not always initiated by the Indians and, as we shall see, the savages are not always red men.

In the preface to the first edition of *The Conspiracy*, Parkman stated that he aimed 'to portray the American forest and the American Indian at the period when both received their final doom'. The way in which this identification of the forest with the Indian affected the narrative has already been glanced at, but to understand its full significance for Parkman we have to turn to his opening chapter, 'Indian Tribes East of the Mississippi'. It begins with the statement: 'The Indian is a true child of the forest and the desert. The wastes and solitudes of nature are his congenial home.' It goes on, drawing on H. R. Schoolcraft's *Oneóta*, J. G. E. Heckewelder's *History of the Indian Nations*, J. F. Lafitau's *Mœurs des sauvages ameriquains*, the *Relations* of several French Jesuit missionaries to the Canadian Indians in the seventeenth century, and other authorities on the subject, to give a brief account of Indian life and Indian beliefs. Pouring scorn on rhapsodic and sentimental versions of the Indian character, Parkman prides himself on a realistic estimate of the limitations of the red man and points to the strange mixture of invincible pride and abject beggary that characterize his dealings with the white man. In its main conclusions, Parkman's judgement follows the common 'savagist' prejudices of his age, deciding that the Indian is doomed to extinction because his 'fixed and rigid quality' makes it impossible for him to learn the arts of civilization. One manifestation of Indian inflexibility that Parkman's authorities had noted was the resistance to Christianity: the refusal to accept the belief in the one, true God in place of the numerous deities of traditional Indian religion. Sharing the dismissive attitude of his contemporaries, Parkman asserts that the religious belief of all the hunting tribes of America 'is a cloudy bewilderment, where we seek in vain for system or coherency' (I. 39), while their understanding of moral good and evil are 'perplexed and shadowy'. But he does recognize that 'to the Indian mind, all nature was instinct with deity. A spirit was embodied in every mountain, lake, and cataract; every bird, beast, or reptile, every tree, shrub, or grass-blade, was endued with mystic influence.' To Parkman, this is 'untutored pantheism' and no more than an arrested stage of religious development, but its implications for the Indian's relationship with nature emerge in important ways throughout the book.

By the time he wrote *The Jesuits in North America* (1867), Parkman knew more about the Iroquois than he had when working on *The Conspiracy*. In the later work he stresses the Indians' awareness of the close relationship between men and the natural world, for he finds in that awareness the explanation of the Indian's need to propitiate the spirit of any animal he must kill for food. In *The Conspiracy*, turning from his survey of the bloody conflict between France and England in the New World between 1700 and 1755, Parkman describes 'The Wilderness and Its Tenants at the Close of the French War, 1755–1763' (ch. v). Here the initial assertion that the Indian is the 'true child of the forest and the desert' and is at home in the wilderness returns in a striking form. A vivid passage shows us the 'nursling of civilization', the city-bred white man, hopelessly lost in the labyrinth of the forest, wandering 'bewildered and amazed' until he dies of hunger and despair. In the forest the civilized man is 'helpless as an infant' (I. 159) and the places on the scale of maturity are dramatically reversed. The white backwoodsman, having learned from the Indian, can eventually excel him at hunting and tracking, but he can never attain to 'that subtlety of sense, more akin to the instinct of brutes than to human reason' that enables the red man to read the meaning of 'the great world of nature' (I. 159–60). The pejorative implications of this judgement are consistent with Bancroft's account of the Indian in his chapter 'The Aborigines East of the Mississippi' in the third volume of his *History* (1839). Bancroft had moved from a recognition that the Indian saw spirits in every concrete particular of the natural world to the conclusion that he lacked the power to conceive an 'absolute substance' or a 'self-existent' deity. The Indian's deficiency, as Bancroft understood it, was a lack of imagination and a lack of 'the faculty of abstraction to lift himself out of the dominion of his immediate experience' (III. 285, 302). Thus the red man was, like the animals, the prisoner of his senses and was so close to nature that 'we may call them savage, just as we call fruits wild' (p. 300). Bancroft was, at the same time, more generous to the Indian than Parkman, insisting that he was also a man, with sufficient moral sense to feel keenly the abuse of his white dispossessor, but though he could explain the Indian's wildness, Bancroft could not project his own imagination into the Indian's relationship with nature as Parkman, for all his prejudices and limitations, so feelingly could.

*

Parkman's prejudices were those of the highly privileged 'nursling of civilization' who belonged to the Brahmin caste of early nineteenth-century Boston. Born in 1823, son of the Reverend Dr Francis Parkman, who was a disciple of William Ellery Channing and minister of the New North Church in Boston, he was, in the words of his biographer, 'born to the purple and with a golden spoon in his mouth'.[3] He was born, in fact, in the family home on Beacon Hill, the most socially desirable area of Boston, and was to live there all his life. But the young Francis Parkman reacted against his family's pious heritage, disliked the great Dr Channing and took no interest in the family-endowed chair at the Divinity School. Parkman first experienced the thrill of contact with the wilderness as a boy, between the ages of eight and thirteen, while holidaying at Five Mile Woods (later Middlesex Fells) at Medford, a wilderness only eight miles from the heart of Boston. In 1841, while a freshman at Harvard, he took a vacation trip to the White Mountains and indulged his desire for adventure by climbing a dangerous avalanche ravine and then exploring the deep forest of what was still the sparsely settled New Hampshire frontier around Lake Umbagog. As early as his sophomore year, Parkman knew what his life-long interest as an historian would be, for in April 1842 he wrote to Jared Sparks, McLean Professor of History at Harvard, asking for information about the military operations around Lake George at the time of the Seven Years War. In the same year, unable to carry out a proposed visit to Mount Katahdin in the Maine wilderness, he visited Lake George, which was also still part of a wilderness area. Parkman's interest had been stimulated by reading Fenimore Cooper's *Last of the*

Mohicans, but he typically sought firsthand experience of the wilds and personal contact with the past. While on this excursion he had the good fortune to meet a certain Captain Patchin, a veteran of the Indian campaigns near Fort Stanwix, and so could gather information from a participant in the story he was determined to tell. These early trips taught Parkman what he was to know of forest and river travel. He depended on them for his understanding of the great explorers La Salle and Champlain in the histories he was to write, for he always liked to work from his own experience when he attempted to recreate the past.

His fascination with the wild began, in Parkman's own account, when he was no more than fifteen or sixteen. Writing about his own past in a letter of 1864 and talking of himself in the third person, Parkman told a friend that at an early age he was seized by a passion for the woods that 'soon gained full control over the course of the literary pursuits to which he was also addicted' (L, I. 176). The word 'addicted' is, of course, revealing; even more so is the statement in the same letter that the passion for the woods was still, in 1864, 'but half gratified'. In his own words, Parkman's 'thoughts were always in the forests, whose features, not unmixed with softer images, possessed his waking and sleeping dreams, filling him with vague cravings impossible to satisfy' (p. 177). Characteristically, he follows this admission with an account of the damage he had done to his health by reckless disregard for it on his excursions into the forest and then goes on to recommend the strenuous life as a remedy for the 'pallid and emasculate scholarship of which New England has had too many examples'. When we find Parkman advising hours in the saddle and on the hunt as a tonic for the 'pale student', it is not difficult to see why Theodore Roosevelt dedicated *The Winning of the West* (1889–96) to him.

Always contemptuous of mental and spiritual culture that went with physical weakness, and always a believer in the virtues of physical toughness and courage, after 1846 Parkman was plagued by psychosomatic maladies that made him an invalid and thus denied him the life of heroic action he desired. Unable to take part in either the Mexican War or the Civil War, he could give expression to his yearning for adventure only in his writings. His illness first took the form of a weakness of the eyes that confined him to a darkened room and made reading and writing virtually impossible for long periods. This impediment to his studies was not all he had to endure, for with the condition of his eyes went a mental disorder that Parkman described as a 'strange undefined torture'. Both conditions seem to have been aggravated by his passion for his historical studies, though Parkman believed that his nervous system had been abnormal from birth. To complete his misery, he was crippled by water on the knee and confined to indoor life after 1852.

Parkman's eyes were already troubling him in the winter of 1845–6 while he worked with furious intensity on the history of Pontiac's conspiracy. It was partly with the intention of resting his eyes that he embarked on the great adventure of his life: his Oregon Trail excursion in the spring and summer of 1846, a trip that had its climax in some weeks spent with a wandering band of completely untamed Oglala Sioux who had had scarcely any contact with the white man. His prime motive in making the expedition, as he recalled it in his autobiographical letter of 1864, was 'to gain an inside view of Indian life' because the knowledge was essential for his literary plans. In the autobiographical letter, more than in the book that resulted from the expedition, Parkman stressed his physical infirmity at the time – 'reeling in the saddle with weakness and pain', he made the arduous journey over hundreds of miles of rough country in search of the Sioux, and when he had found them he had to conceal his weakness or risk provoking the savages' aggression. Yet, weak as he was, he found the rigours of the buffalo hunt a 'tonic' and exerted himself even more than was necessary to earn the respect of the Indians. His policy and his creed was, as the letter makes plain, to combat his physical ailments by forcing himself to violent and dangerous effort. In his words, 'to tame the devil, it is best to take him by the horns'.

The original subtitle of the book that became *The Oregon Trail* was 'A Summer's Journey Out of Bounds'.[4] Nothing could more clearly point to Parkman's motivation. In language uncannily close to Thoreau's account of 'extra-vagance' (see pp. 145, 149), this scion of Brahminical stock reveals his own intense need to go beyond the bounds of the culture in which he firmly and consistently believes with his conscious mind. The most obvious means of escaping the physical confines of Bostonian culture was to go West. The most vivid contrast to the spiritual culture of the Reverend Dr Channing, whose disregard of the physical life seemed to Parkman 'emasculate or fanatical', was provided by the wild life of the completely uncivilized tribe. The great Sioux warrior Mahto-Tatonka, whom Parkman met at the Oglala camp, was 'limbed like an Apollo in bronze' and rode in triumph, his head-dress crested with eagle's feathers, his round white shield hanging at his breast, his quiver at his back, tall lance in his hand, with the scalp-locks of his enemies fluttering from the shaft. 'Balancing with graceful buoyancy to the free movements of his war horse', he seemed to

Parkman to be as 'gorgeous as a champion in panoply' as he rode within the great ring of lodges, watched by the whole admiring village, and sang his song to the Great Spirit before leaving on the war path. To see the Indian as a Greek god in physique and a medieval champion in military prowess is, of course, to dignify him as much as any Romantic could, but Parkman undercuts his own description in the interests of realism: 'Yet, after all, he was but an Indian. See him as he lies there in the sun before our tent, kicking his heels in the air and cracking jokes with his brother. Does he look like a hero?'

Repeatedly in *The Oregon Trail*, Parkman paints the Indian in scenes that are 'striking and picturesque beyond description', giving his readers glimpses of the 'savage multitude, the armed warriors, the naked children, the gaily apparelled girls' moving impetuously through the mountains, or the warriors sitting on horseback, 'savage figures, with quivers at their backs, and guns, lances, or tomahawks in their hands . . . motionless as statues, their arms crossed on their breasts and their eyes fixed in a steady unwavering gaze' on the white men. Self-consciously stressing the aesthetic qualities of such scenes, he invokes the spirit of the favourite painter of the Gothic novelists, Salvator, or the most distinguished writer of historical romances, Sir Walter Scott, as appropriate to his sublime and noble subjects. But just as he both celebrated and demeaned the leading warrior of the tribe, so he sets beside his heroic images of Indian life the boredom, emptiness, futility of their daily round, and insists on the squalid confusion of their life in camp. The old Sioux women are 'hideous'; round the blazing camp-fire flit 'withered, witch-like hags'. Even the warriors behave 'like ungoverned children inflamed with the fiercest passions of men' when they are sold whisky by the white emigrants who pass them *en route* for Oregon. When he came to write of *The Jesuits in North America* (1867), Parkman portrayed with feeling the predicament of the cultivated missionary Le Jeune amid the 'hardship, famine, filth, wickedness' of a Huron camp; clearly, he was again drawing on his own memories. The hunting life, as Parkman knew, could reduce the tribe that followed it to the 'misery and degradation' he described in *The Jesuits*.

In his explicit judgements on the Plains Indians in *The Oregon Trail*, Parkman writes with the condescension and contempt of a highly civilized white man who regards the savages as 'the living representatives of "the stone age" '. If this were all, his book would be no more than a rather clumsily wrought and self-consciously 'literary' travelogue, with the fortuitous historical interest lent by the fact that its writer took part, more or less as a tourist, in the great westward migration to

Oregon in the 1840s. But the main interest of *The Oregon Trail* lies less in its evocations of the sublime scenery of the Rocky Mountains and the occasional glamour of the Indians of the high plains than in the curiously indefinite narrative stance of the author. Angrily rebuffing the crude inquisitiveness of the proletarian emigrants he meets on his journey, the 'I' of the book does not announce his real motive for the trip until he is a third of the way through his story; and even then his language is ambiguous. Hearing of a projected Sioux war-party against the Snake tribe, he says 'I was greatly rejoiced to hear of it. I had come into the country chiefly with a view of observing the Indian character. To accomplish my purpose it was necessary to live in the midst of them, and become, as it were, one of them.' The unashamed delight at the prospect of Indian warfare casts an interesting light on the narrator's role as amateur ethnographer. More significant still is the phrase 'become, as it were, one of them'. Of course no Bostonian of the Brahmin caste could seriously propose to become one of the savages any more than he could identify with the coarse, uncultivated white emigrants who were about to sweep the Sioux to extinction, yet he *does* become 'one of them' as he experiences the thrill of the buffalo hunt, and thus, as his letter of 1864 has it, feels the 'tonic' that revives his failing health and spirits. The joy and exhilaration of the chase is ultimately the joy of the kill, with the added grace that it is a socially sanctioned death-dealing. Parkman did not kill buffalo for food or materials as the Sioux did; he killed for pleasure, and in this, as in his 'motor-mindedness'[5] and *part* of his style of living, he strikingly anticipated some features of Ernest Hemingway's career and some characteristics of his writings.

The chapter entitled 'The Hunting Camp' (ch. 15) is one of the most exciting in Parkman's book. At the end of the preceding chapter, the narrator tells that, ill as he was, 'there was something very animating in the prospect of the general hunt' the next day. When the hunt begins, Parkman leaves camp 'with a philosophic resolution' to remain a spectator, because neither he nor his horse are fit for 'such sport'; but amid the furious movement of the hunt he finds it impossible to sit still, so he drives his exhausted mount to within yards of a desperate buffalo and shoots it in the neck. Returning to the lodge of his Indian host, he falls asleep as quickly as his savage friend who is smeared to the elbows with blood. When he eats the rich, juicy hump-ribs of a slain buffalo cow, against 'all medical experience' he finds that this solid fare agrees with him admirably. He has become one of the tribe in appetite as he never would in conscious thought.

Less dramatic but no less revealing than 'The Hunting Camp' is an incident recorded at the end of 'A Mountain Hunt' (ch. 18). Climbing a mountain alone, Parkman comes, unobserved, across the Indian Mene-Seela 'seated alone, immovable as a statue, among the rocks and trees'. Without announcing his presence, Parkman observes the old Indian for a long time, deciding that 'he was engaged in an act of worship, or prayer, or communion of some kind with a supernatural being'. Knowing that to the Indian 'all nature is instinct with mystic influence', Parkman longs 'to penetrate his thoughts', but has to rest content with speculation. Perhaps Mene-Seela finds his guardian spirit in the old pine-tree at which he stares, for to the Indian it is 'usually embodied in the form of some living thing: a bear, a wolf, an eagle or a serpent'. The white man cannot penetrate this mystery, but when he looks up at the mountain peak, he feels 'impelled' to climb and feels a strange 'strength and elasticity of limb'. Earlier in the narrative, Parkman has written of his desire to 'penetrate' the 'hidden recesses' of the Black Mountains in a sentence whose syntax could make those recesses belong to the 'minds of the Indians' as well as the mountains. Earlier, too, he has noted the 'wonderfully cheering and exhilarating effect' of the proximity of mountains and rushing streams. In this curiously voyeuristic episode in 'A Mountain Hunt', we must surely credit Parkman with an awareness that he is here, as in an earlier chapter with an apt title, 'Hunting Indians' to bring back a spiritual bounty that his system of conscious values cannot acknowledge.

*

The 'true child of the forest and the desert' described in the first chapter of *The Conspiracy of Pontiac* has a mind 'imbued with the spirit of the wilderness'. That spirit gives to the Indian an 'unruly pride and untamed freedom' that are 'in harmony with the lonely mountains, cataracts and rivers among which he dwells'. In making the spirit of freedom the mainspring of the Indian character, Parkman is following an already well-established nineteenth-century tradition. De Tocqueville, in a chapter on the coloured races in *Democracy in America* (vol. I, ch. 18), had contrasted the submissive self-abnegation of the Negro slave with the spirit of utter defiance of white civilization shown by the Indian, who loved his savage life and maintained it as the distinguishing mark of his race. Bancroft, the propagandist for White Anglo-Saxon Protestant liberty, noted in his *History* (vol. III, p. 275), that 'The wild man hates restraint, and loves to do what is right in his own eyes', but saw no generic link between white liberty and savage rejection of all law. Parkman's Indian 'abhors restraint, and owns no other authority than his own capricious will' (I. 2). His spirit of freedom is devalued by repeated association with childishness and with instinctual animal behaviour, for Parkman intends to follow Bancroft in the firm demarcation of savage and civilized liberty, but Parkman *is* aware of a continuity, because he finds it in the materials of his history and in himself.

In the first chapter of *The Conspiracy*, the 'blood-besmeared' Iroquois roam 'like wolves' among the burning settlements of French Canada. Later, as Pontiac and his braves attempt to enter Fort Pitt as friends and then to butcher the garrison, their eyes are 'like those of rattlesnakes' (I. 225); when captured, a savage is no more entitled to quarter than an 'entrapped wolf'. David Levin and Harvey Wish both argue that Parkman is writing of the Indian in the manner of the Puritan historian when he uses this bestial imagery,[6] but no Puritan historian had anything like Parkman's sympathetic response to the wild. When Parkman says that the great mass of Indians who joined Pontiac's conspiracy 'turned against their enemies with as little reason or forecast as a panther when he leaps at the throat of the hunter' (I. 185), he is emphasizing his view that the Indians were driven to desperation by the ceaseless encroachment of the white settlers on their land. At the same time, he is giving a specific application to his theory of the Indian: spontaneous, acting on instinct and without reflection, the savage is a wild animal, acting in perfect freedom of impulse.

Writing of the Canadian fur-trade in the second chapter of *The Conspiracy*, Parkman explains that it produced a class of restless bush-rangers 'more akin to Indians than to white men' (p. 49). He goes on: 'Those who had once felt the fascination of the forest were unfitted ever after for a life of quiet labor; and with this spirit the whole colony [of French Canada] was infected.' The pejorative connotations of 'unfitted' and 'infected' are obvious – as always the verdict is a harsh one – but the passage shows some understanding of the 'infection', for Parkman, as we have seen, had felt the fascination. Of the hunters, traders and scouts who ranged the woods beyond the borders of the English settlements in the 1760s, Parkman writes that they formed a 'connecting link between barbarism and civilization'. Such 'sons of the wilderness' are still to be found in the 1850s, he adds, for the 'lonely trapper' climbs 'the perilous defiles of the Rocky Mountains' in Parkman's imagination even as he writes. The trapper's life is rigorous and dangerous, 'yet his wild, hard life has resistless charms' (I. 159).

One of the most vividly imagined scenes in *The Conspiracy* is the return, in November 1764, of the prisoners captured by the Delawares and Shawanoes. In a note, Parkman first tells the story of Mary Jemison, a white woman captured by the Senecas and twice married to members of the tribe, who hid in the woods to avoid being returned to civilization and 'never lost her attachment to the Indian life' (II. 233), though she lived to an advanced age. He goes on to tell of the many returned prisoners who bitterly resented being forced to 'abandon the wild license of the forest for the irksome restraints of society'. Their recalcitrance, he explains, should not be attributed to moral perversity, for 'many a sound and healthful mind' has felt civilization to be 'flat and stale' when it has experienced 'the reckless independence, the haughty self-reliance, the sense of irresponsible freedom, which the forest life engenders' (II. 237). After such freedom, the pleasures of civilized life are insipid, 'its pursuits wearisome, its conventionalities, duties, and mutual dependence alike tedious and disgusting'. Though Parkman is speaking on behalf of 'the entrapped wanderer', there can be no doubt that such a wanderer is entrapped in Parkman's self. 'His path', we are told, 'was choked with difficulties, but his body and soul were hardened to meet them; it was beset with dangers, but these were the very spice of his life, gladdening his heart with exulting self-confidence, and sending the blood through his veins with a livelier current' (p. 238). What can this be but a vicarious portrait of the historian of the wilderness? It is followed by a passage, in deplorably overblown style, on the symbolic and inspirational value of the desert, mountain and storm to the 'grand and heroic' spirit in man.

Yet Parkman saw himself as the historian of 'progress' in Bancroft's sense of the term. As the defeated and doomed Pontiac skirts Lake Erie (II. 300), our attention is turned from the bleak wilderness to the amazing scene that will shortly appear when commerce works its transformation. Cities and townships will fill the empty waste, and sails will cover the formerly empty waters. When Pontiac is murdered after the failure of his conspiracy, a great city (St Louis) rises over his unmarked grave 'and the race whom he hated with such burning rancor trample [in 1851 and thereafter] with unceasing footsteps' over that grave (p. 313). Commercial development and great cities are, to the nineteenth-century American historian, indisputably signs of a desired march of human progress, yet when Parkman earlier turned his gaze from the beautiful, unspoiled landscape around Fort Pitt in 1759 to the city that grew from its ruins, he saw 'warehouses, and forges with countless chimneys, rolling up their black volumes of smoke' (II. 3). As a young man on his

1841 expedition to the White Mountains and Lake Winnepesaukee, Parkman had deplored the ugliness of a 'disgusting little manufacturing village' (J, I. 9). In his *La Salle and the Discovery of the Great West* (1878; first published as *The Discovery of the Great West* in 1869, then revised and retitled) Parkman noted that the Indian paintings on the rocks above Alton had been replaced by an advertisement for Plantation Bitters when he visited the spot in 1867. He also recorded, in the same book, that the great natural beauty of Minneapolis had been spoiled utterly by two banks and an opera house, while St Anthony had been ruined by a university and a huge spa. Opera houses and universities – if not banks – should have set the seal of civilization on the former wilderness; in Parkman's view they destroyed what he most admired: the natural sublime.

Parkman's introduction to his *Pioneers of France in the New World* (1865), his next book after *The Conspiracy*, begins as if to follow the Bancroft pattern. New England stands for liberty and the spirit of reform; New France represents the spirit of absolutism and is the champion of Roman Catholic reaction against human progress. With the political freedom nurtured in New England goes the material progress that, as in Bancroft's *History*, depends on freedom; in the English settlements every man can advance his fortunes by industry. But even in this opening statement Parkman begins to move away from the scheme of values he has inherited from his eminent predecessor, for he admits that the material progress of New England culture brings with it social conformism, that it is essentially unheroic, and that it produces no great personalities. Reactionary though it is, French culture in the New World gives full scope to the heroic spirit in its aristocracy and produces great men of the stature of Champlain. Soon we find that the bigotry and tyranny of the Roman Catholic Church are represented by Spain rather than France, and attention shifts to the infamous deeds of the Spaniards. Spain under Philip II is the ultimate example of repressiveness; Spain's military leaders in Florida – and the men who serve them – are, like the 'savage' Duke of Alba, crueller and more ferocious than the natives.

Early in *Pioneers of France* Parkman writes of the effect of the wilderness on the French settlers in Florida, explaining a murder that took place at Port Royal in 1562 as a consequence of the awakening of the dormant savage in the breast of the civilized white man. This isolated murder soon pales in significance when followed by the Spaniards' massacre of two hundred French Huguenot prisoners. The 'savage soldiery' of Spain are 'like wolves' in their lust for slaughter and so excel the Indians in ferocity that the French survivors prefer to entrust their lives to the natives rather than put themselves at the mercy of these white butchers. The story of the massacre is one of the most gruesome in all of Parkman's histories of battle and conflict; it is equalled only by an episode in *The Conspiracy* described in a chapter with the appropriate title of 'The White Savage'. That savage is a white man who has lived for some years among the Indians, having been captured by them, and has married a squaw by whom he has had several children. Wishing to return to the settlements and ingratiate himself with the whites, David Owens murders and scalps his Indian wife and half-breed children, intending to collect the bounties offered for them. Labelling this as 'devilish work', Parkman takes the opportunity to comment on the white 'barbarians' who outdo the Indian in savagery. Owens's cold-blooded brutality is not to be understood as a unique aberration of the white psyche, for the Governor of Pennsylvania is himself implicated in the deed: he has proclaimed a bounty on every scalp of an Indian, male or female, over the age of ten. When the 'Paxton Men' slaughter unarmed Conestoga Indians in Lancaster Jail, littering the ground with the mangled bodies of men, women and children, the spirit of the frontier has manifested itself in all classes, from State Governor to uncouth backwoodsman. Though Parkman did not record it until 1869, the message left by French deserters from one of La Salle's expeditions in the 1680s, '*Nous sommes tous sauvages*', could serve as an epigraph for all his stories of New World savagery. Curiously, it was anticipated in one of his first published works: a story called 'The Scalp-Hunter' published in the *Knickerbocker* magazine in April 1845. In this early 'Semi-Historical Sketch' as he called it, Parkman tells of an 'old human bloodhound', a white backwoodsman, who pursues an Indian with a reckless determination that can only be explained by the ten-pound bounty on Indian scalps. In the tale, the Indian is the hunted 'game' that must flee 'like a frightened deer' from the white hunter. He is saved by the spirit of the White Mountains, a 'malignant spirit' in Indian legend, but one that greets with death the first white man to enter the Crawford Notch, who plunges down the avalanche slope that Parkman had himself only just managed to scale on his youthful visit.

That the spirit of the mountain wilderness should destroy the intrusive and destructive white man in Parkman's early fiction is surely appropriate. The Indian, as the historian was later to say, was the 'true child' of the forest and of the wilderness. But Nature was not benevolent even to her own children, as Parkman knew well, for his own experience of the wilderness taught him how precarious was man's hold on life in his savage state. When he came, in *The Jesuits in North America*, to describe the winters on the Great Lakes, he portrayed 'dead Nature' as 'sheeted in funereal white' and the forests as 'silent as the grave' (p. 112). Where the white man would perish, the Indian manages to survive – but barely. Nature is hostile to white advance, but is clearly not protective of the red man. Parkman's delight in the wildness of unimproved nature is a response to its sublimity, not its 'humanity' in the Emersonian sense. Watching the cannibal warfare of some little fishes in a pool among the Laramie Mountains in 1846, Parkman decided that 'life is incessant war' whatever the 'soft-hearted philanthropists' would like to make of it (*Oregon Trail*, ch. 19). In such passages Parkman anticipates the naturalist writers of the 1890s, but, unlike them, he at the same time thought he believed in the high culture of Beacon Hill.

Parkman's 'official' identification with the forces of progress and civilization in their encroachment on the wild is plainly stated in his preface to the first edition of *The Conspiracy*. When he began his researches, so he tells us, 'the field of history was uncultured and unreclaimed', so that the work he had to do was 'like that of the border settler, who, before he builds his rugged dwelling, must fell the forest-trees, burn the undergrowth, clear the ground, and hew the fallen trunks to due proportion' (p. xii). In the same preface Parkman explains that he was aided in the field-work necessary for his history by the 'strong natural taste' that led him 'to the wild regions of the north and west' (p. x). With such a 'natural taste' the historian could hardly avoid ambivalent feelings about his function as tamer of the historical wilderness; his allegiance to the civilization that resulted from the settlement of the wild was, as we have seen, less complete than his explicit ideas would lead us to suppose. At the end of his career, working on the last pages of his *Half-Century of Conflict* in 1890, Parkman wrote in a room kept for him in the Wentworth mansion, a colonial house belonging to his son-in-law. On the wall of his work-room (as Wilbur Jacobs tells us)[7] hung the fringed leather shirt and powder horn that he had used on his 1846 trip to the Oglala Sioux. With him, too, was the saddle he had mounted on his prairie horses on that adventurous expedition. To the end, Parkman 'indulged' (the word is his) a taste for the wild that after 1846 could find expression only in his writings.

Notes

1 The text of the extract is taken from *The Conspiracy of Pontiac and the Indian War after the Conquest of Canada*, sixth edn, rev. with additions, 2 vols,

Boston: Little, Brown, 1870, II. Parenthetic references to *The Conspiracy* throughout the chapter are also to this edition. References to L are to *The Letters of Francis Parkman*, ed. Wilbur Jacobs, 2 vols, Norman: University of Oklahoma Press, 1960.

2 *Howard Doughty, *Francis Parkman*, New York: Macmillan, 1962, p. 97.

3 Mason Wade, *Francis Parkman: Heroic Historian*, New York: Viking Press, 1942, p. 3.

4 *The Journals of Francis Parkman*, ed. Mason Wade, 2 vols, New York: Harper, 1947, II. 386.

5 The term is Howard Doughty's, *Francis Parkman*, p. 97.

6 David Levin, *History as Romantic Art: Bancroft, Prescott, Motley and Parkman*, New York: Harcourt, Brace and World, 1963, pp. 135–6; Harvey Wish, *The American Historian*, Oxford University Press, 1960, p. 91.

7 Jacobs tells the story in his introduction to *The Letters of Francis Parkman*, I.lv.

Further reading

William R. Taylor, 'Francis Parkman', in *Pastmasters: Some Essays on American Historians*, eds Marcus Cunliffe and R. Winks, New York: Harper & Row, 1969.

Harvey Wish, *The American Historian: A Social-Intellectual History of the Writing of the American Past*, New York: Oxford University Press, 1960.

8
Henry David Thoreau (1817–62)

To the sick the doctors wisely recommend a change of air and scenery. Thank Heaven, here is not all the world. The buck-eye does not grow in New England, and the mocking-bird is rarely heard here. The wild-goose is more of a cosmopolite than we; he breaks his fast in Canada, takes a luncheon in the Ohio, and plumes himself for the night in a southern bayou. Even the bison, to some extent, keeps pace with the seasons, cropping the pastures of the Colorado only till a greener and sweeter grass awaits him by the Yellowstone. Yet we think that if rail-fences are pulled down, and stone-walls piled up on our farms, bounds are henceforth set to our lives and our fates decided. If you are chosen town-clerk, forsooth, you cannot go to Tierra del Fuego this summer: but you may go to the land of infernal fire nevertheless. The universe is wider than our views of it.

Yet we should oftener look over the tafferel of our craft, like curious passengers, and not make the voyage like stupid sailors picking oakum. The other side of the globe is but the home of our correspondent. Our voyaging is only great-circle sailing, and the doctors prescribe for diseases of the skin merely. One hastens to Southern Africa to chase the giraffe; but surely that is not the game he would be after. How long, pray, would a man hunt giraffes if he could? Snipes and woodcocks also may afford rare sport; but I trust it would be nobler game to shoot one's self. –

> 'Direct your eye sight inward, and you'll find
> A thousand regions in your mind
> Yet undiscovered. Travel them, and be
> Expert in home-cosmography.'

What does Africa, – what does the West stand for? Is not our own interior white on the chart? black though it may prove, like the coast, when discovered. Is it the source of the Nile, or the Niger, or the

Mississippi, or a North-West Passage around this continent, that we would find? Are these the problems which most concern mankind? Is Franklin the only man who is lost, that his wife should be so earnest to find him? Does Mr Grinnell know where he himself is? Be rather the Mungo Park, the Lewis and Clarke and Frobisher, of your own streams and oceans; explore your own higher latitudes, – with shiploads of preserved meats to support you, if they be necessary; and pile the empty cans sky-high for a sign. Were preserved meats invented to preserve meat merely? Nay, be a Columbus to whole new continents and worlds within you, opening new channels, not of trade, but of thought. Every man is the lord of a realm beside which the earthly empire of the Czar is but a petty state, a hummock left by the ice. Yet some can be patriotic who have no *self*-respect, and sacrifice the greater to the less. They love the soil which makes their graves, but have no sympathy with the spirit which may still animate their clay. Patriotism is a maggot in their heads. What was the meaning of that South-Sea Exploring Expedition, with all its parade and expense, but an indirect recognition of the fact, that there are continents and seas in the moral world, to which every man is an isthmus or an inlet, yet unexplored by him, but that it is easier to sail many thousand miles through cold and storm and cannibals, in a government ship, with five hundred men and boys to assist one, than it is to explore the private sea, the Atlantic and Pacific Ocean of one's being alone. . . .

I left the woods for as good a reason as I went there. Perhaps it seemed to me that I had several more lives to live, and could not spare any more time for that one. It is remarkable how easily and insensibly we fall into a particular route, and make a beaten track for ourselves. I had not lived there a week before my feet wore a path from my door to the pond-side; and though it is five or six years since I trod it, it is still quite distinct. It is true, I fear that others may have fallen into it, and so helped to keep it open. The surface of the earth is soft and impressible by the feet of men; and so with the paths which the mind travels. How worn and dusty, then, must be the highways of the world, how deep the ruts of tradition and conformity! I did not wish to take a cabin passage, but rather to go before the mast and on the deck of the world, for there I could best see the moonlight amid the mountains. I do not wish to go below now.

I learned this, at least, by my experiment; that if one advances confidently in the direction of his dreams, and endeavors to live the life which he has imagined, he will meet with a success unexpected in common hours. He will put some things behind, will pass an invisible boundary; new, universal, and more liberal laws will begin to establish themselves around and within him; or the old laws be expanded, and interpreted in his favor in a more liberal sense, and he will live with the license of a higher order of beings. In proportion as he simplifies his life, the laws of the universe will appear less complex, and solitude will not be solitude, nor poverty poverty, nor weakness weakness. If you have built castles in the air, your work need not be lost; that is where they should be. Now put the foundations under them.

It is a ridiculous demand which England and America make, that you shall speak so that they can understand you. Neither men nor toad-stools grow so. As if that were important, and there were not enough to understand you without them. As if Nature could support but one order of understandings, could not sustain birds as well as quadrupeds, flying as well as creeping things, and *hush* and *who*, which Bright can understand, were the best English. As if there were safety in stupidity alone. I fear chiefly lest my expression may not be *extra- vagant* enough, may not wander far enough beyond the narrow limits of my daily experience, so as to be adequate to the truth of which I have been convinced. *Extra vagance!* it depends on how you are yarded. The migrating buffalo, which seeks new pastures in another latitude, is not extravagant like the cow which kicks over the pail, leaps the cow-yard fence, and runs after her calf, in milking time. I desire to speak somewhere *without* bounds; like a man in a waking moment, to men in their waking moments; for I am convinced that I cannot exaggerate enough even to lay the foundation of a true expression. Who that has heard a strain of music feared then lest he should speak extravagantly any more forever? In view of the future or possible, we should live quite laxly and undefined in front, our outlines dim and misty on that side; as our shadows reveal an insensible perspiration toward the sun. The volatile truth of our words should continually betray the inadequacy of the residual statement. Their truth is instantly *translated;* its literal monument alone remains. The words which express our faith and piety are not definite; yet they are significant and fragrant like frankincense to superior natures.

Conclusion to *Walden* (1854)[1]

* * *

The cosmopolite wild goose breakfasts in Canada, lunches *in* the Ohio River, and takes his feathery rest in a southern bayou. The bison on the western plains move more slowly, yet they do move in step with – at the same pace as – the seasons. The wit that gives the wild creatures human roles also suggests that men often live their lives with an inadequate sense of human nature and its possibilities. Men wall in their lives as they wall in their property; in doing so they set their own narrow limits and seal their own fates. Our notion of 'extravagance' depends, as we are told in the fifth paragraph, on how we, men and beasts, are 'yarded'. The word plays on the double meaning of measured (in yards) and confined in farmyards. In his essay 'Circles', Emerson pictured human life as a 'self-evolving circle' endlessly expanding to form newer and larger circles and endlessly resisting the tendency of ideas to harden into dogma and thus to 'solidify and hem in the life'. Summing up his faith in life as process, Emerson asserted: 'The only sin is limitation.' In *Walden*, as in all his writings, Thoreau's theme is the divine potentiality of human life. He tells us, in the opening pages, that 'man's capacities have never been measured'. But his faith in man's infinite possibilities implies a concern with the actual limits men accept in their lives. Throughout *Walden*, Thoreau is concerned with boundaries and the means of breaking out from them. Emerson, as we have seen, expressed his most profound and passionate ideas in images, yet Thoreau's metaphors in *Walden* have a status and a cumulative force that Emerson's do not, for they arise from a context in which every detail of the literal story – leaving the village, entering the woods, building a house, cultivating the soil, surveying the pond – has an analogical relevance to the measurement of man's capacities and the expression of his life. The Conclusion to *Walden* takes up and restates images and themes that have been announced and developed in earlier chapters. Thus the allusion to fences and walls in the opening paragraph refers us back to the chapter called 'Sounds', where life in the woods is said to be life with 'No yard! but unfenced Nature reaching up to your very sills.' Similarly, the voyages mentioned in the second paragraph depend for their full significance on the thematic discussion of travel in the 'Economy' chapter. Though *Walden* is written in prose, its language has the intensity of poetry.

The wisdom of the doctors, apparently acknowledged in the first paragraph, does not survive the appraisal of tourism in the second. Our real sickness is spiritual, not physical, and will not be cured by sailing in circles, even if the circle sailed is as wide as the globe. The distinction between inward and outward exploration is fundamental to *Walden*, a travelogue in which the actual distance travelled by the 'I' of the story is – as we are told in 'Where I Lived' – about one and a half miles from the village of Concord. At the pond, however, the Thoreau persona says that he is as far from the village-life as if he had settled near the

Pleiades or the Hyades, for it is imagination, not yardage, that gives place its significance. In asking what Africa and the West stand for, Thoreau assumes that the unexplored regions of the globe, still left white on the maps of 1854, are worth the attention of thoughtful men because they correspond to the vast areas of the self that are still uncharted. *Walden* takes as one of its central themes the charting of the unknown self. In 'The Pond in Winter' Thoreau surveys (contemplates, measures) Walden Pond and 'fathoms' it exactly, yet paradoxically, having thus recovered the 'long lost bottom' of the pond, he states that men will continue to believe in bottomless ponds as long as they believe in the infinite. To sound the pond is to probe the depths of the self. The measurements reveal a law, but the discovery of that law is a beginning, not an end, of exploration.

Thoreau had encountered the idea that man is a microcosm, carrying within him the wonders he seeks without, in Sir Thomas Browne's *Religio Medici* (1643), which he read attentively as early as 1837. He had noted Browne's telling phrase 'There is all Africa and her prodigies in us' while still a very young man and made brilliant use of it in his maturity. That use is distinctively Thoreauvian in the movement from the general concept of inward exploration to specific reference to particular explorers and their actual voyages in the world outside the self. Thoreau was so serious a student of the literature of travel that he read at least 172 separate travel accounts and read them from cover to cover, making extensive notes on natural and social phenomena, on scenes, opinions and anecdotes.[2] The Henry Grinnell mentioned in the Conclusion to *Walden* was the sponsor of an American expedition to search for the British explorer Sir John Franklin who was lost in the Arctic. When Thoreau asks whether Mr Grinnell knows where he himself is, however, we think of an earlier chapter, 'The Village', in which the journey back to the pond after a snowstorm makes the road as strange as Siberia and prompts the reflection: 'Not till we are lost, in other words, not till we have lost the world, do we begin to find ourselves, and realize where we are and the infinite extent of our relations' (p. 171). If the comment in the Conclusion seems callous about the fate of Sir John Franklin, Thoreau is no sentimentalist about himself. As we shall see, he uses his own experience at Walden Pond, just as he uses the experience of the lost explorer, for what it can tell us about man's life: its actualities and its possibilities.

Thoreau's reference to the South Sea Exploring Expedition here is followed, in a passage not quoted, by an allusion to the 'Symmes' Hole' that we have already met in Poe's *Narrative of Arthur Gordon Pym*, but, where Poe made Symmes's theory of 'holes at the poles' the occasion for a terrifying imaginative journey of Antarctic exploration ending in a plunge into the gulf of the unknown, Thoreau simply makes the suppositious journey to the hole an analogue for the really important business of getting into one's own unexplored depths. There is no nervous excitability heightened to terror in Thoreau's approach to the journey into the self. He admits that the interior to be explored may be as black as the coast of Africa, but seems undisturbed by the thought. The cool disdain for the effort and expense of the Wilkes Expedition to the South Seas and the undaunted readiness to encounter his own darkest secrets proceed from a confidence in the self and in nature that is antithetical to Poe's anxiety.

The remarks on 'home-cosmography' in the final chapter of *Walden* remind us that, in his opening statements in 'Economy', Thoreau took the tone and the stance of a lecturer reporting on his travels. From 1838, the year in which he gave his first lecture, Thoreau had helped to organize the Concord Lyceum and must therefore have known how popular lectures on exotic places and peoples were. In fact, parts of this first chapter were originally given as a lecture at the Lyceum, in response to enquiries made about his life at the pond. Announcing that he had 'travelled a good deal', Thoreau followed this up with the deflationary words 'in Concord' and at once hinted, through his irony, that his travelling had taken place on more than one level. Moreover, in stating that he had something to say, not about the Chinese or Sandwich Islanders (Hawaiians) but about 'you . . . who are said to live in New England', he broached the question of what it means to *live* in any part of the globe. When in the Conclusion, he tells us why he left the pond after only two years, he again uses travel metaphors to express his Transcendentalist belief that any sort of habitual, routine activity (physical or mental) restricts freedom and deadens the spirit. Making a beaten track for oneself, even in the woods, leads to the danger of falling into a mental rut. Reverting to his nautical metaphor, Thoreau explains that to travel before the mast and on the deck of the world means to him keeping free of any cabin, even, by implication, the house he has built in the woods.

In referring to his stay at the pond as an experiment, Thoreau once more relates *Walden* to Emerson's 'Circles', where the rejection of limits had been followed by the assertion: 'I simply experiment, an endless seeker with no Past at my back.' In his second chapter, 'Where I Lived', Thoreau described taking up residence in the woods as one of a series of 'experiments'. Significantly, the earlier ventures had taken the form of buying farms in his imagination only. By introducing specific details of time and place – 4 July 1845, one and a half miles south of Concord – after paragraphs discussing his imaginative rather than actual possession of the Hollowell and other local farms, Thoreau was indicating to his listeners or readers that the story of the sojourn at the pond was also the story of a spiritual quest. The Conclusion returns to this theme when it draws the lessons from the experiment. To advance in the direction of one's dreams and to build castles in the air could be taken as movements away from reality, retreats from the actual to the realm of the ideal, but the command 'Now put the foundations under them' expresses Thoreau's belief that the ideal can transform the real. To understand the relationship between the foundations and the dreams is to understand *Walden*. That relationship depends upon the theory of expression in the paragraph that follows.

Francis Parkman, as we have seen, called his journey to the Rocky Mountains a summer journey 'out of bounds'. Thoreau's actual journey took him no further than the woods between Concord and Lincoln, Massachusetts, but he does not suggest that wider travel in the wilderness would have been to his purpose. Instead, he says: 'I fear chiefly lest my expression may not be *extra-vagant* enough, may not wander far enough beyond the narrow limits of my daily experience, so as to be adequate to the truth of which I have been convinced.' To speak *without* bounds is to express a life lived 'undefined in front': that is to say, with no limit, no 'finis' sign ahead. Whereas Parkman had acted out his wildness, Thoreau expresses his in the language of *Walden* when its extravagance reaches beyond the 'definite' to signify the realms beyond. In comparing the effect of such language to music, Thoreau may well be drawing on a journal entry he had made in 1845, when he wrote of playing his flute 'as if to leap the bounds [of] the narrow fold where human life is penned' (J, I. 375). Frequently in his writings Thoreau describes his response to music as ecstasy, using the term in its etymological sense of *ex-stasis*, or standing beside oneself, and suggesting by that use the possibility of escaping from the limits of the petty, mundane self to a sense of oneness with nature. At the end of the 'Higher Laws' chapter, John Farmer, the hard-working man whose mind is occupied with his day's labour even when his body is resting, hears the sound of the flute coming to him from a different sphere from that in which he habitually lives. He is awakened to a sense of the 'glorious existence' that is possible. With his faculties thus awakened, John Farmer perceives his material existence as a 'mean moiling life' and understands that the 'same stars twinkle over other fields than these'

(p. 222). In *Walden* we are concerned with actual fields, and in particular with the Bean-Field in which Thoreau toiled, but Thoreau's extravagant language supports more than one order of understandings; it makes the actual field signify the 'other fields', not by denying the actual but by '*translating*' it.

New England Transcendentalists were often supposed, by their unsympathetic contemporaries, to deal in airy abstractions and to hold aloof from the real world, yet in 'The Bean-Field' we have concretions and hard facts aplenty. There were seven miles of bean rows; two and a half acres were planted; the bean seed cost \$3.12½, the potatoes for seed \$1.33; the white line for a crow fence cost two cents. A complete account of expenses is given to set against the income, and to leave a balance of \$8.71½. The activities described in this chapter are earthy enough, for they include much digging and more hoeing. Yet, having associated himself thus with the other farmers of New England, Thoreau says that 'some must work in fields if only for the sake of tropes and expression, to serve a parable-maker one day'. The parable that he is making is quickly served: 'I said to myself, I will not plant beans and corn with so much industry another summer, but such seeds, if the seed is not lost, as sincerity, truth, simplicity, faith, innocence, and the like, and see if they will not grow in this soil.' The New Englander, Thoreau believes, could 'raise other crops' than grain, potatoes and grass. The *agri*-culture described literally in this chapter provides tropes to express the *self*-culture that is Thoreau's theme throughout *Walden*. He loves his rows of beans, he tells us, because they attach him to the earth and give him strength, as Antaeus, the son of Earth, gained strength when he touched his mother; but Thoreau is attached to the earth by the language – the tropes – it provides for his expression. When his hoe strikes the stones, its music yields 'an instant and immeasurable crop'. In this chapter measurable crops serve as tropes for immeasurable crops, just as the Latin word for the ear of wheat, *spica*, relates to *spe* (hope), and the kernel or grain, *granum*, to the word *gerendo* (bearing). At the end of the chapter, the notes on the relationship between the language of material and of spiritual crops are followed by the assertion that the 'true husbandman' will not be concerned with the fruits of his labour but will 'sacrifice' them in his mind. To understand this claim we must recall the account of the cypress tree at the end of the first chapter. Quoting from Sa'di's *Gulistan*, Thoreau takes the cypress to be the symbol of the 'azad, or free man' or 'religious independent' in that it *produces* nothing but is never dry and withered. This parable sums up the meaning of the 'Economy' chapter and of Thoreau's thoughts on productivity and industry, for the implication clearly is that the free man harvests a spiritual crop worth more than whole systems of industry.

In the opening chapter of *Walden* the values and assumptions, or prejudices, of a commercial society are subjected to a radical critique that takes the form of a language game of the utmost seriousness. The method is to take the language of industry and trade, and appropriate it, or by common sense standards misappropriate it, to express Thoreau's 'other levels' of meaning (the mental and spiritual) so that his statements about his own values have ironic references to socially acceptable notions of getting a living. The issue is one of economy, because it concerns nothing less than the way one should 'spend one's life', as Thoreau lets us know when he tells of the 'enterprises' he has cherished (p. 16). To his fellow-citizens, the word 'enterprise' has the meaning it has for Bancroft in his *History*, and for dozens of public orators in the ante-bellum period.[3] Thoreau's cherished enterprises include 'assisting at' the sunrise, in the original sense of 'being present at' but doing nothing to help materially, and acting as the 'intelligence office' (the news office) for the town by staying out in the country and 'trying to hear what was in the wind'. In Thoreau's opinion, as we can tell from his lecture 'Getting a Living' (now known as 'Life Without Principle'), most news gathered and published in the newspapers was no better than gossip, even when it dealt with matters that men take most seriously, but the wind to which he was listening so intently beyond the town was the wind of the spirit, for – as Emerson had stated in the 'Language' section of *Nature* – our very word for spirit derives from the word for wind. The sort of news that Thoreau gathered in his contemplation of nature did not concern the political parties and consequently had no chance of appearing in the Gazette. The only journal to which he acted as a reporter was his private journal, but he kept his accounts faithfully, though they were never audited. Every word is a pun, with a reference both to the public world of financial transactions, accounts and auditors, and to the private world of honest self-analysis and truthful records in the daily account of one's spiritual life, with no audience, or auditors. Describing himself as a 'self-appointed inspector of snow storms and rain storms' and 'surveyor . . . of forest paths', Thoreau – in fact an expert surveyor whose professional services were recognized by his property-owning fellow-townsmen – plays on the words to direct attention from the world of socially acceptable behaviour that includes inspecting and measuring for money to the world of the 'irresponsible' behaviour he indulges in: contemplation, for no material reward.

Thoreau contrasts his private business at the pond with the clipper trade with the Celestial Empire (China) that flourished in New England in the antebellum period. He insists that Walden Pond is a 'good place for business' and that he has a 'trade' to ply there, but his method of suggesting what that private business is does not consist in rejecting the bustle of trade with the Orient; rather, he takes the typical activities of that trade and converts them to the cause of commerce with a different 'celestial empire'. The task, he says, is 'To oversee all the details yourself in person; to be at once pilot and captain, and owner and underwriter; to buy and sell and keep the accounts; to read every letter received, and write or read every letter sent . . . to be your own telegraph, unweariedly sweeping the horizon, speaking all passing vessels bound coastwise', and so on through an immensely long sentence crammed with activities appropriate to the 'new channels, not of trade, but of thought' that he will recommend to the Columbus of the worlds within when he recapitulates the theme in the Conclusion of *Walden*. The link between public and private trade is, of course, '*letters*'. In his extravagant wit, Thoreau becomes the overwriter, not the underwriter, for he addresses himself to the higher faculties of his correspondents.

Early in the 'Economy' chapter Thoreau tells of 'many a poor immortal soul' crushed by its load of possessions. Pointing to the example of the industrious teamster, toiling away a life devoted to the fortunes of his employer, he asks 'How godlike, how immortal, is he?' and suggests, in reply to this rhetorical question, that the man is a slave to his own idea of getting a living. When men live thus, Thoreau argues, they remain in a torpid state, like the snake he saw lying immobile in a pond at the end of March 1845, when he began to cut pines for his new house in the woods. Before we accuse him of arrogance, we should note that he includes himself in the life that has lain torpid all winter and has thus remained in its 'low and primitive condition'. However, when he goes on to say that men 'would of necessity rise to a higher and more ethereal life' if only they would 'feel the influence of the spring of springs arousing them', it is clear that he wants us to take his own awakening, described in *Walden*, as representative of man's capacities. *Walden*, like Whitman's 'Song of Myself', is a very 'egotistical' work, as Thoreau admits in its opening paragraphs, but this spiritual autobiography, like Whitman's, is not merely personal. In the second chapter, 'Where I Lived, and What I Lived For', Thoreau tells us that we still 'live meanly, like ants; though the fable tells us that we were long ago changed into men'. This is followed by the observation that, though we have all agreed on the need for the material improvements that come with better means of communication (telegraph and railway), 'whether we should live like baboons or like men, is a little uncertain'. The first person plural used here is, plainly, deliberate; the speaker includes himself in the ranks of those whose humanity is still in doubt. In 'Reading', the charge is broadened to include man's intellectual life: 'We are a race of tit-men, and soar but little higher in our intellectual flights than the columns of the daily paper.' By the time we come to the battle of the ants in 'Brute Neighbours', the narrator clearly does not count himself one of those human heroes whose ferocity equals that of the ants. He is stirred by the ant-warriors as much as if they had been men, he tells us, adding: 'The more you think of it, the less the difference.' The more you think of it, the more telling those analogies drawn between the human and the animal, or insect, or reptilian worlds throughout *Walden* become. The transformation from caterpillar to butterfly (psyche) in the 'Higher Laws' chapter takes place when mere – or 'gross' – appetite gives way to imagination, Thoreau tells us. Such transformations are possible for 'whole nations' as well as individuals, but most nations remain in the caterpillar state.

In 'Higher Laws' Thoreau contrasts the divine in man with the animal, reptilian, sensual nature that exists in him in inverse proportion to his higher self. In man, he argues, the divine is allied to the bestial; he is a faun or a satyr as much as a demigod. Man's higher nature awakens when he achieves purity but slumbers when he is ruled by his own sensuality. In his personal life Henry Thoreau was so much the ascetic that Emerson characterized him as a man of 'no appetites, no passions' in the funeral oration he delivered in May 1862. Among Thoreau's 'many renunciations', Emerson listed wine, tobacco and meat as well as money and marriage, thus giving the impression that the dominant mode of his friend's life had been one of abstinence. This is a true impression only if we do not confuse abstinence with frugality, for Thoreau's renunciation of money was not the same as a careful, thrifty, miserly attitude to it; he did without it. Further, in doing without so many of the sensuous and sensual pleasures of normal existence, Thoreau followed the Vedantic principles he quotes in 'Higher Laws' in seeking to approach the divine. Certainly there was something daunting and austere in his renunciations, but the converse of the control over the passions that he sought was the experience of ecstasy that is celebrated again and again in his writings. The central paradox of Thoreau's thought lies in his insistence that such ecstasy was not other-wordly but, on the contrary, *this*-wordly. In 'Higher Laws' he claims that the grossest sensuality can be 'transmuted' by purity and devotion rather than denied by it. In *Walden* as a whole he both uses a scale of values that runs from the reptile to the hawk and from John Field's bog-trotting life to John Farmer's momentary awareness of the starry possibilities of existence, and at the same time uses imagery that puts heaven 'under our feet as well as over our heads'.

In 'The Bean-Field' the hawks circling 'high in the sky' correspond to thoughts that rise above our mere earthly existence of getting a living through toil. In 'The Ponds', on the other hand, thoughts of 'vast and cosmogonal themes in other spheres' occur while floating on the pond at night and 'communicating' with the mysterious nocturnal fishes forty feet below the surface by means of a fishing-line. A pull on the line may come to 'interrupt your dreams and link you to Nature again', but it does not destroy the dream; instead it suggests that two fishes can be caught on one hook because the element of water is scarcely more dense than that of air. Walden is 'sky water', it is 'God's drop', but it is also 'earth's eye; looking into which the beholder measures the depth of his own nature'. Like the mind of man, Walden is the middle element: 'Lying between the earth and the heavens, it partakes of the color of both.' The object, then, is not to discover spiritual meaning above and distinct from the earth, but to find it in the thoughts that transform the material by recognizing the spiritual in it.

The ecstatic experience that forms a climax to *Walden* in the 'Spring' chapter is the recognition that 'Walden was dead and is alive again.' The analogy between the pond and Christ in the echo of Luke xv. 24 ('For this my son was dead, and is alive again') is absurd and blasphemous if we have not responded to the carefully eleborated suggestions of a correspondence between the water of the pond and the divine possibilities of the mind of man in the earlier chapter, 'The Ponds'. The water of Walden is 'as sacred as [the water of] the Ganges at least', because 'a field of water betrays the spirit that is in the air'. The life of the spirit is also expressed in the organic life of the natural world,[4] for the grass-blade is 'the symbol of perpetual youth', Thoreau tells us, and the human life that dies down to its root in winter now 'puts forth its green blade to eternity'. *Walden* was published only one year before Whitman's *Leaves of Grass*. It is hardly surprising that Thoreau found Whitman's poem 'very brave and American' and 'exhilarating, encouraging' (*Corresp.*, pp. 444–5).

When Thoreau left the pond on 6 September 1847, he had probably finished the first version of *Walden*, which he had begun to write early in that year or towards the end of 1846. By 1849 he had a version of the book ready for publication, but since he could not find a publisher until 1854 he continued to work on the manuscript, adding most of the quotations from oriental scriptures in the years 1850–1. By the time *Walden* went to press it had been through no less than seven drafts and had doubled its length.[5] Like Emerson, Thoreau drew on his journals for material when composing works for publication. *Walden* contains journal material from the year 1840 and from the early months of 1854, for Thoreau was revising and adding to his book until the spring of the year in which it was published. The final version of *Walden* is much more than the record of the two years its author spent at the pond; it is his most complex and his most successful work of art. It is also his most popular work with modern readers, but if we limit our attention to this one book we inevitably underestimate his achievement. The writings include three other book-length narratives (two of them published posthumously), a number of essays published in periodicals in Thoreau's lifetime, some of them collected after his death in the volume called *Excursions*, fourteen volumes of journals, all published posthumously, and twelve still-unpublished notebooks of materials concerning Indians.

While living at Walden Pond, Thoreau wrote an account of a journey that he and his brother John had made in 1839, when they had travelled by boat and overland from Concord to Mount Washington. *A Week on the Concord and Merrimack Rivers*, published in 1849, is more obviously a travelogue than *Walden*, for it compresses an actual journey of two weeks into a literary voyage in which the chapters are divided into the days of the week. *A Week* is also a more obviously 'literary' work than *Walden*, for within the framework of the actual journey Thoreau includes essays and reflections on topics ranging from the satires of Aulus Flaccus Persius to Chaucer's *Canterbury Tales* and Ossian's verse. Full of allusions to other books, and particularly to the classics, *A Week* is also an exploration of the meaning of 'the wild', for the travellers leave the world of contemporary Christianity, in the 'Sunday' chapter, and the world of contemporary business and commerce, in the 'Monday' chapter, to journey back in time to an America that predates nineteenth-century civilization. In travelling by boat rather than by the railway they announce their independence of the bustling world of industrial and technological progress. In the first sentence of the book, the Concord River is given its Indian name, the Musketaquid: a name that belonged to it before it took its place in 'civilized history'. In the first chapter, the river is said to roll through the plain with the moccasined tread of an Indian warrior, while in the next the Great Meadows beside it are likened to a 'broad moccasin-print'. These allusions to the Indian past are reinforced as the voyagers travel through a landscape that tells the story of the white man's dispossession of the Indian. References to Indian wars and Indian fights remind us of the extermination of the indigenous inhabitants of the land by the representatives of progress. In a general statement of the theme, the 'industrious tribe' of white men are said to have come to 'pluck the wild-flower of [the Indian's] race up by the root' (p. 42). In the 'Sunday' chapter, the Indian's 'intercourse with his native gods' and his occasional attainment of a 'rare and peculiar society with Nature' (p. 55) is contrasted with the alienating religious bigotry of the white Christian. Thoreau expresses his reverence for the true spirit of Christ, but treats the bullying piety of contemporary Christians as a perversion of that spirit. With their intolerance of any infringement of their Sabbath laws, they make religion into a 'ligature' or constricting force. The coarse preacher, roaring out his message, is 'harshly profaning the quiet atmosphere' of Sunday and is, in fact, doing 'dirty work' (p. 77).

As the climax of his allusions to the Indian as the man whose culture was adapted to wild nature, Thoreau tells the story of Hannah Dustan, the white captive who made her escape down the river on which he now sails, a hundred and forty-two years earlier. Hannah murdered and scalped her captors, men, women and children, and then paddled her way through what was to her 'a drear and howling wilderness'. To the Indian, by contrast, the great primeval forest was 'a home, adapted to his nature, and cheerful as the smile of the Great Spirit' (p. 344). If this suggests that Thoreau is writing here as a propagandist for the American Indian, we should note that just before telling the Hannah Dustan story he has offered some generalizing statements on wildness and its relation to culture. Telling us, 'A perfect work of man's art would also be wild or natural in a good sense,' he also states: 'In the wildest nature, there is not only the material of the most cultivated life . . . but a greater refinement already than is ever attained by man' (p. 337). Taken out of context this can seem little more than an empty paradox; taken in the context of *A Week*, and in the light of *Walden*, *The Maine Woods* and *Cape Cod*, the paradox can be seen to contain the essence of Thoreau's thought.

The most obviously 'cultivated' aspect of *A Week* comes in the 'Tuesday' chapter when the account of the ascent of Mount Greylock, or Saddleback Mountain, provides a literal and metaphorical high point of the Transcendental travelogue. The ascent formed no part of the actual journey from Concord to Mount Washington, but the description of dawn on the summit of the mountain is used as a vivid metaphor of spiritual awakening and elevation. The narrator finds himself above the clouds in 'such a country as we might see in dreams with all the delights of paradise'. He feels spiritually lifted above the trivial concerns of man's grovelling existence as he stands in the 'dazzling halls of Aurora' (p. 199). This episode is the most obviously and recognizably Transcendental in *A Week*, for the physical height of the mountain-top corresponds to the spiritual state of the narrator, but, as in *Walden*, the Transcendental vision of Henry Thoreau cannot be adequately expressed in such spatial metaphors. The symbolic meaning of the rivers in the book is combined with images of immense space to suggest a transcendence that is not to be explained as a 'rising above'.

In the 'Monday' chapter, the voyagers are preparing for sleep on the bank of the Merrimack when they hear a drum beating in the dark. In a passage that looks forward to 'Higher Laws' in *Walden*, Thoreau says: 'These simple sounds related us to the stars' (p. 181). They did so by breaking the bonds of 'habitual thinking' and letting the plough of thought break through the crust of the world. Reflecting on the power of music, even the simple music of the drum, Thoreau decides that it is 'the flower of language, thought colored and curved, fluent and flexible, its crystal fountain tinged with the sun's rays, and its purling ripples reflecting the grass and the clouds'. The pun on 'flow' and 'flower' latent in this passage links music, river, organic growth (flowers) and thought. Its implications are developed in an ecstatic description of the river in the 'Thursday' chapter that looks forward to the description of the thawing sandbank in *Walden*. On the return voyage down the Merrimack River, 'all things seemed . . . to flow' and the hardest material seemed 'to obey the same law with the most fluid'. The prose here equates rivers of thought with rivers of rock on the surface of the earth and rivers of ore within its bowels. To the imagination that can perceive the fluidity of all nature, 'the universe is built round about us, and we are central still' (p. 353). Flowing like music and like thought, the river becomes a phenomenon that corresponds to the mind of man.

The idea of the wild in *A Week* may seem remote from any actual wildness, for all the allusions to the American Indian. While he was living at Walden Pond and working on his book, Thoreau made an excursion to the wilderness of Maine, a state that was still largely vacant on the map in the 1840s and 1850s. In September 1846 he travelled to Mount Katahdin, the scarcely explored mountain that Francis Parkman had hoped to visit in 1842. Thoreau's account of his trip, given first as a lecture, was published in the *Union Magazine* in 1848, with the title

'Ktaadn, and the Maine Woods', and was later included in the posthumously published *The Maine Woods* (1864), edited by his friend Ellery Channing. When Thoreau climbed the mountain, it seemed to him 'vast, Titanic', and the effect of this 'inhuman Nature' was to rob man of 'some of his divine faculty' by dissipating his thought. On Mount Katahdin, Thoreau felt that he had encountered 'Matter, vast, terrific, – not his Mother Earth' but Earth made of Chaos and Old Night. With these Miltonic allusions Thoreau combined Emersonian references to the mountain as necessity and fate, for it revealed the limits of man's freedom. Under its influence, even his own body seemed to him alien matter; man's life in nature seemed an impenetrable mystery.

The experience of the wilderness recorded in 'Ktaadn' is not uniform. Thoreau's account of his excursion ends with a passage on the 'inexpressible tenderness and immortal life of the grim forest' where nature is 'blissful, innocent Nature' even in mid-winter. However, the encounter with inhuman nature – with 'a force not bound to be kind to man' – clearly did present a challenge to his conception of the relationship between man and the world of matter. The proper place for man and for the poet, he concluded, was not the vast and Titanic wilderness but the partly cultivated country. This conclusion was a response to a second excursion to the Maine wilderness, in 1853, when Thoreau explored the Chesuncook. His narrative, simply called 'Chesuncook', was published in 1858 and later became the second section of *The Maine Woods*. Closer in time to the experience on Mount Katahdin was the first version of *Walden*, in the final pages of which Thoreau expressed the view: 'We need the tonic of wildness.' He went on to say that 'we must be refreshed by the sight of inexhaustible vigor, vast features and titanic – the sea coast with its wrecks, the wilderness with its living and its decaying trees'.[6] Since this version of *Walden* was written late in 1846 or in 1847, it seems likely that the passage is itself a response to the 'inhuman Nature' on the mountain. In the published version of *Walden* (1854), these words became part of the 'Spring' chapter, as did the following sentence: 'We need to witness our own limits transgressed, and some life pasturing freely where we never wander.' The theme, of course, is the theme that dominates the Conclusion of the book.

Thoreau's account of his third excursion to Maine, in July 1857, introduces Joe Polis, the Indian guide for the trip to the Allegash and the East Branch. The story of this journey into the wilderness is dominated by Thoreau's feeling that in Joe Polis's relationship with the natural world he had proof of an alternative to the alienated white consciousness. Though Polis was not uncontaminated by the white man's culture, his intimacy with the forest and his ability to live in what to the white man was a howling wilderness convinced Thoreau that 'Nature must have made a thousand revelations to [the Indians] which are still secret to us'. Deciding that he had much to learn from the Indian and nothing to learn from the Christian missionary, Thoreau clearly felt that the intuitions he had expressed concerning the Indian in *A Week* had been confirmed. Contrasting the Anglo-Saxon's utilitarian and exploitative attitude to the forest (cutting it down and grubbing it up) with the Indian's ability to 'converse with the spirit of the tree he fells', Thoreau found the Indian's attitude more congenial to the spirit of poetry and mythology. As white civilization advanced, obliterating the forest, the poetic and the mythological were destroyed, just as the Indians' culture had been destroyed.

Typically, Thoreau's interest in the Indian found expression, not only in his excursions into the wilderness or in his uncanny habit of discovering Indian relics in the Massachusetts countryside (a knack of his that many of his friends, among them Hawthorne, found remarkable), but also in his reading. Between 1847 and 1861 Thoreau filled twelve manuscript volumes with over half a million words of notes on his reading connected with the Indian. At some stage of his career Thoreau seems to have intended to write a book about the Indians, but any such project developed no further than the accumulation of facts, with some of his own opinions, in the 'Indian Books'. His own list of the topics that interested him in his reading on the Indians is comprehensive; it includes dress, games, manufactures, superstitions and religion as well as language, painting and music, and he made copious notes on over thirty aspects of Indian culture.[7] His sources included the early anthropologists (Schoolcraft, Heckewelder) whom Parkman also used. Like Parkman, too, he made use of the *Relations* of the Jesuit missionaries to Canada. Much of his reading concerning the Indian overlapped with his travel reading, for the two themes were inseparable from Thoreau's central concern with inner quests and discoveries.

In another series of actual excursions from Concord, Thoreau encountered the wild in a form that had nothing to do with the Indian. In October 1849 he and his friend Ellery Channing walked along the Atlantic shore of Cape Cod and experienced the 'grand fact' of the ocean. They were determined, he wrote, to get 'the resounding sea' into them, to 'associate with the ocean until it lost the pond-like look which it wears to a countryman'. Combining his reflections on this first visit with those he made on subsequent trips to the Cape in 1850 and

1855, Thoreau wrote a travelogue that compressed the three excursions into one and was published, posthumously, with the title *Cape Cod*. The first four chapters had already been published serially in 1855, and Thoreau had lectured on his first visit as early as 1850, but the completed book, though never finally revised by Thoreau, reads as the story of a journey from the south of the Cape to Provincetown, the goal of the travellers. On the sea-shore, they encounter 'naked Nature, – inhumanly sincere, wasting no thought on man'. The shore is a 'rank, wild place, and there is no flattery in it'. In fact, it is a 'vast *morgue*' where 'the carcasses of men and beasts together lie stately up upon its shelf, rotting and bleaching in the sun and waves' (p. 187). On their way to the Cape, the travellers visit Cohasset on the mainland coast, where the wreck of an Irish ship carrying immigrants has taken a hundred and forty-five lives only two days earlier They visit the beach and observe the mangled remains of many of the dead, noting the staring, lustreless eyes of the bloodless, gashed corpses. Once they are on the Cape, the 'savage ocean' becomes the major presence in the narrative. Even when calm and gentle, it does not let man forget that it can 'toss and tear the rag of a man's body like the father of mad bulls' (p. 125). To Thoreau it seems that the ocean is 'a wilderness reaching round the globe, wilder than a Bengal jungle, and fuller of monsters, washing the very wharves of our cities and the gardens of our sea-side residences' (p. 188). It bears no relation to the friendly land, and it teaches him that he is a 'land-animal' to whom the ocean means danger and death. Everywhere on the Cape there are memorials to the dead who have lost their lives at sea.

The ocean in *Cape Cod* is as much a threat as the oceans in Melville's *Moby-Dick*, yet Thoreau finds the sound of the sea an 'inspiriting sound' even when its roar is caused by the death-dealing storm that drowned the would-be immigrants (p. 40). Listening to the 'dirge which is ever played along the shore for those mariners who have been lost in the deep since first it was created', Thoreau hears through its dreariness 'a pure and unqualified strain of eternal melody' (p. 71). His remarkably unsentimental attitude to the deaths of those wrecked at Cohasset, and his rejection of any 'snivelling sympathies' he might have been tempted to feel when on another occasion he reclaimed a body from the sea and found only some bones with a little flesh adhering to them, is explained in part by his extravagant pun on 'inspiriting'. Apropos of the storm that caused the wreck he says: 'The strongest wind cannot stagger a Spirit; it is a Spirit's breath' (p. 13). Here, as in *Walden*, the confidence derives from the Emersonian theory that the physical fact corresponds to and is a symbol of the spiritual fact. Paradoxically, even the natural force that causes human death is a symbol of the life of the soul. Commenting on the failure of the shipwrecked immigrants to reach the New World that Columbus had discovered and the Pilgrims had settled, Thoreau says that 'they emigrated to a newer world than ever Columbus dreamed of' (p. 12). It would seem, then, that he has shifted his hopes for a better life from this world to the promise of the next, yet the opening pages of the book tell us that its theme will be human culture. In fact, the underlying and unifying theme of this travelogue is an appraisal of the state of human culture on the Cape, that mere 'sand-bar in the ocean' (p. 29). Implicit in the observations on the actual state of culture is the suggestion of the possibilities, as yet unrealised, of human life.

Cape Cod is full of references to the Pilgrims who landed there in the seventeenth century. Though less adventurous as explorers than the French who opened up the continent for trade, the Pilgrims 'were pioneers, and the ancestors of pioneers, in a far greater enterprise' (p. 257). Since the inhabitants of the Cape in his own day are, he tells us, the purest descendants of the Pilgrims, the state of their culture reveals the extent to which the great enterprise has succeeded. Thoreau admires the people of the Cape for their honesty and frankness – he notes that there is very little crime among them – but he also expresses his wonder that so many of them can devote so much time and so much of their lives to the mere business of fishing. In terms that relate to his verdict on human busy-ness in the 'Economy' chapter in *Walden* and in 'Life Without Principle', he says: 'It is remarkable what a serious business men make of getting their dinners, and how universally shiftlessness and a grovelling taste take refuge in a merely ant-like industry' (p. 182). The immediate cause for this reflection is the sight of the mackerel schooners rounding the head of the Cape, and later in the narrative Thoreau notes that the 'principle employment' of the inhabitants of Provincetown seemed to be trundling out their fish to dry in the morning and bringing them in at night (p. 213), but the industry that keeps men at the ant stage of development is, as his words make clear, universal. In a general comment on sea-borne commerce, he states that it turns the ocean of eternity into a mere trading flood and turns heaven into the Liverpool docks (p. 106). The ocean, he believes, should lead us to spiritual exploration, not mere trade.

Though the ancient world had regarded the pillars of Hercules as a boundary, Columbus had sailed beyond all known limits to find the New World. The Pilgrims had subsequently made an actual voyage across the Atlantic to pursue a spiritual quest. In his own day, Thoreau tells us, the 'true Hesperia' is no longer the East Coast of America, with its Puritan heritage, but the Far West, 'the only *ne* plus ultra now'. In the last sentence of the book he says that a man may stand on the shore of the Cape and 'put all America behind him'. By this he plainly means that the stage of human development already reached in his own country and in his own day must be taken as a starting point, not a culmination and a terminus of human aspiration. In his essay 'Walking', given as a lecture in the 1850s and published soon after his death in 1862, Thoreau makes the West the fitting direction for the journey that is 'perfectly symbolical of the path which we love to travel in the interior and ideal world' (v. 217). In this essay Thoreau speaks 'a word for Nature, for absolute freedom and wildness' and associates the West with his concept of the imaginatively wild.[8] Two emphases in the essay identify the wildness that is 'the preservation of the world' with the extra-vagance of the Conclusion of *Walden*. In the essay, Thoreau has a vision of nature in which the fences are all burned and the forests allowed to stand: a vision of unbounded existence. In the essay, too, he associates the wildness of the forest animals with the wildness of a strain of music; here, as in 'Higher Laws', music signifies spiritual liberation. The walking Thoreau discusses in his essay is not walking for exercise but rather 'sauntering', making a pilgrimage to the *Sainte-Terre*, to the Holy Land. This was his goal in *Walden* and in all his travelogues.

Notes

1 The text of the extract is taken from the Princeton Edition of *Walden*, ed. J. Lyndon Shanley, Princeton University Press, 1971. Parenthetic references to *Walden* throughout the chapter are to this edition. References to other works by Thoreau are to the Walden Edition of *The Writings of Henry David Thoreau*, 20 vols, Boston: Houghton Mifflin, 1906. Vols 7–20 of the *Writings* are vols 1–14 of the *Journals*. References to J in the text are to the *Journals*. References to *Corresp*. are to *The Correspondence of Henry David Thoreau*, ed. Walter Harding and Carl Bode, New York University Press, 1958.

2 John Aldrich Christie, *Thoreau as World Traveler*, New York: Columbia University Press, 1965, pp. 42–4. Christie's book not only catalogues Thoreau's travel reading but also discusses the uses to which he put that reading in expressing his ideas.

3 Rush Welter, *The Mind of America 1820–1860*, New York: Columbia University Press, 1975, ch. 6, 'Enterprise'.

4 Particularly helpful in his discussion of Thoreau's conception of nature as

both *phusis* (nature pervaded by an animating and unifying spirit) and *kosmos* (the aggregate of things and their relations), is *James McIntosh, *Thoreau as Romantic Naturalist: His Shifting Stance toward Nature*, Ithaca: Cornell University Press, 1974, esp. pp. 71–2, 243–8.

5 For the development of *Walden*, see J. Lyndon Shanley, *The Making of 'Walden'*, University of Chicago Press, 1957, ch. II, 'The Successive Versions of *Walden*'.

6 Shanley prints the first version of *Walden* in *The Making of 'Walden'*. The quoted passage is on p. 207.

7 See Robert F. Sayre, *Thoreau and the American Indians*, Princeton University Press, 1977, p. 120. Chapters 3 and 4 discuss Thoreau's Indian Books.

8 *See Sherman Paul, *The Shores of America: Thoreau's Inward Exploration*, Urbana: University of Illinois Press, 1958, 1972, pp. 412–17. Paul's discussion of 'Walking' and Thoreau's concept of the wild is, as his title suggests, part of a comprehensive study of the theme of exploration.

Further reading

Stanley Cavell, *The Senses of Walden*, New York: Viking Press, 1972.

Frederick Garber, *Thoreau's Redemptive Imagination*, New York University Press, 1977.

9
Henry Wadsworth Longfellow (1807-82)

The Wedding-Day

Forth from the curtain of clouds, from the tent of purple and
scarlet,
Issued the sun, the great High-Priest, in his garments
resplendent,
Holiness unto the Lord, in letters of light, on his forehead,
Round the hem of his robe the golden bells and pomegranates.
Blessing the world he came, and the bars of vapor beneath him
Gleamed like a grate of brass, and the sea at his feet was a laver!

This was the wedding morn of Priscilla the Puritan maiden.
Friends were assembled together; the Elder and Magistrate also
Graced the scene with their presence, and stood like the Law
and the Gospel,
One with the sanction of earth and one with the blessing of
heaven.
Simple and brief was the wedding, as that of Ruth and of Boaz.
Softly the youth and the maiden repeated the words of
betrothal,
Taking each other for husband and wife in the Magistrate's
presence,
After the Puritan way, and the laudable custom of Holland.
Fervently then, and devoutly, the excellent Elder of Plymouth
Prayed for the hearth and the home, that were founded that
day in affection,
Speaking of life and of death, and imploring divine
benedictions. . . .

Meanwhile the bridegroom went forth and stood with the
bride at the doorway,

Breathing the perfumed air of that warm and beautiful morning.
Touched with autumnal tints, but lonely and sad in the sunshine,
Lay extended before them the land of toil and privation;
There were the graves of the dead, and the barren waste of the sea-shore,
There the familiar fields, the groves of pine, and the meadows;
But to their eyes transfigured, it seemed as the Garden of Eden,
Filled with the presence of God, whose voice was the sound of the ocean.

Soon was their vision disturbed by the noise and stir of departure,
Friends coming forth from the house, and impatient of longer delaying,
Each with his plan for the day, and the work that was left uncompleted.
Then from a stall near at hand, amid exclamations of wonder,
Alden the thoughtful, the careful, so happy, so proud of Priscilla,
Brought out his snow-white steer, obeying the hand of its master,
Led by a cord that was tied to an iron ring in its nostrils,
Covered with crimson cloth, and a cushion placed for a saddle.
She should not walk, he said, through the dust and heat of the noonday;
Nay, she should ride like a queen, not plod along like a peasant.
Somewhat alarmed at first, but reassured by the others,
Placing her hand on the cushion, her foot in the hand of her husband,
Gayly, with joyous laugh, Priscilla mounted her palfrey.
'Nothing is wanting now,' he said with a smile, 'but the distaff;
Then you would be in truth my queen, my beautiful Bertha!'

Onward the bridal procession now moved to their new habitation,
Happy husband and wife, and friends conversing together.
Pleasantly murmured the brook, as they crossed the ford in the forest,

Pleased with the image that passed, like a dream of love
through its bosom,
Tremulous, floating in air, o'er the depths of the azure abysses.
Down through the golden leaves the sun was pouring his
splendors,
Gleaming on purple grapes, that, from branches above them
suspended,
Mingled their ordorous breath with the balm of the pine and
the fir-tree,
Wild and sweet as the clusters that grew in the valley of Eshcol.
Like a picture it seemed of the primitive, pastoral ages,
Fresh with the youth of the world, and recalling Rebecca and
Isaac,
Old and yet ever new, and simple and beautiful always,
Love immortal and young in the endless succession of lovers.
So through the Plymouth woods passed onward the bridal
procession.

The Courtship of Miles Standish and Other Poems (1858)[1]

* * *

The wedding morning of Priscilla Mullins and John Alden begins with a splendour that contrasts vividly with the bleakness of the New England landscape and seascape Longfellow has created earlier in his poem. The language of the opening lines of 'The Wedding-Day' has a sensuous richness that transforms the drab, even grim, world of the Plymouth Plantation evoked in 'The Courtship of Miles Standish'. A sun that emerges from its tent of purple and scarlet clouds as a high priest clad in a robe ornamented with golden bells and pomegranates hardly seems appropriate for the marriage of a woman who throughout the poem is described as 'the Puritan maiden'. It is of course fitting that the transfigured scene should be, in Newton Arvin's phrase, 'Hebraic in its gorgeousness',[2] for the imaginative world of the Pilgrims was that of the Bible – they habitually looked for 'types' of their experience in the Old Testament – yet when the newly married pair move to their new home, their image in the stream they cross is 'like a dream of love'. We seem, then, to be close to the 'Merry Mount' of Hawthorne's tale: a story with which Longfellow was familiar, for he had praised his former college friend for his use of New England themes as early as 1837, when he had reviewed *Twice-told Tales* for the *North American Review*. In his poem, written twenty years after his review, Longfellow stresses the severity and the sombre hue of life among the Plymouth Pilgrims as much as Hawthorne had insisted on the gloom of Puritan Massachusetts, but where Hawthorne had attributed the joyless character of their lives to the ethics of the New Englanders, Longfellow's Pilgrims are not sin-obsessed as Hawthorne's Puritans were. Nevertheless, the Pilgrims in the poem have good cause to feel sadness rather than mirth, for the winter preceding the marriage of Priscilla and John has been a terrible one. Many of the Plymouth settlers have succumbed to the climatic rigours of their first winter in the New World.

References to the sufferings and deaths of this first winter run all through the poem that Longfellow called 'an Idyl of the Old Colony times; a bunch of May-flowers from the Plymouth woods' (L, IV. 82). When the *Mayflower* sets out on its return journey to England, the settlers left behind imagine the ship's sail to be a marble slab in a graveyard, marking the burial place of any hopes they might have had of ever leaving the inhospitable shores of Massachusetts. As John and Priscilla gaze after the departing ship, they feel that they have been left in a desert rather than a new homeland. Even as they come from their wedding ceremony they step into a scene that includes the graves of the victims of the winter's severities. Though the morning is warm and beautiful, the sea-shore is a barren waste. 'Touched with autumnal tints, but lonely and sad in the sunshine, / Lay extended before them the land of toil and privation.' This is a world dominated by hard work as well as the threat of premature death. Even on their wedding day, the lovers find their friends impatient of delay in the ceremonies, eager to get the married pair off on their triumphal journey so that the day's real tasks can begin. These young lovers, like the Lord and Lady of the May in Hawthorne's story, are clearly destined for a world of harsh actualities rather than a world of romantic dreams. In the previous section, 'The Spinning-Wheel', we have watched John Alden about the humdrum business of building a simple house. The lines in which his work is described are emphatically pedestrian, almost banal:

> Wooden-barred was the door, and the roof was covered with
> rushes;
> Latticed the windows were, and the window-panes were of
> paper,
> Oiled to admit the light, while wind and rain were excluded.

Though he is a romantic lover who fills his letters home with 'the name and the fame of the Puritan maiden Priscilla', Alden is a patently unheroic figure who flatters his beloved by complimenting her on her thrift, on her hard work at the spinning-wheel. Longfellow's poem is remembered most for the realism that makes Priscilla cut through John Alden's embarrassed proxy-proposal and ask him why he does not speak for himself, but this is only the most striking example of a realism that pervades the story.

The 'dream of love' that the stream reflects in the final verse-paragraph of the poem is the vision that a few lines earlier transfigured the barren sea-shore and the familiar fields, making them 'the Garden of Eden'. There was, as we saw, an 'innocence' in the illusions of Hawthorne's Merry Mount folk as they enacted their Golden Age ceremonies, but in 'The Courtship of Miles Standish' the Edenic associations belong to married life within the Puritan community. The young people are married 'after the Puritan way' and the Elder prays fervently and devoutly 'for the hearth and the home', asking 'divine benedictions' on them. Here, as always in Longfellow's works, the positives are domestic; happiness and blessings are to be found in the home or nowhere. Yet there is a threat to domestic bliss in the poem and it comes from within the Puritan world. It is not, as with Hawthorne, the threat from a sexual guilt that is part of love itself, but is rather the danger from the aggressive impulses represented by Miles Standish.

The Miles Standish who appears like a ghost at the wedding, causing both bride and groom to react with shock, since they thought that he had died fighting the Indians, is no longer the danger that he was in the opening sections of the poem. Nor is he the partly comic figure he was when he acted out the role of the *miles gloriosus* or braggart soldier of comedy, vaunting his own military prowess to the point of comparing himself, with his army of twelve men, to Caesar. Captain Miles Standish is the archetypally martial man, devoted to the god of war, proud of his military exploits and of his warlike weapons. As the epitome of the military character, he is irascible, violent, aggressive. When he learns of the failure of his secretary (and proxy wooer) John Alden to persuade Priscilla to accept his hand in marriage, Standish's rage is intense and dangerous:

> Up leaped the Captain of Plymouth, and stamped on the floor, till his armor
> Clanged on the wall, where it hung, with a sound of sinister omen.
> All his pent-up wrath burst forth in a sudden explosion,
> Even as a hand-grenade, that scatters destruction around it.

When the threat of Indian hostilities diverts his rage from John Alden, Standish's pious comment that war, though a terrible trade, is justified by a righteous cause hardly rings true, for we have learned to recognize him as a man in whom violence rules. In his expeditions against the Indians he proves more ferocious than they are. In response to an insult from Chief Pecksuot, Standish plunges a knife into the savage's breast. Miles is plainly the aggressor, acting as 'the hot blood of his race' determines. The phrase connotes sexual as well as military aggressiveness, as do other phrases that he uses to justify his behaviour. Explaining his reluctance to court Priscilla in person, Miles tells John Alden that he dare not 'march up to a woman with such a proposal', though he can 'march up to a fortress and summon the place to surrender'. The comic awkwardness Standish displays should not obscure the fact that his attitude to the woman is latently aggressive. Even his fear of a 'thundering "No!" point-blank from the mouth of a woman' suggests, in its confusion of military and sexual reference, that one of his wars is the war of the sexes.

After his victory over the Indians, Standish brings back the head of the slain chief Wattawamat to display on the roof of a building in Plymouth that is, appropriately, both church and fortress. The association between Puritanism and militarism has been made earlier in the poem, when Miles has referred to his howitzer on the roof of the church as 'a preacher who speaks to the purpose, / Steady, straight-forward and strong, with irresistible logic, / Orthodox, flashing conviction right into the hearts of the heathen.' In response to the threat from the Indians, only one member of the council at Plymouth is for peace; the rest follow their captain in identifying the apostolic tongues of fire with the flames of the cannon. As Hawthorne had taken Endicott, the man of steel, to be the archetype of the Puritan, so Longfellow here uses the armour-clad Miles Standish to stand for one aspect of Puritanism. The Elder who marries the lovers, of course, represents a contrasting quality in the faith.

The John Alden of 'The Courtship' is a gentle, delicate, scholarly man as well as a builder of simple, prosaic houses. Whereas the historical John Alden was robust enough to have been a master cooper, Longfellow's Alden is 'a maker of phrases' where Miles Standish is a 'maker of war'. Alden is a scribe, which means – to the military mind of the Captain – that he has 'the graces of speech, and skill in the turning of phrases'. The conflict between the writer and the soldier in the poem has led one recent critic to argue that it expresses Longfellow's anxiety about his role as poet at a time of approaching national crisis.[3] 'The Courtship' was written in 1857 and 1858, years when the danger of sectional conflict was looming large as a result of the Kansas-Nebraska Act (see pp. 226–34). The threat of violence was brought home to the poet by the brutal beating inflicted on his close friend

Charles Sumner on the floor of the United States Senate on 22 May 1856. Sumner, a leading spokesman for the anti-slavery cause in Congress, had been attacked by Congressman Brooks of South Carolina in an incident that seemed to Longfellow an 'infamy to the country' and a 'wound to Liberty'. Though he believed that the one good result of Brooks's outrage was that it made 'Freedom and Slavery stand face to face in the field as never before' (L, III. 549), Longfellow resisted attempts to engage his art directly in the political debate over slavery. His own anti-slavery poems, published in 1842, had shown – in Walt Whitman's words – that 'his very anger [was] gentle', and his response to hostile criticism had been to call for 'all gentleness and Christian charity' in the effort to change the hearts of the Southerners (*Life*, II. 8). Possibly, then, Longfellow saw something of himself in his portrait of a man of sensibility who is daunted by the overbearing will and threatened by the anger of the man of action, but if this is so it is also true that the gentle writer triumphs in the comedic story.

There can be no doubt that the personal growth to maturity of John Alden is associated in the poem with the movement towards national maturity. From a boyish submissiveness to the will of the father-surrogate – the Captain – and from a regressive impulse that had produced fantasies of finding a grave close by his mother's side in Old England, Alden develops into a man determined to stay in the New World and defend the woman he loves. When eager to escape Standish's anger and his own responsibilities, the young man had hurried to the Plymouth Rock with the other Pilgrims, planning to take the ship back to England. But the rock was 'to their feet a door-step / Into a world unknown, – the corner stone of a nation'. Private and public rites of passage are enacted in the decision to stay and face the challenges of the New World.

If we take John Alden to be Longfellow's portrait of the artist as a young Puritan, we must examine John's relationship with his muse, Priscilla, as well as with the authoritarian figure of Captain Standish. We learn more of Priscilla's psychology than we do of John's, and this too is significant, for 'The Courtship' reveals its author's enlightened interest in the woman's feelings. To Priscilla, Captain Standish's proxy-proposal reveals a typically male attitude to women. Commenting on it to John Alden she says:

> 'That is the way with you men; you don't understand us, you
> cannot.
> When you have made up your minds, after thinking of this
> one and that one,

Choosing, selecting, rejecting, comparing one with another,
Then you make known your desire, with abrupt and sudden
avowal'.

She is shocked by the fact that Alden, who as she well knows loves her himself, should speak for another man, but her words clearly apply to the social code that assumes the woman's role in courtship to be submissive. Not only does she reject outright the idea that 'by fighting alone you could win the heart of a woman'; she also, and more interestingly, rejects the superficially gallant language with which John Alden attempts to deflect the force of her sincere and deeply felt expression of emotion. In her words, woman's fate is to be patient and silent until 'some questioning voice dissolves the spell of its silence'. As a result, women cannot express their own deepest feelings:

'Hence is the inner life of so many suffering women
Sunless and silent and deep, like subterranean rivers
Running through caverns of darkness, unheard, unseen and
unfruitful,
Chafing their channels of stone, with endless and profitless
murmurs.'

To this John Alden replies inanely that the rivers always seem to him 'More like the beautiful rivers that watered the garden of Eden / More like the river Euphrates, through deserts of Havilah flowing.' This is precisely the 'elegant language' that Miles Standish expected the scribe John Alden to use on his behalf. Priscilla rejects it because it insults as it flatters. Such empty compliments, she says, reveal how little John really cares for her. She has spoken frankly, from the depths of her heart, and is offended by the 'common and complimentary phrases / Most men think so fine, in dealing and speaking with women'. If Alden is the type of the poet in the story, then Priscilla's comment has an obvious aesthetic and critical significance.

The central symbol of the poem is Priscilla's distaff. With it she seems to John Alden, who is an incorrigible payer of compliments, 'Bertha the Beautiful Spinner . . . the queen of Helvetia'. In response to this piece of flattery, Priscilla's foot moves more quickly on the treadle and makes the spindle utter 'an angry snarl', yet she is nevertheless pleased that the man she loves should praise her thrift. In this section, called 'The Spinning-Wheel', the relationship between the sexes is significantly altered, for the woman is not the submissive object of choice or the grateful recipient of compliments. In fact, when Priscilla makes John hold out his hands so that she can wind the thread from them, he becomes the passive one; she is now in control and dominates him. When her hands brush against his, for – as the poet asks us archly – 'how could she help it?', she sends 'electrical thrills through every nerve in his body'. Though the sight of Priscilla at the distaff suggests the virtuous woman of Proverbs to the pious John Alden, the verse leaves no doubt that her power over him is sexual. Watching her at the spinning wheel, John also imagines that she is spinning the thread of his life and fortune. She is, in the story, the Fate to whom he will submit. It is possible that the first version of the wedding procession, in which Priscilla rides on John Alden's snow-white steer, seemed to its author to contain the possibility of an irony that was too destructive of John's virility. For whatever reason, the snow-white steer of the first (1858) edition of the poem was later replaced by a snow-white bull, both in 'The Wedding-Day' and in 'The Spinning-Wheel' sections.

*

The chief strength of 'The Courtship of Miles Standish' is the controlled and gentle humour with which the relationship between the lovers is treated. That humour is possible only because Longfellow has freed himself from romantic stereotypes in his poem. When he wrote *Kavanagh* (1849), a novel set in contemporary New England, his theme was the power of real life to inspire art. Kavanagh, the Minister, explains to the would-be romancer, Mr Churchill, that the painter Raphael found inspiration for his Holy Family in the simple peasant mother at her cottage door with her children. Yet in the love of the young Minister for the beautiful and rich Cecilia Vaughan, daughter of a judge and therefore a member of the social élite of the village in which she lives, Longfellow offered only idealized, and thoroughly conventional, sentiment. There was nothing of real human interaction in this love story. It seems that the poet needed the distancing effect of history before he could treat sexual relationships with any degree of realism.

In the second of his *New England Tragedies*, *Giles Corey of the Salem Farms*, which was written in 1868, something of the authenticity of the John Alden–Priscilla Mullins relationship returns in the glimpse Longfellow gives us of the marriage between Giles and Martha Corey. In Act Two, Scene Two, we watch the rather solemn, pompous and superstitious Giles, who is considerably older than his wife, assert his authority over the young woman, who is evidently neither submissive nor docile. More sensible and less superstitious than her husband, Martha defies him and thus provokes the insinuation of witchcraft.

Though Corey makes an impassioned defence of his wife's character at her trial, insisting that she has been dutiful, virtuous and industrious, his superstitious reaction to earlier losses of his cattle is used by the relentless Judge Hathorne (Nathaniel Hawthorne's ancestor) to incriminate Martha. She is therefore correct when she tells Giles that he has sworn away her life. In this verse drama, as in 'The Courtship of Miles Standish', Longfellow shows us an independent woman threatened by the aggressive and intolerant force of a Puritanism that is, necessarily, represented by the men of iron for whom Judge Hathorne speaks.

In the first of his *New England Tragedies*, *John Endicott*, an early version of which had been written in 1857, though the published version was not written till 1868, Longfellow tells the story of the Puritans' persecution of the Quakers in the 1660s. His 1837 review of Hawthorne's *Twice-told Tales* had stated that 'the puritanical times begin to look romantic in the distance' and that the old days in New England offered 'many quaint and quiet customs, many comic scenes and strange adventures, many wild and wonderous things, fit for humorous tale, and soft, pathetic story'. Yet in *John Endicott* there is nothing humorous. The only 'romantic' element is the love of John Endicott's son (a fictitious son, invented for the drama) for the young Quaker woman his father is persecuting. The gentle and sensitive son rebels against the intolerant creed of his Puritan father, invoking the memory of his mother when he intercedes on behalf of the Quaker woman. The father, however, is inflexible: he cannot be moved by appeals to emotion. As his son later says: 'There is no pity in his iron heart.' Like Hawthorne, then, Longfellow sees in Endicott the 'iron' Puritan fanatically sure of his own righteousness. Hawthorne had attributed fanaticism to the Quakers as well as to the Puritans in 'The Gentle Boy', but in Longfellow's simpler version the Quakers are presented as totally good, self-abnegating and loving. Further, in making Edith Christison the most emotionally engaging of the Quaker martyrs, Longfellow developed the association between independence and femininity that we have already noticed in 'The Courtship'. Edith Christison's bid for freedom is spiritual. She defies the authority of the Puritan ministers because, as she claims, the Lord commands her to obey his word and that word is a 'burning fire' in her heart. There is no suggestion in the play that her religion of the heart might be self-indulgent or that she might be deluded. John Norton, the least attractive of the Puritans, rebukes Edith as a 'babbling woman' who should submit to the Pauline doctrine that women should be silent in the churches. As in *The Scarlet Letter*, religious intolerance and cold-heartedness are male characteristics.

These are works of the late 1850s and 1860s. In them Longfellow shows an interest in the feelings of women that takes him beyond many of the conventional pieties of his day, yet his most popular heroine, the Evangeline who gave her name to the poem he published in 1847, hardly prepares us for Priscilla Mullins or Edith Christison. The story he used in *Evangeline* appealed to the poet as soon as he heard it because it seemed to him a supreme illustration of the 'faithfulness and constancy of woman'. In his prologue Longfellow addressed readers who believed, with him, in 'the beauty and strength of a woman's devotion'. In the 1840s this was a large readership, for the dominant 'cult of true womanhood' insisted on the submissiveness and devotedness of the female.[4] Praised by Hawthorne, Whittier and countless other readers, this poem sold nearly 36,000 copies within ten years (a great sales success by the standards of the day) and was hailed by the British *Fraser's Magazine* as the first great American poem. Its popularity suggests that it reinforced conventional views of the woman's role instead of challenging them, yet for the student of Longfellow the poem reveals an overriding commitment to an ideal of domestic bliss.

The pathos of *Evangeline* results from the repeated frustrations of the heroine's longings. Separated from her betrothed, Gabriel Lajeunesse, Evangeline devotes her life to the search for him, to meet with success only when Gabriel, by now an old man, is dying of fever. In a less sentimental age than Longfellow's, the elusiveness of Gabriel and the repeated disappointment of Evangeline are more likely to provoke mirth than a sympathetic response in the reader, but the poem is more than a sentimental journey, for it offers a distinctively American version of Longfellow's perennial theme: the exile of the modern consciousness from its Edenic state of harmony with nature. The poem begins with an account of a peasant community in the village of Grand-Pré in Acadia (now Nova Scotia). The setting of the village is the 'happy valley' that is perfectly appropriate for the idyllic picture of rural life that Longfellow creates. Smoke rises from the hearths of 'homes of peace and contentment', while the village street is a meeting place for matrons and maidens. As the tale begins, the village is bathed in the light of an Indian summer that is so dreamy and magical that the landscape seems 'new-created in all the freshness of childhood'. In this perfectly harmonious world, 'rest and affection and stillness' reign. This is a world of childhood safety and security, centred in the home. The house of Evangeline Bellefontaine and her father is an integral part of the rural scene, for at its entrance there are woodbine and sycamore, while orchard and meadows are close by. The barns of the Bellefontaines are full of hay. In the dovecots that are part of the house there are 'innocent inmates / Murmuring ever of love'. Benedict Bellefontaine, as his name suggests, is blessed with peace and contentment on his sunny farm. In harmony with nature, he trusts in the goodwill of his fellow men.

Into this happy valley of love and domestic contentment come the British troops to drive the innocent French Canadians out of their Eden. Longfellow's source was history here, for the Acadian removal had occurred in 1755, as a punishment for their supposed loyalty to the French king. The poem treats the historical events allegorically, describing the British as a storm that lays waste the harvest in its fury and contrasting the brutal militarism of the British with the brotherly love of the Acadians. The parallel with Bancroft's treatment of the British blockade of Boston harbour is instructive. Though both writers see the British as destructive in their belligerence, where Bancroft contrasts British aggression with American industry and commercial enterprise, Longfellow offers an idyll of rural and static harmony as the antithesis of the brutal force of the military. Burning homes and farms, the British troops drive the gentle and loving peasants into exile, causing the death of Evangeline's father and her separation from her lover. In his prefatory note, Longfellow described the Acadians as 'primitive, simple-minded' folk, without apparently intending any pejorative connotations, for their simplicity is portrayed as a primal innocence. Theirs is a prelapsarian world; the evil that destroys it is an external evil.

The happy valley theme returns in the second part of the poem when Evangeline and the priest with whom she is travelling reach the new home of Basil Lajeunesse, the father of her betrothed Gabriel, after wandering friendless through the land. On the banks of the River Têche, in the Opelousas, Basil has recreated the blissful domestic world that was lost when the Acadians were banished. His new house has all the natural and fruitful associations of the houses at Grand-Pré; it bears the insignia of domestic love, for it has dovecots at each end, and these are 'love's perpetual symbol', providing 'scenes of endless wooing'. Reunited in this new home, the Acadians recreate their lost idyll. Immediately, old friendships revive and they dance 'like children delighted . . . / Dreamlike, with beaming eyes' to the music of the fiddler.

Evangeline's tediously pathetic story is given more than sentimental force by Longfellow's rehearsal of the archetypally Romantic theme of the fall from innocent harmony with nature to self-conscious alienation from the natural world. In his *Lectures on Dramatic Art and Literature*, translated by John Black in 1815, August Wilhelm Schlegel had defined Greek poetry as the poetry of enjoyment, modern poetry as the poetry of desire. Whereas the former had its foundation in the present scene, the latter, according to Schlegel, hovered between recollection and hope. Though Longfellow knew Schlegel's works before they were translated and had visited the German scholar in 1835, it is not necessary to suppose that *Evangeline* is a deliberate illustration of his particular formulation of the difference between classic and modern sensibility. Yet illustrate it, it does. Every reader of Longfellow has recognized that he wrote most feelingly when his theme was the frailty and the evanescence of human happiness. In his tale of woman's constancy he found an opportunity to explore the theme of loss.

Since the loss in this poem was the loss of the happy valley, it also offered the occasion for an American travelogue. In *Outre-Mer: A Pilgrimage Beyond the Sea* (1833–4), Longfellow had entertained his readers with sketches of a Europe that he knew at first hand. In *Evangeline*, he relied on other men's reports for his views of the American landscape. Unlike Francis Parkman, who felt the need to visit the scenes of his historical narratives, Longfellow was content to have the scenes come to him. In December 1846, while he was working on the poem, John Banvard's diorama of the Mississippi came to Boston, much to the poet's delight. Looking at the canvases, he felt himself to be sailing down the great river and made use of his impressions in the poem. In a letter to a friend, he wrote that he had tried to give the various descriptions of American scenery in the poem 'the true and peculiar coloring of Nature' (L, III. 142), but his descriptions of the lower Mississippi country were dependent on Charles Sealsfield's *Life in the New World* (1844), while his account of Evangeline's journey to the West made use of J. C. Frémont's *Expedition to the Rocky Mountains* (1845).[5] From Frémont he took the family name of Evangeline's betrothed. The actual Lajeunesse was one of Frémont's party and was tomahawked to death by marauding Indians in one of the many violent episodes recounted in the travelogue. Reading it, Longfellow wrote in his journal on 3 December 1846: 'What a wild life, and what a fresh kind of existence!' Typically, he added: 'But, ah, the discomforts!' Though the fascination of the wild could not lure him beyond his study, he did go on to state that Frémont had particularly touched his imagination (*Life*, II. 65–6).

In *Hiawatha* (1855) Longfellow turned his attention to the wild once more when he made Indian legends his theme. To treat the Indian in an elegiac mode was already a literary convention by the time that

Longfellow wrote his early poems linking the Indian with death ('The Indian Hunter', 'Lover's Rock', 'Jeckoyva', 'The Burial of the Minnisink'), but when he decided that he had found a way to 'weave together their beautiful traditions' – a decision he recorded in 1854 – he clearly believed that his poem would do more than evoke the pathos of the Indian's fate.

The introduction to *Hiawatha* explains the author's plan as that of showing that 'in even savage bosoms' there are yearnings and strivings for 'the good they comprehend not'. The Indian legends incorporated in the poem reveal, so the poet believes, that the pagan Indian was 'groping blindly in the darkness' toward the true light of Christianity. Even before he was vouchsafed that light, the savage could be lifted up and strengthened when he touched God's right hand, but the final sections of the poem show the arrival of the Christian missionaries to complete the grand scheme of spiritual enlightenment. The unlikelihood that an Indian chief would welcome the white strangers, as Hiawatha does, even though he has had a vision of the obliteration of his own people and their culture, plainly does not disturb Longfellow.

In preparing himself to write *Hiawatha*, Longfellow read those anthropological works on which any student of the Indian past had to some extent to rely in mid-nineteenth-century America.[6] Like Parkman and Thoreau, he depended on Henry Rowe Schoolcraft's work for some of his information, but he was less critical of Schoolcraft than Parkman was soon to become. In December 1855 he sent a copy of *Hiawatha* to Schoolcraft with a covering letter stressing that he had 'adhered very faithfully to the old myths' (L, III. 509), clearly meaning to affirm his allegiance to Schoolcraft. Some of the poem's departures from Indian tradition are, in fact, the direct result of that allegiance, for Longfellow's principle source was not as reliable as he believed it to be. Longfellow removed from his Indian hero features that were essential to the Indians' conception of the demigod. Manabozho was a complex figure in the legends on which Longfellow drew, for as well as a leader of his people he was also a trickster and a dupe. Further, he combined the character of a man with the forms of animals, particularly the Great Rabbit, but this would have worked against Longfellow's systematic humanization of his Indian culture-hero and was omitted from the poem. The Hiawatha we encounter in Longfellow's version of the legends is sent by the Gitche Manito, the Lord of Life, to reconcile the previously warring tribes and to preach them the gospel of love and peace. There is, as Van Wyck Brooks noted, something of William Ellery Channing in this Hiawatha; in the poem, therefore, the less benevolent aspects of Manabozho's character are displaced on to Pau-Puk-Keewis, Hiawatha's antagonist.

When the Gitche Manito warns the belligerent tribes that their 'danger is in discord' and asserts that their strength is in their union, as he does in the first canto of the poem, he is preaching lessons that have an obvious relevance to the United States of 1855. As the champion of peace and love, Hiawatha is plainly Longfellow's spokesman. Sent by the Lord of Life to guide the Indian nations, Hiawatha furthers the work of reconciliation among the tribes by marrying a Dacotah squaw, though he is an Ojibway chief. Closely connected with his mission as peace-bringer is his role as instructor of his people in the arts of peace: in agriculture and in picture-writing. The relevance of these lessons to Longfellow's contemporary America is less obvious, yet there is a sense in which these aspects of Hiawatha's altruism connect with the poet's own fundamental beliefs.

In the fifth canto of the poem, 'Hiawatha's Fasting', the chieftain wins the knowledge that will free his people from dependence on hunting and fishing by means of a vigil fast that culminates in his vision of the corn-god Mondamin. Hiawatha is granted the boon that will transform the lives of his people precisely because his prayers are altruistic, because he does not seek for renown. Mondamin, the spirit of the maize, visits Hiawatha, engages in a series of ritual struggles with him that lead to the death, ritual burial and rebirth of the maize, and thus teaches the secret of cultivation of the soil. In Schoolcraft's *Algic Researches* this story was associated not with Manabozho but with another hero named Wunzh, but in transferring the legend to Hiawatha Longfellow was thoroughly consistent with his purpose of creating a culture-hero who would represent the spirit of love and harmony, for the idyllic life of the tribe is expressed in the poem in terms of an ideal agricultural community. In the thirteenth canto, 'Blessing the Corn Fields', Hiawatha and his wife Minnehaha, having unified their tribes by marriage, live in a blissful setting where

> All around the happy village
> Stood the maize-fields, green and shining
> Waved the green plumes of Mondamin,
> Waved his soft and sunny tresses,
> Filling all the land with plenty.

We could well imagine ourselves in the 'happy valley' of Evangeline Bellefontaine and the Acadian innocents before their exile. In the happy village of the Ojibways, the poem tells us, the women are the chief agriculturalists. The ceremony of blessing the corn fields, in which Minnehaha draws a magic circle round the fields to protect the grain from harm by walking naked round them at night, is taken, as Longfellow's note tells us, from Schoolcraft's *Oneóta*, and is as authentic as the account of Hiawatha's vigil fast. The poet was indeed being faithful to the legends here, even though he transposed the central myth from one hero to another, and the episodes concerned with the cultivation of the maize are among the most successful in the poem. Yet Longfellow gives them his own distinctive emphasis and significance in firmly linking the fruitfulness he evokes with the ideal of romantic love and the domestic happiness that, in his scheme of values, is the consummation of that love.

All appraisals of the 'Indian' qualities of *Hiawatha* agree that the poem is furthest from the spirit of its legendary sources in the treatment of Hiawatha's courtship of Minnehaha, in the 'love story' that offered Longfellow's readers an acceptably sentimentalized view of the Indian hero. In 'Hiawatha's Wooing', the sun smiles benignly on Hiawatha, telling him to 'Rule by love', while the moon whispers to Minnehaha, advising her to 'Rule by patience', and a note of realism is sounded in the moon's admission that man is 'imperious, woman feeble'. We do not witness the imperious side of Hiawatha's married conduct, however; we learn only of his loving devotion to his wife. At the wedding-feast, Chibiabos, the poet-musician

> Sang in accents sweet and tender,
> Sang in tones of deep emotion,
> Songs of love and songs of longing.

Chibiabos is always described as 'gentle' in the poem; his songs, when we first hear of them, are described as songs of 'love, and longing'. In *Hiawatha*, a romantic, yearning love, leading to an idyllic domestic happiness – though that bliss is to be destroyed by the famine and death that destroy the rural Eden – replaces the Dionysian elements of the historical Algonquins. At the wedding-feast, the representative of the wild, ecstatic impulse is not Chibiabos but Pau-Puk-Keewis, whose whirling, frenzied movement contrasts with the gentle, sentimental songs of Hiawatha's friend.

Hiawatha is not, of course, merely saccharine, even if it does tame the Indian wildness. Death enters the poem when the musician Chibiabos, who has claimed that the love-song is the 'most potent spell of magic', is destroyed by the power of the Evil Spirits, who tempt him on to the ice of Lake Superior and drown him. Hiawatha's other close friend, Kwasind, is later, in the eighteenth canto, drowned as a result of the malice of the cunning Little People, and this death is followed by the appearance of ghosts in Hiawatha's wigwam, souls of the departed who have come to warn of future disasters. The great disaster is the famine that kills Minnehaha and destroys Hiawatha's happiness before the advent of the first white man. In fact, for all the 'official' optimism of its conclusion, *Hiawatha* is a profoundly pessimistic poem. Not only does it show us the ephemerality of the idyllic world of Hiawatha and Minnehaha; it also looks forward to the total obliteration of the Indian culture that is supposedly evolving into Christian civilization. More revealing of Longfellow's own feelings than anything else in the poem are the lines in which the dying chief imagines the 'westward marches' of the nations that will displace his own people. The men who will build the cities in the valleys and put steamboats on the rivers will be 'Restless, struggling, toiling, striving' men of Longfellow's own day. As the public poetic voice of his age, Longfellow gave Hiawatha further lines that should neutralize his own most telling words: the energetic, competitive, restless new Americans will have 'one heart-beat in their bosoms' although they will speak many tongues. This, of course, is Longfellow's own heartfelt wish and his message to his nation in the 1850s, but Hiawatha's vision of white civilization in America sounds remarkably like the young Longfellow's in his 'Defense of Poetry', an article he had published in the *North American Review* in 1832. There he argued that the spirit of the age was obsessed with schemes for gain and gloried in material progress at the expense of moral and spiritual well-being. In contrasting the materialistic ethos of his day with the 'true glory of a nation' in the realms of intellect and spirit, Longfellow made what in 1832 was already a conventional defence of American poetry. For the rest of his own poetic career, he associated the true spirit of poetry with the peace of domestic love that was always threatened by the 'restless' modern spirit and was the victim of an aggressive materialism whose ultimate expression was war.

Notes

1 The text of the extract is taken from the first edition of *The Courtship of Miles Standish, and Other Poems*, Boston: Ticknor & Fields, 1858. Parenthetic references to L throughout the chapter are to *The Letters of Henry Wadsworth Longfellow*, ed. Andrew Hilen, 4 vols, Cambridge, Mass.: Harvard University Press, 1966–72. References to *Life* are to *The Life of*

Henry Wadsworth Longfellow, with Extracts from His Journals and Correspondence, ed. Samuel Longfellow, 2 vols, London: Kegan Paul & Trench, 1886.

2 *Newton Arvin, *Longfellow: His Life and Work*, Boston: Little, Brown, 1963; repr. Westport, Conn.: Greenwood Press, 1977, p. 179.

3 Robert A. Ferguson, 'Longfellow's Political Fears: Civic Authority and the Role of the Artist in *Hiawatha* and *Miles Standish*', *American Literature* 50: 2 (May 1978), 187–215.

4 Barbara Welter, *Dimity Convictions: The American Woman in the Nineteenth Century*, Athens: Ohio University Press, 1976. See especially ch. 2, 'The Cult of True Womanhood: 1800–1860'.

5 Murray Gardner Hill, 'Some of Longfellow's Sources for the Second Part of *Evangeline*', *PMLA* 31 (1916), 161–80.

6 Useful information on Longfellow's adaptation of his sources, and on the unreliability of Schoolcraft as a source, can be found in Stith Thompson, 'The Indian Legend of Hiawatha', *PMLA* 37 (1922), 128–40, and Rose M. Davis, 'How Indian is Hiawatha?' *Midwest Folklore* 7 (1957), 5–25. A general discussion of Longfellow's interest in the Indians' attitude to nature forms part of Christabel F. Fiske's 'Mercerized Folklore', *Poet-Lore* 31 (1920), 538–75.

Further reading

Lawrance Thompson, *Young Longfellow, 1807–1843*, New York: Macmillan, 1938, repr. New York: Octagon Books, 1969.

10

Herman Melville (1819-91)

'Captain Ahab,' said Starbuck, who, with Stubb and Flask, had thus far been eyeing his superior with increasing surprise, but at last seemed struck with a thought which somewhat explained all the wonder. 'Captain Ahab, I have heard of Moby Dick – but it was not Moby Dick that took off thy leg?'

'Who told thee that?' cried Ahab; then pausing, 'Aye, Starbuck; aye, my hearties all round; it was Moby Dick that dismasted me; Moby Dick that brought me to this dead stump I stand on now. Aye, aye,' he shouted with a terrific, loud, animal sob, like that of a heart-stricken moose; 'Aye, aye! it was that accursed white whale that razeed me; made a poor pegging lubber of me for ever and a day!' Then tossing both arms, with measureless imprecations he shouted out: 'Aye, aye! and I'll chase him round Good Hope, and round the Horn, and round the Norway Maelstrom, and round perdition's flames before I give him up. And this is what ye have shipped for, men! to chase that white whale on both sides of land, and over all sides of earth, till he spouts black blood and rolls fin out. What say ye, men, will ye splice hands on it, now? I think ye do look brave.'

'Aye, aye!' shouted the harpooneers and seamen, running closer to the excited old man: 'A sharp eye for the White Whale; a sharp lance for Moby Dick!'

'God bless ye,' he seemed to half sob and half shout. 'God bless ye, men. Steward! go draw the great measure of grog. But what's this long face about, Mr. Starbuck; wilt thou not chase the white whale? art not game for Moby Dick?'

'I am game for his crooked jaw, and for the jaws of Death too, Captain Ahab, if it fairly comes in the way of the business we follow; but I came here to hunt whales, not my commander's vengeance. How many barrels will thy vengeance yield thee even if thou gettest it, Captain Ahab? it will not fetch thee much in our Nantucket market.'

'Nantucket market! Hoot! But come closer, Starbuck; thou requirest a little lower layer. If money's to be the measurer, man, and the accountants have computed their great counting-house the globe, by girdling it with guineas, one to every three parts of an inch; then, let me tell thee, that my vengeance will fetch a great premium *here*!'

'He smites his chest,' whispered Stubb, 'what's that for? methinks it rings most vast, but hollow.'

'Vengeance on a dumb brute!' cried Starbuck, 'that simply smote thee from blindest instinct! Madness! To be enraged with a dumb thing, Captain Ahab, seems blasphemous.'

'Hark ye yet again, – the little lower layer. All visible objects, man, are but as pasteboard masks. But in each event – in the living act, the undoubted deed – there, some unknown but still reasoning thing puts forth the mouldings of its features from behind the unreasoning mask. If man will strike, strike through the mask! How can the prisoner reach outside except by thrusting through the wall? To me, the white whale is that wall, shoved near to me. Sometimes I think there's naught beyond. But 'tis enough. He tasks me; he heaps me; I see in him outrageous strength, with an inscrutable malice sinewing it. That inscrutable thing is chiefly what I hate; and be the white whale agent, or be the white whale principal, I will wreak that hate upon him. Talk not to me of blasphemy, man; I'd strike the sun if it insulted me. For could the sun do that, then could I do the other; since there is ever a sort of fair play herein, jealousy presiding over all creations. But not my master, man, is even that fair play. Who's over me? Truth hath no confines. Take off thine eye! more intolerable than fiends' glarings is a doltish stare! So, so; thou reddenest and palest; my heat has melted thee to anger-glow. But look ye, Starbuck, what is said in heat, that thing unsays itself. There are men from whom warm words are small indignity. I meant not to incense thee. Let it go. Look! see yonder Turkish cheeks of spotted tawn – living, breathing pictures painted by the sun. The Pagan leopards – the unrecking and unworshipping things, that live; and seek, and give no reasons for the torrid life they feel! The crew, man, the crew! Are they not one and all with Ahab, in this matter of the whale? See Stubb! he laughs! See yonder Chilean! he snorts to think of it. Stand up amid the general hurricane, thy one tost sapling cannot, Starbuck! And what is it? Reckon it. 'Tis but to help strike a fin; no wondrous feat for Starbuck. What is it more? From this one poor hunt, then, the best lance out of all Nantucket, surely he will not hang back, when every foremast-hand has clutched a whetstone? Ah! constrainings seize thee; I see! the billow lifts thee! Speak, but speak! – Aye, aye!

thy silence, then, *that* voices thee. (*Aside*) Something shot from my dilated nostrils, he has inhaled it in his lungs. Starbuck now is mine; cannot oppose me now, without rebellion.'

Moby-Dick (1851)[1]

* * *

The Ahab we meet in the 'Quarter-Deck' chapter (ch. 36) of *Moby-Dick* is not the 'poor old whale-hunter' Ishmael refers to in 'The Speck-synder' (ch. 33), but the 'grand, ungodly, god-like man' that Captain Peleg describes in 'The Ship' (ch. 16). The language Ishmael now uses to describe Ahab's actions, together with Ahab's own rhetoric, gives him a status and a force that is more than human. His shout of mingled rage and sorrow is like the 'terrific' sob of a stricken moose; his imprecations are 'measureless' in the sense that he swears to pursue the whale beyond the limits of the oceans as far as hell itself. Earlier in this chapter, Ahab has seemed to the crew to be like the weather horizon when a storm is coming up. The simile is Ishmael's, but it is developed in Ahab's own speech to Starbuck when the Captain warns his mate that no solitary sapling can withstand the hurricane – a storm, he implies, generated by himself. Rejecting the charge of blasphemy, Ahab says that he would not submit to insult even from the sun. Rather than submit, he would strike at the sun itself. The words are vainglorious to the point of absurdity if we see Ahab as nothing more than an old whaling captain maddened by the misfortune that made a cripple of him, but Melville's treatment of this dramatic scene within the frame of Ishmael's narrative clearly develops the possibilities of the narrator's earlier assertion (in 'The Ship') that a Quaker sea-captain can be a 'mighty pageant creature, formed for noble tragedies'. In changing from the narrative to the dramatic mode, Melville makes Ahab an immediate presence in the fiction. Previously, his character has been mediated to the reader by Ishmael, who – in a chapter called simply 'Ahab' – has already associated the Captain with Perseus, the destroyer of the Gorgon, and with the thunder-struck but dauntless Satan of *Paradise Lost*. In that chapter Ishmael's rhetoric has amplified the character it described, attributing to Ahab 'an infinity of firmest fortitude, a determinate, unsurrenderable wilfulness' and a 'nameless regal overbearing dignity of some mighty woe'. Now Ahab's speech reminds us of Shakespeare's tragic heroes; its incoherent phrases evoke through their rhythms the world of Elizabethan drama rather than that of Nantucket whaling captains.

Apologizing to Starbuck, Ahab sounds like Hamlet disowning his own mad deeds to Laertes. Further, Ahab's phrase 'Commend the murderous chalices' is an unmistakable echo of Macbeth's when he reflects on the justice that 'Commends the ingredients of our poison'd chalice / To our own lips.' The allusions are blatant; they insist that the reader adjust his expectations, abandoning those of the realistic novel for those of tragic drama.

Within the scene, the crew's reaction validates Ahab's rhetoric. Responding to their captain's appeal with a shout of excitement, the wild crewmen move as one to take part in the diabolic ceremony Ahab instigates, drinking liquor 'hot as Satan's hoof', their eyes like serpents' eyes as they feel its effects. These are also the eyes of prairie wolves, mad for the blood of the bison. Later (in ch. 38), Starbuck describes the heathen crew as 'whelped somewhere by the sharkish sea' and thus associates them with the most ferocious of all creatures. Since the ship in which they sail is named after an Indian tribe, the Pequots, and since one of the harpooneers is an Indian, while all three who appear in this scene are savages, it is clear that the crew of the *Pequod* represent wild, or savage, society. Ahab appropriately calls them 'my braves'. Though the leader of the desperate crew is a Quaker captain from civilized Nantucket, that captain is the fiercest of the 'Anacharsis Clootz deputation from all the isles of the sea, and all the ends of the earth' that sailed in the *Pequod*. Writing of savages in his first book, *Typee* (1846), Melville had stated that 'the white civilized man [is] the most ferocious animal on the face of the earth'. The ship's name in *Moby-Dick* does not merely allude to the Pequots, it also recalls their extermination by the white Christians of New England. On board that savage-civilized ship, Ahab's satanic ceremony is followed by an orgiastic scene in which the crew's violence keeps pace with the natural violence of a squall (ch. 40). It ends in a fight between a Spanish sailor and Daggoo, the black harpooneer, and in the prayer of the little black cabin-boy Pip: 'Oh, thou big white God aloft there somewhere in yon darkness, have mercy on this small black boy down here; preserve him from all men that have no bowels to feel fear!'

Ahab, plainly, has 'no bowels to feel fear', yet in talking of the 'mighty pageant creature, formed for noble tragedies', Ishmael had described a man 'with a globular brain and a ponderous heart': a man capable of majestic emotions as well as intense thought. Rejecting Starbuck's argument that the *Pequod*'s mission should be financial profit rather than vengeance on a brute beast, Ahab does indeed appeal to the heart when he states that the 'great premium' or reward will be found in his breast. Yet, as Stubb notes, that breast 'rings most vast, but hollow'. Ahab's great heart has been hollowed by his dedication to hate and by his monomaniac pursuit of revenge. Just before he commits ship and crew to the final, fatal chase, Ahab will have an opportunity to renounce his vengeance and sail for home, family and love. In 'The Symphony (ch. 132), Starbuck will appeal for the last time to Ahab's humanity, but the Captain will reject this appeal and Ishmael, in another phrase that evokes Milton's version of the Fall of Man, will describe Ahab as a 'blighted fruit tree' casting 'his last, cindered apple to the soil'. The implications of Ishmael's words are clear: Ahab's quest for the fruit of the forbidden Tree of Knowledge has 'blighted' his own life and consumed it in his own destructive fire. Throughout *Moby-Dick* Ahab is associated with the fires of hell. In 'The Try-Works' (ch. 96) his soul will be identified with the flames of the fire that heats the whale's blubber to turn it into boiling oil. These 'snaky flames' make a 'red hell' in whose light the crew glare 'like devils'. To Ishmael, the *Pequod*, 'freighted with savages, and laden with fire, and burning a corpse, and plunging into that blackness of darkness' will seem 'the material counterpart of her monomaniac commander's soul'. Ahab's monomania, as we learn in 'The Chart' (ch. 44), is the purpose that can grimly live and burn in him with a kind of self-assumed, independent being, taking possession of him and consuming him just as the fire of the try-works consumes the whale's body. That purpose is the vengeance of which Starbuck talks in 'The Quarter-Deck', calling it both madness and blasphemy.

Judged by common-sense standards, Ahab's obsession with revenge on a whale is absurd rather than blasphemous. In 'Leg and Arm' (ch. 100), the *Pequod* encounters the English whaler, the *Samuel Enderby*, whose captain has lost an arm in giving battle to the White Whale. Captain Boomer's arm was ripped open by the barb of a harpoon that had caught in his shoulder and carried him down below the waves when Moby Dick dived. Far from bearing malice against the dumb brute that caused his mutilation, Boomer thanks 'the good God' for the escape that cost him an arm, states that the White Whale is welcome to what he took, and resolves to leave so dangerous an antagonist alone in future. Captain Boomer's ship's surgeon, an irrepressibly jolly former-clergyman named Bunger, tells Ahab that 'what you take for the White Whale's malice is only his awkwardness'. Moreover, Bunger attributes the fact that the whale cannot digest even a man's arm to the Divine Providence that has so 'inscrutably constructed' the whale's digestive organs. To the jovial English captain, Ahab's mania for revenge makes him seem distinctly 'crazy', while even the facetious Bunger thinks of the 'foul fiend' when he sees how Ahab's blood is 'boiling'. Neither Boomer nor Bunger, themselves comic figures whose facetiousness allows them to see only the bright side of life, could comprehend the 'lower layer' of meaning to which Ahab had directed Starbuck's attention in 'The Quarter-Deck'. To that we must now turn, since without the lower layer of meaning Ahab's quest would be only a parody of Jacobean revenge-tragedy.

In stating that 'all visible objects' are merely 'pasteboard masks', Ahab is attempting to explain his rage with a 'dumb brute' that may well act unknowingly, without conscious malice. If the White Whale is not itself the 'principal' or originator of the malice Ahab finds in all things, it is the 'agent' of a power that lies behind the visible world and 'puts forth the mouldings of its features' in the 'masks' that constitute the phenomenal world. Ahab's language recalls Thomas Carlyle's in *Sartor Resartus*: 'All visible things are emblems . . . Matter exists only spiritually, and to represent some Idea, and *body* it forth.' It also recalls the Emersonian doctrine, in the 'Language' section of *Nature*, that 'Particular natural facts are symbols of particular spiritual facts' and that 'Nature is the symbol of spirit.' The difference between Ahab's symbolic interpretation of the natural world and those of the Transcendentalists is, of course, that Ahab believes the idea or spirit behind or above the world of appearances to be a power that is malevolent. In matching the supposed malice of that power with his own hate, Ahab is prepared to hate both the mask and whatever is hidden behind the mask. To hate 'the inscrutable thing' is to hate both phenomenon and noumenon – if the appearance is inscrutable, the ground or cause of that appearance must necessarily be inscrutable too. Ahab will wreak his hatred in an act of revenge against the White Whale that tore off his leg with its 'outrageous strength', yet his anger seems to be caused as much by the inscrutability of the whale as by its destructiveness. In the chapter devoted to Moby Dick (ch. 41), Ishmael tells us that Ahab came to identify the whale not only with his bodily woes but also with 'all his intellectual and spiritual exasperations'. When Ishmael says that the White Whale became the 'monomaniac incarnation' of all the malicious agencies that some deep men feel 'eating in them', he not only gives Promethean connotations to Ahab's sufferings but also a new force to Carlyle's metaphor of 'bodying forth' the spiritual.

Before Ishmael met his captain, he was warned by Captain Peleg that Ahab had 'been in colleges, as well as 'mong the cannibals; been used to deeper wonders than the waves; fixed his fiery lance in mightier, stranger foes than whales'. Ahab's rage, clearly, is metaphysically motivated. When he says that the whale is a wall that imprisons him, we remember that, in the playful section called 'Etymology' that stands as a preface to the novel, Melville called our attention to the relationship between words and the things they signify. His lexical high spirits were not confined to including the 'Feegee' and 'Erromangoan' words for whale – 'Pekee-Nuee-Nuee' and 'Pehee-Nuee-Nuee' – for he also cited Hackluyt to the effect that 'the letter H . . . almost alone maketh up the signification of the word', and followed this with a list of verbal equivalents for the English 'whale', including among them the Dutch 'wal'. Near the end of his quest, Ahab will refer to the 'dead, blind wall' that 'butts all inquiring heads at last' (ch. 125). By that time, we will have watched Ishmael's attempts to 'read' the sperm whale's brow (in 'The Praire') and will have heard Ishmael refer to the sperm whale's head as a 'dead, impregnable, uninjurable wall' (in 'The Battering-Ram', ch. 76). Ishmael, too, will prove to be a prisoner, hemmed in by the wall of the whale's vast presence, yet even when he admits the impossibility of scrutinizing the 'dead, blind wall' of the whale's head, Ishmael also states that 'unless you own the whale, you are but a provincial and sentimentalist in Truth'. To 'own' the whale must mean to admit or acknowledge its significance, even when one cannot grasp what it signifies. To Ishmael, it is clear, the whale is a wall that butts enquiring heads and it is a veil like that which veiled the goddess at Sais ('The Battering-Ram'), but it is also the whole meaning of life for which man is bound to seek, though he will never attain his goal. (In 'Etymology' we were informed – or misinformed – that the Anglo-Saxon word for whale was 'whœl', an obvious anagram for 'whole'.) Refusing to accept the limits of human knowledge, Ahab becomes a 'fiendish man', an 'ungodly old man', as Ishmael tells us in the 'Moby Dick' chapter. He also becomes a *mad* man, with a madness like that of Shakespeare's King Lear, as Melville conceived it in his 'Hawthorne and His Mosses' essay: 'Tormented into desperation, Lear, the frantic king, tears off the mask, and speaks the sane madness of vital truth.'

The sanity of Ahab's madness consists of his awareness that there is a 'lower layer' of meaning in his own pursuit of the White Whale, for that allows us to interpret his rage as a desire to *know*. Yet before Ahab hints at the symbolic meaning of Moby Dick, Ishmael the narrator has given a symbolic significance to the sea itself. In 'Loomings', the opening chapter, Ishmael states that 'meditation and water are wedded forever'. All men, he claims, are fascinated by rivers and oceans because they see themselves in them. In this they are like Narcissus, who plunged into the water and was drowned because he could not grasp 'the tormenting, mild image' he saw in it. As Ishmael interprets the Narcissus myth, the image that attracts and torments man when he gazes into the water is 'the image of the ungraspable phantom of life'. When he comes, in the 'Moby Dick' chapter, to try to explain the readiness with which the wild crew shared its captain's hate for the White Whale, Ishmael uses a phrase that clearly connects that hate with his interpretation of Narcissus' story. The crew, he says, found the idea of the whale insufferable because they associated it with 'the gliding great demon of the seas of life'. Narcissus was tormented by his inability to grasp the image (of the self) that he saw in the reflecting water of thought. Ahab is driven mad by the inscrutability of the 'thing' that confronts him, or the wall (whale) that imprisons him.

Gazing at the severed head of a whale in 'The Sphynx' (ch. 70), Ahab asks this sphinx-like head to tell him its secret. His belief that the whale has a secret derives from the fact that for him the whale has dived deeper than any other creature (in the waters of thought) and has seen more of the world's mysteries as it moved 'amid this world's foundations'. Typically, Ahab supposes that the mysteries are horrors, that knowledge of them would be enough to make even Abraham an infidel; yet he ends his address to the whale-sphinx with an assertion of his belief in the emblematic value of the material world: 'O Nature, and O soul of man! how far beyond all utterance are your linked analogies! not the smallest atom stirs or lives in matter, but has its cunning duplicate in mind.' This sounds so remarkably like the Emersonian doctrine of correspondence between nature and spirit that we may well wonder why – with such a belief – Ahab finds the material world inscrutable. In 'The Doubloon' (ch. 99) we will, in fact, see Ahab interpreting one set of signs: those on the Ecuadorian coin he nailed to the mast of the *Pequod* in the ceremony of hate on the quarter-deck. When he treats the three mountain peaks on the coin as emblems, Ahab sees them as emblems of his own soul. The tower that tops one peak, the volcano spurting from the second, and the cock that crows from the third summit, all (to Ahab) signify aspects of his own character, for he believes that the terrestial globe, 'like a magician's glass, to each and every man in turn but mirrors back his own mysterious self'. In *Nature*, Emerson had claimed that the relationship between the mind and matter was not dependent on the poet's fancy but stood 'in the will of God'. Substituting his own will for that of any God, Ahab finds himself in a totally solipsistic world, with no possibility of escape from the prison of his own mind. Even his antagonist – even the White Whale – must, then, be a projection of his own mind, for Ahab-Narcissus is self-tormented.

Ahab's symbolic reading of the doubloon's meaning is followed by Starbuck's Christian interpretation of the same symbols. The mighty peaks that to Ahab stood for the self, seem to Starbuck faint earthly symbols of the Trinity. After the Christian mate, in quick succession, the jocular and spiritually irresponsible Stubb, the trivially materialistic Flask, the superstitious Manxman, the Pagan Queequeg and the heathen Fedallah all interpret the doubloon in terms of their own, contrasting, views of life. Pip, now crazed by his own thought-diving when left alone in the immensity of the ocean (in 'The Castaway'), does not offer a symbolic reading of the coin; instead he provides a comment on the interpretive process itself: 'I look, you look, he looks; we look, ye look, they look.' Pip's sane madness is a dramatic restatement of ideas that Ishmael has explored – with less pathos but with no less emotion – in his reflections in the chapter 'The Whiteness of the Whale' (ch. 42). Noting that whiteness has been associated with innocence, with the greatest human dignity and power, and with supernatural or divine majesty, Ishmael associates first awe and then terror with the colour. In puns that give his thoughts a terrible force, he states that whiteness intensifies the effect of 'things the most appalling to mankind' because it makes the universe seem as 'palsied' as a leper. Whiteness suggests the pall of death and annihilation because it is both an absence of colour and the 'concrete of all colours'; that is, it is the light whose refraction leads men to attribute to objects the colours that (in the Lockean theory of perception) exist only in the mind of the beholder. This subjectivist epistemology is expressed in terms that are beyond the apprehension of Ahab's wild crew and in a discourse more reasoned than any the Captain offers, yet Ishmael's conclusion refers us back to the ceremony we have witnessed on the quarter-deck: 'And of all these things the Albino whale was the symbol. Wonder ye then at the fiery hunt?'

The hunt is most fiery in 'The Candles' (ch. 119), when Ahab defyingly worships the fallen Mother – Sophia – to whose influence the Gnostics attributed the evil they found in the material world.[2] In this scene, Ahab's harpoon actually burns in the unholy fire of the lightning; it burns 'like a serpent's tongue'. Ahab has already baptized the barbs destined to pierce Moby Dick's body in the name of the Devil ('The Forge'); now he claims that his whole crew is bound by the oath given on the quarter-deck, as he is himself bound. Thus 'The Candles' completes the diabolic ceremony of dedication to revenge. It seals the fate of the *Pequod*, consigning it to the flames of which Ahab spoke in his vaunting speech – 'perdition's flames'. Yet Ahab is not only a diabolic figure, linked with Milton's Satan. When he first appeared on the quarter-deck of the *Pequod*, as we have noted, Ishmael linked him with Perseus, the heroic slayer of the Gorgon. In the 'Moby Dick' chapter, when telling of Ahab's mutilation, Ishmael refers to the Captain's 'Egyptian chest' and thus associates him with Osiris, the priest-god-king who hunted Typhon and was dismembered by that enemy of man in an annual ritual that to the Egyptians symbolized the annual death of the vegetation.[3] In 'The Candles' the typhoon strikes the *Pequod* directly ahead, as if to warn captain and crew from their quest of the White Whale. One great wave smashes the boat in which Ahab will attack Moby Dick and destroys the very part of the boat on which Ahab will stand. Thus when Ahab, just before he begins his final chase for the White Whale, sees himself as 'Adam, staggering beneath the piled centuries since Paradise' (in 'The Symphony'), he gathers together several strands of mythic connotation to dramatize his role as the representative – and champion – of man; of man the victim of divine (or diabolic) displeasure.

Unlike the mythic Osiris, Ahab will not rise again in a seasonal renewal of life; his death in combat with Moby Dick will form the last act of his drama. Yet his quest has given him heroic stature, for he is man's champion, not only in his struggle with the 'gliding great demon of the seas of life', but also in the very fact of his voyaging. In 'The Lee Shore' (ch. 23), apropos of the helmsman Bulkington, Ishmael unambiguously identifies ocean-voyaging with the quest for ultimate truths. Bulkington is a demigod who leaps up to his apotheosis from the sea; he perishes because he shuns the safety of the shore. In Ishmael's words, 'all deep, earnest thinking is but the intrepid effort of the soul to keep the open independence of her sea', for 'in landlessness alone resides the highest truth, shoreless, indefinite as God'. The world of Captain Ahab and his crew is the landless world of 'The Lee Shore', but in Ahab's case the metaphysical voyaging costs him his humanity as well as his life.

In 'The Symphony', reviewing his forty years of whaling, Ahab stresses the desolate solitude of his life at sea as well as its perils. He contrasts the horrors of the deep with the peaceful pleasures of the land and then pictures his existence as a walled town cut off from the sympathies of the green country beyond its bounds. Here, as elsewhere in *Moby-Dick*, the ocean world of thought is contrasted with the pastoral world of love. To dissuade Ahab from going on with the hunt, Starbuck adds his own yearnings for the wife and child he has left at home to his captain's momentary regrets for his abandoned world of domestic happiness. But Ahab rejects all natural lovings and longings even while admitting that they are natural; instead he devotes himself to the purpose that controls him, and goes on with the relentless quest. Earlier, as the *Pequod* entered the great South Sea, Ishmael was moved to thoughts of Pan by the mysteries of the Pacific Ocean, with its 'sea-pastures, wide-rolling watery prairies', for the ocean that evoked these pastoral images also suggested the world-soul, the heart of the earth, to this pantheistic gazer from mast-heads. But there were few thoughts of Pan in Ahab's mind; instead there were images of the White Whale rolling in its own blood. As he entered the mild ocean, Ahab stood on deck like an iron statue ('The Pacific'). A spell of mild weather on that ocean inspires Ishmael with such tender feelings that he imaginatively transforms the sea into the flowery earth or grassy prairies again, even making the waves into domestic creatures ('The Gilder'). The metamorphosis of waves into cats purring by the hearthstone is the product of an extravagant play of Ishmael's fancy occasioned by the influx of a 'filial, confident, land-like feeling' towards the temporarily mild and maternal sea. Already – in 'The Grand Armada' – the experience of maternal love and filial trust has intruded on the landless world of the *Pequod*, offering to the awe-struck crew glimpses of the domestic life and loves of the whale beneath the watery surface. Yet, though Ishmael claims that he has an area of serenity at the centre of his being analogous to the charmed circle of the nursing whales, his ferocious fellow-whalers quickly destroy the peaceful scene of 'young Leviathan amours in the deep', killing and wounding all the whales they can reach. To hunt for the whale is to be the implacable foe of the 'dalliance and delight' witnessed in 'The Grand Armada'. Such hunting is possible only to men who have rejected, or spurned, their filial relationship with nature. Like Ahab, though, they may feel that their stepmother nature has cast them off.

In the last of the 'gams', just before the final chase begins, the *Pequod* meets the *Rachel* (ch. 128), whose captain has lost his son and begs for help in the search for him. Though, in his desperate attempt to move Ahab's heart and thaw his 'iciness', the distraught captain reminds Ahab that he too is a father, nothing can reach the feelings of the monomaniac captain of the *Pequod*; he stands 'like an anvil, receiving every shock, but without the least quivering of his own'. In this scene, Ahab's inhumanity is dramatized – it is acted out before the reader – but it is also interpreted by Ishmael in language that connects the incident with the crucial scene on the quarter-deck. In subjugating the crew to his will, Ahab attempted to shock into them the accumulated magnetic force that was in him; to make them feel his 'own electric thing'. The man whose will attained an occult and sinister power over others when he induced them to share his rage and take his oath now proves himself a man of iron, impervious to the electrical charge of human sympathy. Beneath the contrast lies a fundamental continuity of character, for in the quarter-deck scene the electrical metaphors for Ahab's will were associated with the suggestion that his vitality had a *mechanical* hum to it. The implication that Ahab's relentless and remorseless purpose had made a machine rather than a man of him is developed in the soliloquy that follows the oath-swearing ceremony, a soliloquy in which Ahab talks of the iron rails of purpose on which his soul is grooved to run. Thus he identifies himself with the railway engine, the symbol of soulless force to nineteenth-century writers who, like Melville, knew their Carlyle. The iron crown of Lombardy that Ahab imagines himself to be wearing, is emblematic of his loss of humanity. Ishmael's later references to his captain's iron nature confirm the judgement. More than a mere man in the quarter-deck scene, Ahab is also less than a man in his denial of the human heart. Yet where Hawthorne's Puritans became men of iron or of adamant in their moral bigotry, Melville's Ahab becomes a fiend in his intellectual fanaticism. When he describes his ideal man to the carpenter (ch. 108), Ahab asks for a man fifty feet high, with a massive chest, a forehead of brass, a quarter of an acre of brains and no heart at all. In its hyperbolic way, this is a picture of the Captain himself, the man dedicated to the inhuman quest for knowledge.

Ahab's icy, inhuman rejection of the appeal by the *Rachel*'s captain is dramatically powerful because we have witnessed the human kindness of which he is capable only a few chapters earlier, in his dialogue with Pip (ch. 125). Pip's madness touches Ahab in his inmost centre, because the poor boy's love contrasts with the heartlessness of the gods and because the boy stands for all mankind in his very ignorance of what he does. Pip lost his wits, as Ishmael told us in 'The Castaway', when he saw God's foot on the treadle of the loom and spoke to it. In attaining to 'heaven's sense' men must wander from mortal reason. Ishmael's words connect Pip's experience with the 'deep earnest thinking' of which he spoke in 'The Lee Shore', for the black boy's soul was drowned when he was left alone on the heartless immensity of the ocean. In other words, Pip involuntarily experienced the very landlessness that for Bulkington was synonymous with the highest truth. When Ishmael also states that it was the 'intense concentration of self in the middle of such a heartless immensity' that made Pip's situation unbearable, he prepares us for the crucial ironies of Ahab's relationship with Pip. The mad boy is the mad captain's spiritual son because he has dived deepest into the ocean of the self. As the 'ringed horizon' expanded around the lonely castaway, Pip experienced the ultimate sensation of boundlessness. On the quarter-deck, Ahab claimed that no bounds could exist to his pursuit of the White Whale. To the crew of the first ship he met ('The Albatross', ch. 52) Ahab boasted vaingloriously that the *Pequod* was 'bound round the world'. By this Captain Ahab meant that his ship was bound for no mere port, as other vessels were, but was dedicated to the pursuit of his revenge around the globe. As the story of the fiery hunt unfolds, the unintentional irony of Ahab's boast becomes ever more apparent. In his boundless quest for knowledge – a quest that involves the rejection of sacred human bonds – Ahab is bound to the circle of the self and destined, with his crew, for death. In terms of the Faustian association of boundless human aspiration with limitless space, the voyage shows us the collapse of space – the disappearance of the 'other' without which the self can not obtain knowledge.[4] In other words, the very 'landlessness' of the voyage indicates a self-destructive subjectivism.

Ahab is the great tragic hero of *Moby-Dick* and his pursuit of the White Whale gives shape to Melville's story. Yet long before we meet Captain Ahab in the chapter with the dramatic title 'Enter Ahab; To Him, Stubb' (ch. 29), and long before we even hear of Ahab, Ishmael the narrator has told us of his own desire to embark on an ocean voyage. In 'Loomings' (ch. 1), Ishmael explains his motives for voyaging in terms reminiscent of Poe's Arthur Gordon Pym. Attracted by the perils as well as the wonders of whaling, he loves 'to sail forbidden seas, and land on barbarous coasts'. Like Pym, he anticipates disaster and seems to relish the prospect, for he believes that horror is as much a part of human life as what is good. Unlike Pym, Ishmael is aware of the symbolic significance of his attraction to the sea, for, as we have seen, he associates water and meditation. When, much later, Ishmael imagines himself boarding the Argo-Navis, the ship in which Osiris sailed against Typhon, and sees himself hunting for Leviathan in the heavens (ch. 57), he clearly links his own role with Ahab's, for he explains his imagined voyage as a quest to discover 'whether the fabled heavens with all their countless tents really lie encamped beyond my mortal sight!' His quarry then, like Ahab's, is knowledge of what lies beyond the wall – or behind the inscrutable mask – of appearances in the world. Yet unlike Ahab and the rest of the crew of the *Pequod*, Ishmael survives the final encounter with Moby Dick. Since Ahab's voyage is to a considerable extent interpreted for us by Ishmael as narrator – since it is a voyage within a voyage – to understand *Moby-Dick* we have to understand the meaning of Ishmael's quest and of his survival.

In 'The Lee Shore', as we have seen, Ishmael identified all 'deep, earnest thinking' with 'the intrepid effort of the soul to keep the open independence of her sea'. Later, in 'Of the Monstrous Pictures of Whales' (ch. 55), he expresses pride in his profession of whaling because, as he claims, the living whale can only be seen 'in his full majesty and *significance*' (my emphasis) at sea on the unfathomable waters of the ocean. Artists and naturalists who have not hunted the whale themselves create only 'monstrous pictures', for the only way to discover what the whale really looks like is to go whaling yourself, but to do that is to risk destruction. Developing the idea in 'Measurement of the Whale's Skeleton' (ch. 103), Ishmael states that it is foolish for 'timid untravelled man' to try to understand the 'wondrous whale' merely by examining its skeleton. 'Only in the heart of quickest perils; only when within the eddyings of his angry flukes; only on the profound unbounded sea, can the fully invested whale be truly and livingly found out.' Ishmael's quest, then, is to 'find the whale out' by the most intrepid voyaging on the profoundest waters of thought. Paradoxically, though, to find the whale out 'livingly' means to engage in the whaling man's hunt to kill whales. In 'The Lamp' (ch. 97), Ishmael gives an obviously allegorical interpretation of whaling when he claims that a whaling man seeks the 'food of light' (the sperm oil that was used for lamps) and 'lives in light' while he is aboard the whaler. In 'The Affidavit' (ch. 45), he warns his landlubberly readers against reducing Moby Dick to a 'hideous and intolerable allegory', but at the same time he tells them to be economical with the lamps and candles by which they read, for that illuminating oil has cost men's blood.

When the voyage has begun, but before the *Pequod* is lost in the 'unshored, harbourless immensities' of the ocean, Ishmael begins his own quest for the meaning of the whale in a chapter entitled 'Cetology' (ch. 32). Even before Ishmael introduced himself in the first sentence of the opening chapter of his narrative, the whale 'Etymology' and the 'Extracts' called attention to the relationship between whales and words, whaling and books. Now Ishmael sets out to classify a field of knowledge that has hitherto been mere confusion or chaos and has been covered, he says, by an 'impenetrable veil'. Reminding himself of God's taunt to Job – 'Canst thou draw out leviathan with an hook?' – he nevertheless determines to write the hitherto unwritten life of the sperm whale. He will try to bring the whale to *life* in his book since, as he says, it 'lives not complete in any literature'. In this, then, his quest is the reverse of Ahab's, for whereas the Captain vows death to the White Whale and binds his crew with an oath that leads them to death, Ishmael resolves to give literary life to the 'endless processions of the whale' and to the 'one grand hooded phantom' of which he spoke in 'Loomings'. His initial attempt to bring the whale to life in letters results in an amusing but dead classification into folio-, octavo- and duodecimo-sized whales. This proclaims the bookishness of the endeavour, without bringing us any nearer to the living significance of the whale.[5] By Ishmael's own later admission, true knowledge of the whale can only be found when the quester has voyaged far beyond the bounds already established in existing literature.

Quite early in the voyage, in 'The Spirit-Spout' (ch. 51), when the mysterious silvery jet of the whale seems to tempt the crew of the *Pequod* to pursue the hunt, Ishmael has intimations of the divinity of the majestic creature. In the rays of the moon the spout seems celestial, as if 'some plumed and glittering god' were rising from the waves. Much later, on the first day of the final chase, when Moby Dick appears to the crew, his vastness seems to be combined with such joyousness and gentleness that Ishmael feels moved to describe him as a god. In doing so, Ishmael offers analogies that are important for our understanding of the White Whale's significance. One is the great Natural Bridge of Virginia, which to nineteenth-century Americans was synonymous with the natural sublime. This allusion makes Moby Dick both wonderful and terrible; being sublime he is necessarily mysterious. The other anology Ishmael uses is with the white bull in whose form Jupiter carried off Europa. From the sublime we have moved to the erotic with the suggestion that the knowledge and power connected with the great whale – and with all sperm whales – cannot be dissociated from sexuality. Ishmael's earlier puns (in 'Cetology') linked the light-giving oil of the whales with their sperm; in 'The Pequod Meets the Virgin' his reference to the parable of the Wise and Foolish Virgins acts ironically on the central themes of *Moby-Dick* when Ishmael tells of the slaughter of an old, sick whale. The poor creature is mercilessly murdered for the oil that will be used to illuminate not only churches where peace and love are taught but also 'gay bridals'. Sacred and profane love – spiritual and sexual knowledge – are inextricably joined in the symbol of the whale.

The god-like attributes of the whale are stressed in 'A Bower in the Arsacides' (ch. 102) when Ishmael claims to have entered the belly of the whale and thus to have come closer to Jonah's condition than any other man has come. At last Ishmael has gone deeper than skin-deep, but the irony now is that the whale beneath whose ribs he has penetrated has no skin; it is a skeleton merely. Yet this skeleton is considered holy by the barbarian King Tranquo, whose priests use it as a temple. Ishmael, too, feels awed at the sight of the great white skeleton that supports a flourishing vegetable *life*. The interwoven live plants and dead bones suggest that the whale is a source of the life that surrounds it. This makes Ishmael think of the 'weaver god' whose incessant creativity makes him deaf to mortal questionings. When, in 'The Tail' (ch. 86), Ishmael admitted that he could go no more than 'skin deep' however he dissected the whale (analysed its meaning), he made the whale speak with the voice of God and say – as God said to Moses – 'Thou shalt see my back parts . . . but my face shall not be seen.' To this Ishmael adds that he cannot completely know even the tail of the whale. The punning and rhyming talk of the tail (tale) of the whale sounds facetious, but we must take Ishmael seriously here. His notion of the divine is antithetical to that we have encountered in William Ellery Channing's sermon. Far from being 'like' man as a father is like his child, the God of whom Ishmael speaks is to be comprehended only by negating all human attributes.

In 'The Battering Ram', as we have seen, Ishmael spoke in Ahab's terms when he admitted that the sperm whale's head was a dead, blind wall to him. In 'The Praire', attempting a physiognomical reading of the whale's head, Ishmael had to admit the impossibility of deducing character-traits from so featureless a brow. Yet the very featurelessness of the whale's brow makes him sublime; it gives him a god-like dignity. Stating that the whale *dumbly* lowers with doom for men and their boats, Ishmael notes that the ancient Egyptians deified the crocodile because it was tongueless. Silence, then, is itself a god-like attribute. It follows, as Ishmael was ready to recognize in 'The Albatross', that pursuit of the 'demon phantom' of the whale that 'swims before all human hearts' will take the quester on voyages round the globe and will either lead him 'in barren mazes' or leave overwhelmed in the middle of his course. Circumnavigation of the world of thought, Ishmael tells us, though glorious, only brings us back to the place where our voyaging began: the place where less adventurous souls were all the time secure.

Ishmael's survival can be partly explained in terms of his loving relationship with the savage Queequeg, since it is Queequeg's coffin that provides him with his life-buoy. In 'A Bosom Friend' (ch. 10), Ishmael tells us that the soothing savage with whom he has formed a 'cosy, loving pair' has redeemed a world that has hitherto been 'wolfish' and has maddened him. Yet this homosexual romance hardly solves Ishmael's metaphysical problems, for the cetological chapters, in which Ishmael searches for the whale's meaning by scrutinizing its physiology and physiognomy, are all subsequent to his bridal embrace with Queequeg. At the end of his failed attempt to explain even the mystery of the whale's spout, in 'The Fountain' (ch. 85), Ishmael explains that he has both doubts and intuitions: 'Doubts of all things earthly, and intuitions of some things heavenly.' He continues, 'this combination makes neither believer nor infidel, but makes a man who regards them both with equal eye'. The great difference between the monomaniac captain and the speculative crewman who interprets his quest is that Ishmael can live with doubt. As the fate of the *Pequod* makes plain, for the intellectual voyager to live at all he must live thus. Ahab's refusal to accept any limits to human knowledge leads to his own loss of humanity and to his total destruction.

*

Ahab is Melville's grandest voyager, his quest is the most dramatic and the most significant of Melville's fictional quests, but Ahab is not, of course, the first of Melville's thought-voyagers. The protagonists of all five works that preceded *Moby-Dick*, from *Typee* to *White-Jacket* (1850), are wanderers on the oceans. All Melville's major characters are homeless wanderers, from 'Tommo' to Billy Budd, for those whose careers begin at home – Redburn, Pierre Glendinning, Israel Potter – soon leave their homes for a friendless, perplexing world, whether in pursuit of absolute truth (in the case of Pierre) or at the whim of fortune (in the case of Israel Potter). Tommo's desertion of his ship translates into action his alienation from the white 'Christian' culture of whose ferocity the black hulls of the French warships in Nukuheva Bay are emblems. To Tommo, Typee provides a glimpse of the gardens of Paradise. Before the Europeans intrude upon it with their civilized wickedness, the valley of the Typee is a pre-lapsarian world where 'the penalty of the Fall presses very lightly'. But in this happy valley Tommo cannot find a home that is any more permanent than the homes of Longfellow's Acadians in their Eden. His mysterious ailment is obviously enough related to his mental dis-ease in the society of the uncivilized, unsophisticated natives. In *Omoo* (1847), Tommo's appraisal of white civilization is even more severe than it had been in *Typee*. His contempt for the white missionaries shows how little sympathy he has with attempts to convert the Polynesians from their uninhibited, because unfallen, sensuality. His beach-combing shows how slight are his ties to any home. The visit to Tamai, a Tahitian community still unspoiled by European influence, provides another glimpse of an ideal community, though it could never be a home for the drifting Tommo, who is exiled from the white community, however lightly he takes his exile.

Redburn (1849) begins with the youthful illusion that travel means romance, but the young narrator is disabused as soon as he leaves home. Much more obviously than Ishmael, Redburn feels the wolfishness of the world in his splintered heart, for he meets with nothing but disdain from the rich travellers he encounters, cunning deception on the part of Captain Riga, malevolence on the part of most of the crew of the *Highlander*, and a peculiarly satanic or infernal malice on the part of Jackson, the sailor who holds the crew in thrall. When he arrives in Liverpool, the great commercial centre in whose docks all countries should embrace, so Redburn believes, 'under the beneficent sway of the Genius of Commerce', he finds all that is dishonourable to civilization and to humanity in the terrible pauperism of the masses. Redburn acquires knowledge on his travels, but it is knowledge of man's inhumanity to man. In *White-Jacket* (1850), the whole world is represented by the man-of-war, and the articles of war with their threat of death to the man who disobeys them seem to 'White Jacket' the true index of civilization.

In Melville's third book, *Mardi* (1849), the voyage became a symbolical rather than a real voyage, for his impatience with the actualities of seafaring in his fictions led Melville to plume his powers for flight and let 'the romance and poetry of the thing . . . grow continually'. Lacking the ballast of the actual world of ships and sailing men that was to give the voyage of the *Pequod* its distinctive quality, Taji's quest for Yillah takes flight all too readily into the realm of allegory. Though less engaging than *Moby-Dick*, *Mardi* introduces the themes that give the later book its interest. Claiming that he has launched boldly for the deep waters, Taji asserts that those who hug the shore will find nothing new. It is 'better to sink in the boundless deeps' without having gained the haven than to have floated on vulgar shoals, he argues, and thus anticipates Ishmael on Bulkington. Moreover, Taji also argues that the world he seeks is stranger than that sought by Columbus, for it is the world of the mind. Like Henry Thoreau, Melville had read Thomas Browne on exploring the continents within. Like Thoreau, Melville's theme was always exploration, but he never shared the Transcendentalist's confidence that the process could be triumphant.

Closer in theme to *Moby-Dick* than any of Melville's other works, and far more disturbingly pessimistic than any of the others, is *Pierre* (1852). Though the action takes place on land rather than on the oceans of the world, *Pierre* is the story of the most fanatic search for truth. Here the quest begins in a domestic setting, in the traditional home of the Glendinnings, where Pierre dotes on his lovely mother. The truth Pierre seeks is not embodied in a symbol as comprehensive as that of the White Whale; in fact, the truth is at first a truth about his own family and, particularly, his own father. The domestic bliss that Pierre enjoyed was, in any case, meretricious, but true or false it could not long survive Pierre's uncompromising quest. Later he decides that the appetite for God destroys household peace, turning the Delectable Mountains into the Mount of Titans. Like Ahab, Pierre will feel hemmed in by a wall, will determine to 'tear all veils' in order to see all hidden things, for to Pierre all life will partake of the 'unravelable inscrutableness of God'. Yet, unlike Ahab, Pierre can find nothing to strike – no great antagonist, no worthy object for the rage caused in him by the inexplicable mysteries or ambiguities of life. His journey of inner exploration convinces him that 'Appalling is the soul of a man! Better might one be pushed off into the material spaces beyond the utmost orbit of our sun, than once feel himself fairly afloat in himself.' Not only is the soul vast, it is also 'appallingly vacant'. To penetrate into the depths of the soul is like groping one's way into the central room of a pyramid, joyfully spying the sarcophagus, lifting the lid and finding that 'no body is there!' A corollary of this emptiness is Pierre's belief that, though nature is an alphabet (as Coleridge had said that it was), man has to supply the meaning. Melville's satirical portrait of Emerson as Plotinus Plinlimmon in *Pierre* is far less significant than the fact that – in its disturbed and disturbing way – the book takes the themes and the vocabulary of Transcendental optimism and finds in them cause for despair.

Notes

1 The text of the extract from ch. 36, 'The Quarter-Deck', of *Moby-Dick* is taken from the Norton Critical Edition, eds Harrison Hayford and Hershel Parker, New York: W. W. Norton & Co., 1967.

2 For the meaning of the 'sweet mother' in the 'Candles' chapter, see Thomas Vargish, 'Gnostic *Mythos* in *Moby-Dick*,' *PMLA* 81 (1966), 272–7.

3 See H. Bruce Franklin, *The Wake of the Gods: Melville's Mythology*, Stanford University Press, 1963, ch. 3, 'Moby-Dick: An Egyptian Myth Incarnate'.

4 See Gustaaf Van Cromphout, '*Moby-Dick*: The Transformation of the Faustian Ethos', *American Literature* 51: 1 (March 1979), 17–32.

5 On the significance of Ishmael's 'bookishness' see Edgar A. Dryden, *Melville's Thematics of Form*, Baltimore: Johns Hopkins University Press, 1968, pp. 92–4.

Further reading

Warner Berthoff, *The Example of Melville*, Princeton University Press, 1962.

Merlin Bowen, *The Long Encounter: Self and Experience in the Writings of Herman Melville*, University of Chicago Press, 1960.

Martin E. Pops, *The Melville Archetype*, Kent State University Press, 1970.

I I

Walt Whitman (1819-92)

[*Song of Myself*]

[*5*]

I believe in you my soul. . . . *the other I am must not abase
itself to you,
And you must not be abased to the other.

Loafe with me on the grass. . . . loose the stop from your throat,
Not words, not music or rhyme I want. . . . not custom or
lecture, not even the best,
Only the lull I like, the hum of your valved voice.

I mind how we lay in June, such a transparent summer
morning;
You settled your head athwart my hips and gently turned over
upon me,
And parted the shirt from my bosom-bone, and plunged your
tongue to my barestript heart,
And reached till you felt my beard, and reached till you held
my feet.

Swiftly arose and spread around me the peace and joy and
knowledge that pass all the art and argument of the earth;
And I know that the hand of God is the elderhand of my own,
And I know that the spirit of God is the eldest brother of my
own,
And that all the men ever born are also my brothers. . . . and
the women my sisters and lovers,

* Ellipses are Whitman's own punctuation for the first edition (1855) to indicate a pause; he used them instead of conventional punctuation marks.

And that a kelson of the creation is love;
And limitless are leaves stiff or drooping in the fields,
And brown ants in the little wells beneath them,
And mossy scabs of the wormfence, and heaped stones, and elder and mullen and pokeweed.

[*6*]
A child said, What is the grass? fetching it to me with full hands;
How could I answer the child?. . . . I do not know what it is any more than he.

I guess it must be the flag of my disposition, out of hopeful green stuff woven.

Or I guess it is the handkerchief of the Lord,
A scented gift and remembrancer designedly dropped,
Bearing the owner's name someway in the corners, that we may see and remark, and say Whose?

Or I guess the grass is itself a child. . . . the produced babe of the vegetation.

Or I guess it is a uniform hieroglyphic,
And it means, Sprouting alike in broad zones and narrow zones,
Growing among black folks as among white,
Kanuck, Tuckahoe, Congressman, Cuff, I give them the same, I receive them the same.
And now it seems to me the beautiful uncut hair of graves.

Tenderly will I use you curling grass,
It may be you transpire from the breasts of young men,
It may be if I had known them I would have loved them;
It may be you are from old people and from women, and from offspring taken soon out of their mothers' laps,
And here you are the mothers' laps.

This grass is very dark to be from the white heads of old mothers,
Darker than the colorless beards of old men,
Dark to come from under the faint red roofs of mouths.

O I perceive after all so many uttering tongues!
And I perceive they do not come from the roofs of mouths for
nothing.

I wish I could translate the hints about the dead young men
and women,
And the hints about old men and mothers, and the offspring
taken soon out of their laps.

What do you think has become of the young and old men?
And what do you think has become of the women and
children?

They are alive and well somewhere;
The smallest sprout shows there is really no death,
And if ever there was it led forward life, and does not wait at
the end to arrest it,
And ceased the moment life appeared.

All goes onward and outward. . . . and nothing collapses,
And to die is different from what any one supposed, and
luckier.

Leaves of Grass (1855)[1]

* * *

In the first edition of *Leaves of Grass* (1855) the opening words of the first (untitled) poem were 'I celebrate myself'. Virgil began the *Aeneid* by announcing that he would 'sing' of arms and the man, of heroic military deeds; Milton began *Paradise Lost* by calling on the muse to 'sing' of man's first disobedience and its consequences. In a later addition to his opening line, Whitman made his departure from epic tradition more obvious by adding 'and sing myself'. In the preface to the first edition, Whitman explained that the expression of the American poet was to be transcendent and new; it was to be 'indirect and not direct or descriptive or epic'. What he meant by indirect is not at once clear, but his discussion of the term involves the relationship between the body and the soul, between the material and the spiritual. As some resounding phrases in the preface have it, 'folks expect of the poet to indicate more than the beauty and dignity which always attach to dumb real objects . . . they expect him to indicate the path between reality and their souls'.

The 'I' who addresses the reader in the opening lines of 'Song of

Myself' says that he leans and loafs at his ease. This is plainly not a traditionally bardic stance – it is much too casual, too informal – yet the poet assumes both an intimacy with the reader and a wisdom and authority that suggest the poet-prophet. In the second section he promises to reveal the origin of all poems and to enable his reader to 'possess the good of the earth and sun'. The title-page of the 1855 edition had no author's name on it, but the opposite page carried a portrait of a bearded man, casually dressed in a shirt open at the neck, wearing no coat, his hat at a rakish angle, one hand in a pocket, the other on a hip. From his appearance he could well be loafing. The 'I' of the poem is identified in section 24 as 'Walt Whitman, an American, one of the roughs, a kosmos, / Disorderly fleshy and sensual.' Among his activities are listed, 'eating drinking and breeding'. Early reviewers took the point. Charles Eliot Norton, a genteel man of letters who would later teach the History of Art at Harvard, decided that the author was probably an omnibus driver or a fireman. From the style of the poem, from the writer's 'scorn for the wonted usages of good writing', Norton had no difficulty in believing that Walt Whitman was disorderly. The style suggested to Norton 'a compound of the New England transcendentalist and New York rowdy'. With an implied raising of aristocratic eyebrows, he wrote: 'That he was one of the roughs was . . . tolerably plain; but that he was a kosmos, is a piece of news we were hardly prepared for.'[2] This reviewer was clearly shocked by the arrogance of a poet who claimed so much for himself and by the flagrant lack of good taste in the sexual references in the poem. It could not, Norton decided, be read aloud to a mixed audience. By the standards of social and literary decorum that ruled in mid-nineteenth-century America, a poem that 'celebrated' the poet's self by rhapsodizing about his genitalia – as this poem does in its second section – was distinctly beyond the pale.

In an unsigned review of his own book that he published in 1855, Whitman offered his readers help by explaining that the poet 'substitutes his own decorums' for the old decorums that he discards. According to this anonymous self-critique, in teaching that the body is beautiful and that sex is beautiful, Walt Whitman 'makes audacious use of his own body and soul' to exemplify a new school of poetry and new laws of literature. The new literature is to be the expression of American life, of its democratic vigour. The new poet is neither classic nor romantic, so the review states, 'nor a materialist any more than a spiritualist'. The claims relate closely to the opening sections of the poem, for the first section asserts that the 'I' of the poem is the representative man, while the next two sections work to establish the equal status, or rather the equivalence, of the material and the spiritual. The second section not only celebrates the sexuality of the poet, but also vividly evokes the world of the senses. All the senses contribute to what the poet calls 'the song of me' in this section, from the most intimate (the taste of the atmosphere in the mouth and the feeling of breath in the lungs) to the more objective (the sight of 'The play of shine and shade on the trees as the supple boughs wag'). Here the spiritual is equated with the material when the poet celebrates his 'respiration and inspiration', for Whitman, like Thoreau, knew Emerson's derivation of spirit from breath, or wind, and even repeated it in a paraphrase of the 'Language' section of *Nature*.[3] The metaphoric significance of inspiration – literally 'breathing in' – is so commonly accepted that the metaphor is dead. By making both inspiration and respiration a cause for delight in the self, Whitman is revivifying the metaphor and suggesting that the physical life is itself spiritual. Further, he is introducing the metaphor on which the whole poem is built, for the 'self' of the poet is throughout constituted by a process of taking in experience (inspiration) and giving forth words or songs (respiration).

Whitman's characteristic insistence that the material and the spiritual are one – that the spiritual can be found *in* the material – is present in the third section of the poem. Metaphors taken from house-building, a trade at which the poet had himself worked, are paradoxically applied to the physical self and to the soul at the same time:

> Sure as the most certain sure. . . . plumb in the uprights, well
>   entretied, braced in the beams,
> Stout as a horse, affectionate, haughty, electrical,
> I and this mystery here we stand.

The last line claims as much certainty for 'this mystery' as it claims for the physical self. The paradox will be restated in almost the same words at the end of section 44: 'Now I stand on this spot with my soul.' In section 3 we are told that the unseen is 'proved by the seen', that neither can exist without the other. If the poet's delight in his own body seems to make him vulnerable to the charge of narcissism (as well as bad taste) in the opening sections of the poem, we should note that in the fourth section he distinguishes between the social self, the merely personal self that forms intense emotional relationships, and 'the Me myself' – the self that is also the soul.

In the fifth section the soul and 'the other I am' come together in a contact that is unmistakably erotic. In the tradition of the Christian mystics, Whitman uses sexual metaphors to present the encounter between the human and the divine. In this ecstatic experience the soul is equated with God; it touches the self as the tongue of a lover touches the beloved. In the language used to convey the sense of God's love, the apparent casualness of the opening sections modulates into a solemnity that is liturgical: 'the peace and joy and knowledge that pass all the art and argument of the earth'. Equally solemn is the phrase 'a kelson of the creation is love', yet the term 'kelson' is drawn from shipbuilding (it means a beam running above the keel) and evokes the world of labouring men and practical activities. There is obviously a sustained attempt in the opening sections of the poem to avoid any compartmentalization of experience; the sacred and the profane are interpenetrating realms. The revelation of God's love brings the recognition that 'limitless are leaves stiff or drooping in the fields, / And brown ants in the little wells beneath them'. No logical link with the knowledge of God's familial relationship with the self is given, but it is clear that these humble forms of life have been transformed by the poet's direct contact with the divine. In section 31 he will make his profession of faith: 'I believe a leaf of grass is no less than the journeywork of the stars, / And the pismire [ant] is equally perfect, and a grain of sand, and the egg of the wren'. Telling us that 'a mouse is miracle enough to stagger sextillions of infidels', Whitman announces his belief that all life is miraculous, that it 'proves' the unseen. The phenomena listed in section 31 – the pismire, the grain of sand, the wren's egg, the tree-toad, the blackberry – together with the heaped stones, elder and poke-weed of section 5 occur in the first preserved manuscript fragments of the poem (*Uncollected*, II. 70). Then there follows the announcement: 'I am the poet of little things and of babes / Of gnats in the air, and of beetles rolling balls of dung.' From the beginning, it seems, Whitman was concerned with the poetic vision that gives dignity to the whole gamut of creation.

In the preface to his pamphlet *As a Strong Bird on Pinions Free*, published in 1872, Whitman said that when he began to elaborate the plan of his poems 'one deep purpose underlay the others, and has underlain it and its execution ever since – and that has been the Religious purpose' (*Reader's Edition*, p. 742). In a note that was published only after his death, in *Notes and Fragments*, Whitman asked himself what name should be given to his poems and gave the answer 'Religious Canticles'. These, he said, 'perhaps ought to be the *brain*, the *living spirit* (elusive, indescribable, indefinite) of all the "Leaves of Grass" Hymns of ecstasy and religious fervour' (p. 170). To his death he remained convinced that

Leaves of Grass was 'the most religious book, crammed full of faith' (WWWiC, I. 372), and that his work could not be understood unless its religious purpose was seen to be more important than any aesthetic aims.

The problem, of course, is to know what he meant by faith and by religion. When he prepared some notes for a projected lecture on religion, he wrote that 'there is nothing in the universe any more divine than man. All gathers to the worship of man' (*Workshop*, p. 43). We know that Whitman admired William Ellery Channing's works: when he reviewed 'Self-Culture' in the Brooklyn *Daily Eagle* on 28 June 1847, he called it an 'unsurpassed piece'. Whitman's religion of humanity sounds very like the 'idolatrous' interpretation of Channing's theory of 'Likeness to God' that Orestes Brownson had come to reject as the great heresy of the age a decade before the first edition of *Leaves of Grass* was published. But though Whitman believed that 'Out of Christ are divine words' (*Primer*, p. 1) he was no more content to regard even a heterodox version of Christianity as an adequate expression of his religious purpose than Emerson had been in the 1830s.

When Thoreau read the 1856 edition of *Leaves of Grass* – the edition that had as a preface an open letter to Whitman's 'dear Friend and Master' Emerson – he considered it 'wonderfully like the Orientals'. Thoreau expressed surprise that, when he asked Whitman if he had read them (Thoreau visited the poet in that same year), he replied, 'no tell me about them'.[4] While he was elaborating his plans for his book, Whitman may in fact have acquired considerable knowledge of Eastern religious thought from the many articles on that subject available to him in the periodical literature of the day, but, whether his insights came from his reading or by intuition, the similarities were indeed remarkable. Whitman's belief that the central reality can be known in a state of pure immediacy is so close to the Vedantic idea that the *brahman* can be known by a fusion of the knower and the known, by a sort of intuitive identification, that one scholar has argued persuasively for an approach to the poems in terms of Vedantic mysticism.[5] Such an approach can, however, distract attention from Whitman's conception of the *poetic* function. The possible disingenuousness of Whitman's reply to Thoreau may have signalled his belief that the religious meaning of his work could best be understood in terms of the poems as poems. In section 41 of 'Song of Myself' the poet claims to have taken the exact dimensions of Jehovah, to have lithographed Kronos, Zeus, Hercules, to have bought drafts of Osiris, Isis, Belus, Brahma, Adonai, and to have placed Manito, Allah and Christ in his portfolio. The astonishing arrogance comes to a climax in the statement that the gods 'bore mites as for unfledged birds who have now to rise and fly and sing for themselves', but this assertion is the key to it all, for it treats the gods as singers (poets) and implies that any true poet is a god.

After the experience of union with God that forms the first climax of the poem, the poet responds to the child's question 'What is the grass?' At first he disclaims any special knowledge. This must surprise us, after the emphatically noetic quality of the mystical experience – 'And I know . . . And I know' – but the tentative answers, when they come, explain the hesitancy. Beginning with the colloquial phrase 'I guess', the poet offers symbolic interpretations of the grass: the 'flag' of his own disposition; the 'handkerchief' of the Lord; the 'babe' of the vegetation. We are back in a dualistic system of thought in which the symbol operates to bring together two distinct realms of being. This is not the mystic's intuition of the identity of the material and spiritual (or of the self and soul) but the poet's imaginative effort to unify the two realms in his symbols. The poet in this poem is the Emersonian 'liberating god', but he is also presented as a seeker who must endeavour to interpret signs. Where Ahab's attempt to interpret the 'linked analogies' of nature led him to a solipsistic reading of the doubloon and of the White Whale in terms of himself, Whitman's poet both claims to be divine and to read the symbol of the grass as a 'remembrancer' of a Lord who must be other than the self.

Interpreting the grass as 'itself a child', the poet associates it with life. He then makes it a democratic symbol, understanding its ubiquity as a sign that the distinctions between regions and social classes are not worthy of his attention. The grass makes the French Canadian (Kanuck) and the Tidewater Virginian (Tuckahoe) equal; it makes Congressman and Negro slave (Cuff) one. But from the birth of babes the poet's mind moves to their deaths and to all deaths. Responding to the vision of the grave, he again seems hesitant, uncertain: 'I wish I could translate the hints about the dead young men and women'. Even the confidently colloquial phrase 'they are alive and well' is followed by the rather blank 'somewhere', which seems an admission of the limits of his knowledge, and of his assurance. By the end of the section the grass has become a symbol of rebirth, showing that 'there is really no death', but the tone is still muted, the mood exploratory, the style conversational rather than vatic. To say that death is 'different from what anyone supposed, and luckier' is not to speak with the resonance of the prophet.

The tone changes in the next section, with the claim that the poet *knows* that it is 'lucky' to die, that he is 'immortal and fathomless'; and that all men are as immortal and fathomless as he. Now he claims the power to 'pass' birth and death with those who are born and those who die, and to find all objects in the universe 'good'. This statement acts as a prelude to the celebration of America and of its people in the body of the poem. The eighth section gives a series of glimpses of life, from birth to love-making to violent death. Beginning with individuals, it proceeds to the crowds and bustle of the city. In subsequent sections we are taken on imaginative journeys over the continent, for the poet describes scenes of rural life, of the wilderness and of the city. In section 15 we come to the first great catalogue of American life, with dozens of human activities, each represented in a single image of a man or a woman at work or at leisure. At much greater length, the list does what the uniform hieroglyphic of the grass did in the sixth section; it suggests the equal worth to the poet of the varied human life he observes, from prostitute to President, from deck-hand to connoisseur of fine art. It also suggests the sheer richness and volume of diverse American life, for the cumulative effect of the list of occupations, each given its simple declarative statement, is to evoke immense vitality. With the poet we range from the New England mill, where the factory girl works, to the stream where the Wolverine (the inhabitant of Michigan) is setting his traps, to the regions drained by the Tennessee and Arkansas rivers, where the coon-hunters are at work. The second great catalogue, in section 33, is prefaced by the statement that the poet now sees that what he guessed at when he loafed on the grass is true. Now the poet is a presence in the diverse scenes he evokes, for he is 'afoot with [his] vision' and roams over the vast continent, participating in the life he observes, feeling with those who suffer. Beginning with a vivid, if seldom particularized, evocation of place, the second catalogue moves through images of teeming vegetable, animal and human life to focus on scenes of disaster, injury, suffering and death. The poet claims to *be* the hounded slave, the wounded person, the injured and trapped fireman.

Two sections of conventionally epic material – the slaughter of Texan troops by the Mexicans at Goliad and the sea-fight between the British *Serapis* and the American *BonHomme Richard* – lead to the section in which the poet assumes the role of Christ, experiencing his 'own crucifixion and bloody crowning' in the sufferings of those he observes. In this section, too, he experiences his own resurrection and presents it in terms that are integral to his conception of the poetic function. When he says that 'The grave of rock multiplies what has been confided to it, or to any graves' and that he comes forth 'replenished with supreme power', he is ready to claim that he can save the dying. In section 40 he acts the role of saviour – 'I dilate you with tremendous breath' – and of begetter of life – 'On women fit for conception I start bigger and nimbler babes, / (This day I am jetting the stuff of far more arrogant republics.)'. The following section is the most arrogant and the most outrageous. Not only does he claim to have superseded the old gods, he also values 'The most they offer for mankind and eternity' at 'less than a spirt of my own seminal wet'. This line – like several other of the more shockingly sexual references – was dropped from later editions of *Leaves of Grass*, but in omitting it Whitman weakened his poem, for the claim he makes for poetry in the 1855 edition is no less than that implicit in the sexual metaphor: poetry can generate life.

To understand what Whitman means by this claim for his verse we need to return to his metaphors of respiration and inspiration in the second section. At the end of his first catalogue, the poet said that all the people and the activities listed 'tend inward to me, and I tend outward to them'. Later in the poem, claiming to be 'deathless', he says: 'To me the converging objects of the universe perpetually flow, / All are written to me, and I must get what the writing means.' The claim comes in section 20, where the poet rejects the idea of conventional religions, of praying, venerating, and being 'ceremonious'. A few sections after this, he decides to do nothing but listen for a long time, 'and accrue what I hear into myself. . . .and let sounds contribute toward me'. In all these statements, the receptive, inspirational function of the poet is stressed, but the converse and corollary function is respirational or expressive. In the very first list of observed life in the poem (section 8), commenting on the city crowds and the unseen 'souls moving along' in the city streets, he exclaimed: 'What living and buried speech is always vibrating here.' When he introduced himself as 'Walt Whitman, an American, one of the roughs, a kosmos' in section 24, he also claimed to be the outlet for 'many long dumb voices, / Voices of the interminable generations of slaves'. Summing up his role as poet near the end of the poem, he both sees himself as the endless quester, the *homo viator*, tramping 'a perpetual journey', never able to rest content with the knowledge he has already attained, and claims to 'act as the tongue' of his reader – 'it was tied in your mouth. . . .in mine it begins to be loosened'. The procreative function of the poet is, then, his expressive function. Repeatedly the 'self' of the poem is equated with the 'song'. As poet, or singer, he comes 'Magnifying and applying' the life that he has absorbed with his 'omnivorous words'. Those words, as he tells us in section 42, are 'of a questioning, and to indicate reality'.

'Song of Myself' is an extremely difficult poem to understand because the 'self' it 'sings' is body and soul, the personal self (conditioned by early life, social status, personal involvements) and the 'Me myself' that stands apart. To add to the complexity, the voice that speaks to us in the poem claims that the self for which it speaks is divine 'inside and out' (in section 24) and proceeds to worship that divine body, yet though it repeats, near the end of the poem, that 'nothing, not God, is greater than one's self is', that same voice returns to the notion that the world is full of signs of God's presence. In section 48, the 'letters from God dropped in the street' take us back to the 'handkerchief' and 'remembrancer' of the Lord that the poet found to be one possible meaning for the grass. The arrogance that claims to have superseded all the gods (in section 41) is followed by the return to tentative hopefulness in section 50: 'There is that in me. . . . I do not know what it is. . . . but I know it is in me.' Moreover, not only are the values of that 'self' so uncertain that the 'singer' accepts the idea of his own self-contradiction ('Very well then. . . . I contradict myself') but also the tone of the poem varies disturbingly. From the solemnity of the fifth section, with its stately liturgical rhythms, we shift to the colloquial familiarity of section 20, where the poet asks 'How is it I extract strength from the beef I eat?' and tells us that he does not 'snivel' the belief 'That life is a suck and a sell, and nothing remains at the end but threadbare crape and tears'. In the final section, sounding his 'barbaric yawp over the roofs of the world', the poet tells his readers: 'If you want me again look for me under your bootsoles.' So startling are the changes of tone and so extreme are the claims made for the self in the assertive passages that Richard Chase argued that the poem should be read as a great comic poem in the tradition of the serio-comic bragging of frontier humour.[6] Yet Chase assumed that the bathos of 'Song of Myself' implied a failure to sustain the role of the Emersonian poet. He might more helpfully have suggested that the new 'decorums' and the 'audacious use of his own body and soul' of which the poet spoke in his self-review indicate that he could not wish to 'sustain' such a role; rather, the 'song' of the 'self' shows us a process of transformation: of the mere self into the poetic self, or of the self into the singer.

The poem we now know as 'Song of Myself' (it was given that title in the 1881 edition) is longer than the other eleven poems of the first *Leaves of Grass* together. In some of the shorter poems the voice that speaks is less that of 'the poet' of the new epic of indirection and more that of 'a poet' whose experience has a general significance but is personally felt. In the poem beginning 'There was a child went forth every day', we follow the speaker's development from the securities of childhood, with its spontaneous and untroubled feeling of identity with the world experienced, through the terrible doubt that the world may be unreal, illusory, a projection of the mind, and on to a new ability to perceive the world as distinct from the self without feeling the terror of alienation. 'To Think of Time' is a meditation on death that ends with confidence, but it is a muted confidence, hedged by the admission of the limits of knowledge. This poem alone should be evidence enough to refute the notion that the poet of the 1855 *Leaves* had only one voice. If further evidence were needed, 'I wander all night with my vision' ('The Sleepers') would suffice, for it is an intimately personal statement of confusion and shame. A night-time reverie, or fantasy, this poem does not display the assurance that the poet can *become* the lives he observes; rather his longings suggest the 'hunger' that divides childhood and manhood.

In his reflections on language, posthumously published with the title *An American Primer*, Whitman wrote that he considered *Leaves of Grass* 'only a language experiment'. In 'A Backward Glance O'er Travel'd Roads' (1888) he stated that the book and its theory were 'experimental, – as, in the deepest sense, I consider our American republic to be, with its theory'. The analogy between his book and his country was plainly central to Whitman's thought, for in the years between the first and last editions of *Leaves*, he added poems that dealt with the great events in the life of the nation as well as poems that expressed his own personal development. From the slim volume of 1855 with its twelve poems, *Leaves of Grass* grew to the massive 'Deathbed' edition of 1892 with its three hundred and eighty-three poems.[7] The book was Whitman's life's work and was, in literary terms, his life, for it evolved as his life evolved. Though the first edition sold hardly any copies, Whitman brought out a second edition in the following year and included in it twenty new poems and (without permission) a letter from Emerson, greeting the poet 'at the beginning of a great career' and stating that the first edition had contained 'incomparable things said incomparably well'. He also included an open letter to Emerson, expressing his 'perfect faith' in America and stating that 'the work of my life is making poems'. Some of the new poems expressed the doctrine that 'sex contains all, bodies, souls' ('A Woman Waits for Me') or dealt explicitly with physical love-making ('Spontaneous Me'), while others celebrated the American Republic. 'Song of the Broad Axe' (called 'Broad-Axe Poem' in 1856) was a hymn of praise for westward expansion and the material progress of the United States, while 'By Blue

Ontario's Shore' (the verse equivalent of the 1855 Preface, and called 'Poem of Many in One' in 1856) celebrated the 'great Idea' of the Republic – 'the idea of perfect and free individuals'. The best of the new poems in the 1856 *Leaves* belonged to neither of these groups. 'Crossing Brooklyn Ferry' (then called 'Sun-Down Poem') takes the passing of time and the relationship of the ephemeral material world to the soul of man as its theme, exploring its ideas through the vividly imagined scene as the poet, delighting in the material and human world seen from the ferry, feels in the flow of the tide the flux of time that carries him with it from his present moment towards a future in which he will have passed from the world of appearances. Addressed to future readers, the poem speaks of the poet's physical existence in the past tense, projecting a future in which he will be present only in his verse. The poignancy of the verse derives from the intensity of his response to the 'glories' of a world that is, in the time-scheme of the poem, already passed, for the beauties of the sea-scape, the busy life of the bay and the industrial life of the city – all vividly particularized – are presented in phrases with verbs in the past tense. In the final section we learn that the world of appearances is a 'necessary film' that envelops the soul; that the 'dumb, beautiful' objects of material existence are 'ministers' to the soul and 'furnish' their parts toward eternity and to the soul. They also, of course, furnish their parts toward the poem we are reading, itself a witness to the poet's triumph over death.

In the third edition of *Leaves of Grass* (1860), Whitman not only added 146 new poems but also began to arrange the whole volume in groups of poems linked by theme. In later editions the groups would be rearranged and some poems transferred to other and new 'clusters'. Most significant of the groups in the 1860 *Leaves* was the 'Calamus' group, forty-five numbered, but untitled, poems whose dominant theme was a more personal, private love than that celebrated in 'Song of Myself'. Declaring, in the first 'Calamus' poem, that he is 'no longer abashed', the poet goes on to sing his 'chant of lovers' and to suppose that it is also a chant 'for Death'. The love of which the poems sing is such that it makes the poet indifferent to 'the grandeur of The States, and the example of heroes' and even indifferent to his own songs, as he says in the eighth 'Calamus' poem. It is a love of comrades, a homosexual love, that replaces the public themes, giving the poet more happiness than success or fame could give and reassuring him when he confronts 'the terrible question of appearances', yet the poems of satisfied love are balanced by others that express a sense of loss and yearning. One of the most powerful – 'I saw in Louisiana a live-oak growing' –

suggests the anguish of loneliness that prevents creativity. The new sense of the limits of the poet's powers is not confined to the 'Calamus' group. One of the group of poems called simply 'Leaves of Grass' tells of the poet's silence when he looks at all the sorrows of the world and observes the suffering caused by natural and by man-made disasters. Beginning with the words 'I sit and look out', this poem does not offer to raise up the fallen or 'dilate' them with the life-giving breath of the poet. Instead, the poet observes human misery and is silent. Another poem in the same group takes the 'trail of drift and debris' on the shores of Paumanock (Long Island) as emblems of the poet and of his lines. From his 'dead lips' come, not the spermatic words of 'Song of Myself', but the 'ooze exuding at last'. Though the poem promises that the flow of the tide will return, the later title, 'As I Ebb'd with the Ocean of Life', indicates the mood of quiescence and near-death expressed here.

In the *Passage to India* cluster added to the fifth edition of *Leaves of Grass* (1871–2), Whitman placed the poem that became 'As I Ebb'd' in a new grouping with the title 'Sea-Shore Memories'. The first in this group was another poem about the sea, with the title 'Out of the Cradle Endlessly Rocking'. (It had first been included in *Leaves of Grass* in 1860, under the title 'A Word Out of the Sea'.) The increasing importance of the sea as a symbol in Whitman's verse is clear from the fact that the third of a new group called 'Inscriptions' at the beginning of the fifth edition was 'In Cabin'd Ships at Sea'. Calling his thoughts 'voyagers' thoughts', Whitman addresses them to sailors; his poem, he says, is 'Ocean's poem'. Standing as it does in the introductory section, this poem seems to suggest that the whole volume should be considered 'Ocean's poem'. Certainly, 'A Word Out of the Sea' was a major addition to *Leaves of Grass* when it was added in 1860. Its position in the annexed *Passage to India* group gave it prominence – an importance that was confirmed in the final (1881) grouping called 'Sea-Drift, for there too it was the first poem. It told of the growth of the poet's mind as an awakening from a peaceful childhood state to a new realization that 'the cries of unsatisfied love' would 'Never more' be absent from him. The immediate cause of his awakening is his response to the plangent song of bereavement and loss sung by a mocking-bird that has lost its mate. Listening to the bird's lament, the boy who is to become a poet is roused to an awareness of his own 'unknown want'. The message to the child is that love means suffering and loss. It is combined with the word that the sea whispers to the listening child: the word 'Death'. Yet paradoxically the awakening poet's response is not despairing but 'ecstatic'. The song of the 'lone singer' on the sea-shore, though he sings 'Death's carols', calls the child to his destiny as the 'bard of love'. His tongue has been 'sleeping', but when he hears the mournful notes of the bereaved lover, 'a thousand singers – a thousand songs, clearer, louder, more sorrowful' than the mocking-bird's start to life within the poet 'Never to die'. To understand fully the importance of this poem in *Leaves of Grass* we have to think back to the 'uttering tongues' of the sixth section of 'Song of Myself'. Those tongues, too, were associated with death, for they were the tongues of those who had never achieved expression in their lives. In both poems, it is the poet's song that makes life out of death. The major difference is that, in the 1860 *Leaves*, death and loss are realized with a more personal, a less generalized, intensity.

During the Civil War, Whitman lived in Washington, DC, where he supported himself by work in a government office and devoted his energies to visiting and comforting the wounded and sick Union soldiers in the many hospitals there. He had first gone to the war zone in 1862, to search for his brother George, who had been wounded at the Battle of Fredericksburg. His glimpses of the battlefields moved Whitman deeply, as his later poems indicate, but it was his prolonged encounter with suffering and death in the hospitals that constituted the real experience of the war for him. Much later, in 'A Backward Glance' (1888), Whitman stated that *Leaves of Grass* would not have existed if it had not been for his experiences in the war years. This can be taken to mean that his self-appointed role as 'wound-dresser' – soothing the wounded and dying, doing what he could to alleviate their sufferings – offered Whitman a way out of the crisis in his emotional life that had found expression in the 1860 *Leaves*. Clearly, in the poem called 'The Wound-Dresser', the poet presents himself as a father to the sick young soldiers, unashamedly accepting their filial love. But Whitman's statement on the crucial importance of the war for his book must also be understood in terms of his belief that *Leaves of Grass* was the autobiography of the nation as well as his own life's story. To the fourth edition, published in 1867, he added *Drum-Taps* and *Sequel to Drum-Taps*, previously published as separate volumes in 1865 and 1866. Dealing with the war and its aftermath, these collections necessarily break new ground for Whitman, though as we have seen the theme of death was central to his work from the first edition of his book. Among the most powerful of the *Drum-Taps* poems are 'Vigil Strange I Kept on the Field One Night' and 'A Sight in Camp in the Daybreak Gray and Dim', both poems in which the poet imagines himself directly confronting the fact of death. Though the former, unlike the latter, is not based on his own experience, both reveal a psychological pattern that is characteristic of Whitman's best verse. The more closely he engages with the idea of human death, the more intensely his feeling of love for the victim is expressed. In the second poem, the dead soldier seems to the poet to be Christ himself, 'Dead and divine and brother of all'. To suggest his hopes for the future reconciliation of North and South, Whitman borrowed from his 'Calamus' poems on the love of comrades. He slightly adapted the fifth of the 1860 sequence to make it 'Over the Carnage Rose Prophetic a Voice', a poem in which Northern and Southern states are brought together and their sons joined in bonds of love. In one of the new poems in the *Sequel to Drum-Taps*, the speaker recognizes his dead enemy as 'a man divine as myself'. Appropriately, the title of this poem is 'Reconciliation'.

The greatest of the poems connected with the Civil War was 'President Lincoln's Burial Hymn' ('When Lilacs Last in the Dooryard Bloom'd'). We know from his prose writings that Whitman often saw Lincoln in his Washington years. Though he had no social contact with the president, Whitman seems to have felt that some sort of special relationship existed between himself and the man he saw as the embodiment of the principle of Unionism in its struggle against Secession. In *Specimen Days and Collect*, reminiscences published in 1882, Whitman wrote of Lincoln as the 'most characteristic, artistic, moral personality' in American biography and history. In his great elegy, the poet gives the murdered president a mythic status, linking him in his death with the 'powerful western fallen star'. There is a naturalness about the symbols in Whitman's poem, for Venus was low in the western sky at the time of Lincoln's death and the lilac, the symbol of the poet's love for the dead man, was actually in full bloom where Whitman was staying at the time of the assassination. Using the historical fact of the funeral journey from Washington to the burial in Springfield, Illinois, Whitman's art makes the actual procession – like the natural facts – take on the significance of a symbolic ceremony. We watch the coffin 'Passing the yellow-spear'd wheat, every grain from its shroud in the dark-brown fields uprisen, / Passing the apple-tree blows of white and pink in the orchards'. With no explicit references to any myths and with no intrusive commentary, the poet has given the murdered president the dignity of a god sacrificed for the continued life of the land and its people. As his own gift to the lost leader, Whitman offers images of the beauty and of the rich, continuing life of America. The poet's song merges with the third symbolic element of the poem, the song of the hermit-thrush, becoming both 'Death's outlet song' and a 'song of life'. Like the song of the mocking-bird in 'Out of the Cradle', this is a song sung by a solitary singer; it too finds cause for joy in its very sadness. Even a vision of the Civil War battlefields with their 'myriads' of corpses is assimilated into the poem's faith in the renewal of life. Lincoln's own address at the Gettysburg battlefield inevitably comes to mind. The music of the Lincoln elegy is less obviously operatic than that of 'Out of the Cradle', where the transitions from aria to recitative are clearly marked, but the modulations of style and tone are equally effective. From the solemnly emphatic rhythm of the opening lines, 'When lilacs last in the dooryard bloom'd / And the great star early droop'd in the western sky in the night', we move to the anguished apostrophe of the second section – 'O powerful western fallen star! / O shades of night – O moody, tearful night!' – and on to the absolutely calm simplicity of the following lines: 'In the dooryard fronting an old farm-house near the white-wash'd palings, / Stands the lilac-bush tall-growing with heart-shaped leaves of rich green'. The assurance of tone here is the result of the complete integration of the public with the private theme. There is not the least sense of straining after representative significance in private grief; the 'solitary singer' is the national poet.

In the 1867 edition of *Leaves of Grass*, Whitman not only added new poems and clusters but also revised some of the groups that already formed part of the whole. Particularly significant were his alterations to the 'Calamus' group of 1860. As Gay Wilson Allen has suggested,[8] there seems to have been a revision of purpose here, as the poet dropped those poems that had been most morbidly confessional. At the same time, he reaffirmed his confidence in himself as poet-prophet, for the omitted poems were those in which the desire to turn from public to private life had been most evident. The title poem of the *Passage to India* volume, published separately in 1871 and then bound with the second issue of the fifth edition of *Leaves*, offered another example of Whitman's engagement with public themes, for it celebrated great events of the previous decade. The opening of the Suez Canal in 1869, the completion of the transcontinental American railway in the same year, and the laying of the Atlantic cable (completed in 1866) are all taken as the occasion for a poem on the progress of man from his beginnings in the 'gardens of Asia'. Whitman sings what he calls a 'worship new', that of 'captains, voyagers, explorers, . . . engineers . . . architects, machinists', and he takes Columbus as the representative of the 'awaken'd enterprise' that broke the bounds of feudalism and allowed humanity to make its way forward. Whitman's faith in human progress was a faith in democratic man that relates him closely to the Bancroft of the 1835 oration 'The Office of the People' and of the whole *History of the United States*. Whitman had claimed in the Preface to the 1855 *Leaves*: 'The Americans of all nations at any time upon the earth have probably the fullest poetical nature'; in an essay published in 1881 that became 'Poetry Today in America' (*Specimen Days and Collect*) he still asserted that 'All serves our New World progress' and argued that 'the ship, upon the whole, makes unmistakably for her destination', in spite of set-backs and squalls. Yet in 'Passage to India' the new worship of explorers, engineers and machinists is 'not for trade or transportation only, / But in God's name, and for thy sake O soul'. The epigraph to the poem in the annex to the 1871–2 *Leaves* referred to the 'Voyage of the Soul' through time and space. The concluding section calls on the soul to launch out on the trackless seas and 'steer for the deep waters only'. We are here in the realm of trade with the 'celestial empire' that was Thoreau's alternative to the commercial enterprise of the nineteenth century. Whitman stands between Bancroft and Thoreau in his attitude to material progress, for whereas Thoreau defined spiritual advances by negative analogies with the practical and material gains of his century, Whitman persisted in his faith that the one was not only compatible with the other but would lead to it. In 'Passage to India', he treats the 'great captains and engineers', the 'noble inventors' and scientists as precursors of the 'poet worthy that name, / The true son of God' who will come 'singing his songs'. All the progress he celebrates in the poem is interpreted as a physical spanning of the earth with means of communication that will make spiritual union between East and West possible and thus achieve 'God's purpose from the first'. The ultimate triumph will be the union not only of all mankind but also of man and nature. Completing the work of the explorers and scientists the poet will 'absolutely fuse' nature and man so that the anguish of man's alienated consciousness will be relieved and his soul will be satisfied. This faith was certainly not naive. In *Democratic Vistas*, published in the same year as *Passage to India*, Whitman offered shrewd and biting observations on the hollowness of heart, lack of faith in humanity, and hypocrisy that he felt characterized the United States in the post-war years. At the very end of his life, in the essay 'American National Literature' published in 1891, Whitman conceded that his own country had not yet produced the first-rate poetry he had expected of it, but had been occupied with practical and material concerns. This essay ends with the 'terrible query' whether there can ever be an American national literature. Only one year earlier, in a speech at the celebration of his seventy-first birthday, Whitman had replied to religious doubts expressed by Colonel Robert Ingersoll by asserting that there was 'something' behind the material vigour and progress of American life. That 'something', as Whitman also suggested, was 'the spiritual' that lay behind material existence and gave it meaning.[9] His purpose in writing *Leaves of Grass* had been, he said, to express both.

Notes

1 The text of the extract from the poem that was later entitled 'Song of Myself' is that of the first edition of *Leaves of Grass* (1855). The text of the 1855 edition of the poem is reprinted in the Viking Compass Edition of *Leaves of Grass*, ed. Malcolm Cowley, New York: Viking Press, 1959, repr. 1968; and in the revised *Viking Portable Whitman*, 1974; Harmondsworth, Middx.: Penguin Books, 1977. The text of the final (1881) version of the poem can be found in the 'Comprehensive Reader's Edition' of *Leaves of Grass*, ed. Harold W. Blodgett and Sculley Bradley, New York University Press, 1965; repr. New York: Norton, 1968). Parenthetic references to *Uncollected* throughout the chapter are to *The Uncollected Poetry and Prose of Walt Whitman*, ed. Emory Holloway, 2 vols, New York: Doubleday, 1921; repr. Gloucester, Mass.: Peter Smith, 1972. References to *Notes and Fragments* are to the volume with that title, ed. Richard Maurice Bucke, London, Ont., 1899; repr. Darby, Penn.: Folcroft Library Editions, 1972. References to *Workshop* are to *Walt Whitman's Workshop*, ed. Clifton Joseph Furness, Cambridge, Mass.: Harvard University Press, 1928; repr. New York: Russell and Russell, 1964. References to WWWiC are to Horace Traubel's *With Walt Whitman in Camden*, 3 vols, New York: Rowman & Littlefield, 1961. References to *Primer* are to *An American Primer*, ed. Horace Traubel, Boston: Small Maynard, 1904; repr. San Francisco, City Lights Books, 1970.

2 Norton's review, originally published in *Putnam's* Magazine, is reprinted in *Walt Whitman, The Critical Heritage*, ed. Milton Hindus, London: Routledge, 1971, pp. 24–7. Whitman's anonymous self-review, quoted in the next paragraph, is also reprinted in Hindus's book.

3 See Whitman's 'Slang in America', *North American Review*, CXLI (1885). repr. in *Prose Works 1892*, ed. Floyd Stovall, 2 vols, New York University Press, 1963–4, II, *Collect and Other Prose*, p. 573.

4 *The Correspondence of Henry David Thoreau*, ed. Walter Harding and Carl Bode, New York University Press, 1958, pp. 444–5.

5 V. K. Chari, *Whitman in the Light of Vedantic Mysticism: An Interpretation*, Lincoln: University of Nebraska Press, 1965. One of the first modern scholars to stress Whitman's 'orientalism' was Malcolm Cowley, in his introduction to his Viking Compass edition of the 1855 *Leaves of Grass*.

6 Richard Chase, *Walt Whitman Reconsidered*, London: Gollancz, 1955, ch. 2.

7 For a detailed and helpful study of the evolution of *Leaves of Grass*, see *Gay Wilson Allen, *The New Walt Whitman Handbook*, New York University Press, 1975, ch. 2.

8 *New Walt Whitman Handbook*, p. 121.

9 *Prose Works 1892*, ed. Stovall, II. 687.

12
Abraham Lincoln (1809-65)

Look at the magnitude of this subject! One sixth of our population, in round numbers – not quite one sixth, and yet more than a seventh, – about one sixth of the whole population of the United States are slaves! The owners of these slaves consider them property. The effect upon the minds of the owners is that of property, and nothing else – it induces them to insist upon all that will favorably affect its value as property, to demand laws and institutions and a public policy that shall increase and secure its value, and make it durable, lasting and universal. The effect on the minds of the owners is to persuade them that there is no wrong in it. The slaveholder does not like to be considered a mean fellow, for holding that species of property, and hence he has to struggle within himself and sets about arguing himself into the belief that Slavery is right. The property influences his mind. The dissenting minister, who argued some theological point with one of the established church, was always met by the reply, 'I can't see it so.' He opened the Bible, and pointed him to a passage, but the orthodox minister replied, 'I can't see it so.' Then he showed him a single word – 'Can you see that?' 'Yes, I see it,' was the reply. The dissenter laid a guinea over the word and asked, 'Do you see it now?' [Great laughter.] So here. Whether the owners of this species of property do really see it as it is, it is not for me to say, but if they do, they see it as it is through 2,000,000,000 of dollars, and that is a pretty thick coating. [Laughter.] Certain it is, that they do not see it as we see it. Certain it is, that this two thousand million of dollars, invested in this species of property, all so concentrated that the mind can grasp it at once – this immense pecuniary interest, has its influence upon their minds.

But here in Connecticut and at the North Slavery does not exist, and we see it through no such medium. To us it appears natural to think that slaves are human beings; *men*, not property; that some of the things, at least, stated about men in the Declaration of Independence apply to them as well as to us. [Applause.] I say, we think, most of us, that this Charter of Freedom applies to the slave as well as to ourselves, that the class of arguments put forward to batter down that idea, are also calculated to break down the very idea of a free government, even for white men, and to undermine the very foundations of free society. [Continued applause.] We think Slavery a great moral wrong, and while we do not claim the right to touch it where it exists, we wish to treat it as a wrong in the Territories, where our votes will reach it. We think that a respect for ourselves, a regard for future generations and for the God that made us, require that we put down this wrong where our votes will properly reach it. We think that species of labor an injury to free white men – in short, we think Slavery a great moral, social and political evil, tolerable only because, and so far as its actual existence makes it necessary to tolerate it, and that beyond that, it ought to be treated as a wrong.

Now these two ideas, the property idea that Slavery is right, and the idea that it is wrong, come into collision, and do actually produce that irrepressible conflict which Mr. Seward has been so roundly abused for mentioning. The two ideas conflict, and must conflict.

Again, in its political aspect, does anything in any way endanger the perpetuity of this Union but that single thing, Slavery? Many of our adversaries are anxious to claim that they are specially devoted to the Union, and take pains to charge upon us hostility to the Union. Now we claim that we are the only true Union men, and we put to them this one proposition: What ever endangered this Union, save and except Slavery? Did any other thing ever cause a moment's fear? All men must agree that this thing alone has ever endangered the perpetuity of the Union. But if it was threatened by any other influence, would not all men say that the best thing that could be done, if we could not or ought not to destroy it, would be at least to keep it from growing any larger? Can any man believe that the way to save the Union is to extend and increase the only thing that threatens the Union, and to suffer it to grow bigger and bigger? [Great applause.]

Whenever this question shall be settled, it must be settled on some philosophical basis. No policy that does not rest upon some philosophical public opinion can be permanently maintained. And hence, there are but two policies in regard to Slavery that can be at all maintained. The first, based on the property view that Slavery is right, conforms to that idea throughout, and demands that we shall do everything for it that we ought to do if it were right. We must sweep away all opposition, for opposition to the right is wrong; we must agree that Slavery is right, and we must adopt the idea that property has persuaded the owner to believe – that Slavery is morally right and socially elevating. This gives a philosophical basis for a permanent policy of encouragement.

The other policy is one that squares with the idea that Slavery is wrong, and it consists in doing everything that we ought to do if it is wrong. Now, I don't wish to be misunderstood, nor to leave a gap down to be misrepresented, even. I don't mean that we ought to attack it where it exists. To me it seems that if we were to form a government anew, in view of the actual presence of Slavery we should find it necessary to frame just such a government as our fathers did; giving to the slaveholder the entire control where the system was established, while we possessed the power to restrain it from going outside those limits. [Applause.] From the necessities of the case we should be compelled to form just such a government as our blessed fathers gave us; and, surely, if they have so made it, that adds another reason why we should let Slavery alone where it exists.

If I saw a venomous snake crawling in the road, any man would say I might seize the nearest stick and kill it; but if I found that snake in bed with my children, that would be another question. [Laughter.] I might hurt the children more than the snake, and it might bite them. [Applause.] Much more, if I found it in bed with my neighbor's children, and I had bound myself by a solemn compact not to meddle with his children under any circumstances, it would become me to let that particular mode of getting rid of the gentleman alone. [Great laughter.] But if there was a bed newly made up, to which the children were to be taken, and it was proposed to take a batch of young snakes and put them there with them, I take it no man would say there was any question how I ought to decide! [Prolonged applause and cheers.]

That is just the case! The new Territories are the newly made bed to which our children are to go, and it lies with the nation to say whether they shall have snakes mixed up with them or not. It does not seem as if there could be much hesitation what our policy should be! [Applause.]

New Haven *Daily Palladium*, 7 March 1860[1]

* * *

The language of the first paragraph of the extract from Lincoln's speech at New Haven, Connecticut, on 6 March 1860 is at first glance transparently simple and direct. He asks his audience to do no more than 'Look at the magnitude' of the subject of slavery. In the preceding paragraphs he has asserted that the question of slavery is the all-absorbing question of the day and has argued that all attempts to solve it have failed because they have underestimated the size of that question. They have been, as his metaphor has it, 'small cures for great sores – plasters too small to cover the wound'. Moving from emotive imagery to the language of statistics, Lincoln now talks of the magnitude of the subject in terms of the numbers involved: almost a sixth of the whole population of the United States are slaves. But far from being transparent, this language is dense with an irony that transforms numerical into moral issues. The word 'population' derives from the Latin *populus* and means, of course, 'the people'. By including the slaves in the tally of 'our population' Lincoln implicitly gives them the status of members of 'the people' for whom the Declaration of Independence spoke – yet this status was precisely what the champions of slavery-extension denied to the Negro. Throughout his campaign to restrict the spread of slavery in the United States, Lincoln took his stand on an interpretation of the Declaration that included the Negro among those for whom inalienable rights were claimed. Since the authors of the Declaration claimed those rights for all men, it might seem self-evident to us that they intended them to apply to the Negro, but this was by no means self-evident to all Americans in Lincoln's day – in fact it was explicitly denied by the pro-slavery forces. In the second paragraph we are told that it 'appears natural' to Northerners to think that slaves are human beings, to think that the Declaration applies to them, and to therefore think that slavery is a great moral wrong. The size of that wrong is commensurate with the size of the enslaved population, but it only *appears* so to men whose vision is not obscured by money. The central theme here is the effect of property values on moral vision.

Lincoln enforces his own moral judgement by means of an anecdote that occasioned 'Great laughter' according to the newspaper report of his speech. Anecdotage was one of the staples of his rhetorical strategy and was thoroughly consistent with the 'vernacular ease' that Jacques Barzun has identified as a leading characteristic of Lincoln's style.[2] The purpose served by the laughter here is, of course, deeply serious, for Lincoln's illustrative tale makes his audience *see* the morally vitiating effect of property on the mind of the slave-owner. When the guinea that obscured the biblical word is magnified to become '2,000,000,000 of dollars', we feel the immensity of the 'pecuniary interest' and register its 'influence' on the minds of those who own slaves. To call it a 'pretty thick coating' might seem an inappropriate display of vernacular ease on Lincoln's part, until we realize that the euphemistic relaxation of tension is entirely apt, for, while determined to carry his audience with him in his moral judgement, Lincoln clearly does not want to stir up righteous anger against the slave-owner. Though the moral stand is firm and clear – 'we think Slavery a great moral, social and political evil' – the tone is not at all vituperative and the method is not denunciatory. In fact, by sharing for a moment the predicament of the orthodox minister who finds the word blotted out by the guinea, we briefly share the point of view of the slave-holder who *cannot see* the humanity of the slave because he can see the property value. Unlike the abolitionists, who denounced slave-owners as evil men, Lincoln never depicted them as corrupt or cruel. Throughout his campaign against the spread of slavery, Lincoln sought to deflect any animus that his moral condemnation brought with it; though the institution was labelled 'evil', the men involved in it were treated as reasonable, well-intentioned human beings who found themselves in a situation they had not created and for which they were not responsible.

In the 1850s the slave appeared as property not only to the Southern plantation-owner or slave-dealer but also to the Supreme Court of the United States. In March 1857 the Court had decided in the case of a Negro slave named Dred Scott, who had been taken by his master from Missouri (a slave state) into Illinois (a free state) and then into Wisconsin Territory. Scott had sued for his freedom by arguing that his residence in free territory had made him a free man. Speaking for the majority of the justices, Chief Justice Taney had declared that no Negro of slave ancestry could be a citizen of any state and that Congress had no authority to prohibit slavery in the territories because to do so would be to violate the *property* rights of American citizens guaranteed in the Fifth Amendment to the Constitution.[3] The Missouri Compromise of 1820 was thus declared unconstitutional. By the terms of that Compromise, Congress had allowed Missouri into the Union as a slave state to balance the entry of the free state of Maine and had prohibited slavery in the remainder of the territory acquired from France in the Louisiana Purchase (1803) north of the line 36° 30′. Between 1820 and 1854, when territories that had been organized north of that line came into the Union, they came in as free states and could only come in so. Effectively, then, the extension of slavery had been limited by the Compromise, but the Dred Scott decision seemed, to Lincoln and to others who opposed it, to threaten to nationalize slavery. That decision also seemed to complement the work of Stephen Douglas's Kansas-Nebraska Act (passed in May 1854), for as Lincoln stated in his 'House Divided' speech in 1858, if slavery were allowed to spread into the vast new territories of Kansas and Nebraska, as it could under the terms of the act, then the great moral evil of slavery would quickly become much greater still, for the property value of slaves would rise higher as the scope of slavery increased.

In an autobiographical sketch he wrote in 1860, Lincoln remembered that the repeal of the Missouri Compromise in 1854 'aroused him as he had never been before'.[4] When Stephen Douglas spoke in defence of his act at Springfield, Illinois, in October of that year, Lincoln delivered the first of a series of speeches that answered Douglas. That speech, given first at Springfield on October 4, was repeated at Peoria, Illinois, on October 16 and became known as the Peoria Address. In it Lincoln argued that the Missouri Compromise had been consistent with the intentions of the founding fathers of the nation in restricting the spread of slavery. In 1787, Congress had passed an ordinance prohibiting slavery in the entire North-West Territory, and had thus ensured that when the future states of Ohio, Indiana, Illinois, Michigan and Wisconsin were formed from it they would enter the Union as free states. In rejecting Douglas's doctrine of 'popular sovereignty' – his belief that the settlers in Kansas and Nebraska should be left to decide for themselves whether or not they would adopt slavery – Lincoln based his argument on an appeal to the intentions of the founders of the nation, as he understood them. For him, to resist the spread of slavery was to be faithful to the spirit of the great men of the Revolutionary generation; of the framers of the Constitution and the authors of the Declaration of Independence. When Douglas accused him of endangering the Union by his resistance to the Kansas-Nebraska Act, Lincoln replied – as he does in the fourth paragraph of his New Haven speech – that the threat to the Union came from slavery itself. Thus Lincoln presented himself as the true son of the founding fathers, the true defender of the Union, and the genuinely pacific leader with no plans to attack slavery where it existed: that is, in the slave states.

In admitting that even a new government would find it necessary to accept the existence of slavery within the slave states and to allow the slave-holder entire control in those states, Lincoln was distinguishing his position clearly from the abolitionists. Where they saw the suppression of slavery in all states as a moral duty, Lincoln admitted that he had no 'right' to touch slavery 'where it exists'. The key to his attitude and to his political campaign against the Kansas-Nebraska Act can be found in his use of the word 'right', for Lincoln's whole case rested on his belief that legal rights and the morally right were in harmony under the American Constitution. It was Lincoln's consistent purpose, throughout his public career, to encourage respect for the law and submission to its authority. Even when he considered a legal ruling to be unjust – as in the Dred Scott case – he considered himself bound by it, though he also felt it his duty to speak out against such a legal decision and to work for its reversal. Admitting the legality of slavery in those states whose constitutions endorsed the institution, Lincoln at the same time claims the 'power' to restrain it from going outside the limits of those states. His conception of moral duty clearly involves the use of the power to which one has a right. While denying that he has any aggressive intentions, Lincoln accepts the idea of a conflict; in a conflict of ideas – in a moral conflict – he is determined to stand firm.

In his parable of the children and the snakes, Lincoln is plainly not out to conciliate the Southern pro-slavery forces. Slavery is a venomous snake that may kill the children and ought to be killed itself. The assumption that the speaker should take the nearest stick and kill the reptile seems to corroborate Southern suspicions that Lincoln and the 'Black Republicans' were, after all, belligerent, that they *did* threaten the Union. Yet the fable of the snake actually extends the metaphor of children to the Southern slave-owners and treats them as potential victims of the snake's venom. As in the story of the minister and the biblical word, in Lincoln's illustrative tale of his neighbour's children all animus is diverted from the whites involved with slavery to the loathsome institution itself. The children must be protected, whether in the Southern slave states or in the new territories of Kansas and Nebraska that are as yet hardly infested with the snakes, but the father-figure in the fable will exercise only a controlled power. If there is any danger to his neighbour's children, it will not be from his stick. Far from suggesting enmity between the sections, the fable draws North and South together in its domestic imagery and in its familial connotations. In doing so it develops some implications of the opening paragraph of the speech, where Lincoln spoke of the duty of the Republican Party to 'attend to all the affairs of national house-keeping' if ever it had the 'national house entrusted to its keeping'. Lincoln's 'House Divided' speech provided the most celebrated example of his use of the domestic metaphor for the Union, yet this was only one of many speeches in which he employed familial and domestic imagery to express his conception of the unity of the American nation. Repeatedly accused by Douglas of causing division in the national 'house', Lincoln took the opportunity provided by the last of his debates with Douglas in 1858 to assert that slavery was itself breaking the nation apart, whereas national unity was being encouraged by trade between the sections (III. 309).

In talking of the nation as a household and of its people as a family,

Lincoln was conforming to a convention of American public speech in his day. As several recent historical studies have shown, between the War of Independence and the beginning of the Civil War public speakers and orators habitually conceived of the Republic in these terms. In the eighteenth century the family had acted as an integrating institution in American life, and by the time of the Revolution it had become a *lingua franca* that influenced men's conceptions of their political relations.[5] But in the first half of the nineteenth century America was transforming itself from a family-household society to a society based on a market economy, and the forces of that transformation were profoundly disturbing to the national life. As Lockean contractual theory replaced patriarchy in the United States, new tensions arose from the attempt to retain the spirit of family brotherhood – of 'sacred society' – within a framework based on freedom of contract. The very prevalence of references to familial unity in public speeches can be taken as testimony to the strain imposed on that unity by centrifugal forces within society. Thus the cult of Washington as father of the nation – a cult whose durability is witnessed by the success of Edward Everett's speech 'The Character of Washington' in the years 1856 to 1860, when he delivered it 129 times – can itself be taken as a reaction to a sense of threatening change. The national commitment to equality and progress in Jacksonian America meant that all 'privilege' associated with inherited rank and fortune was under attack, not only by the Democrats, but also – in their public rhetoric – by the Whigs. Consequently, the one archaic, hierarchical institution that was compatible with national ideals was the family.

Lincoln's political filiopiety – his reverence for the fathers of the nation – predates his campaign against the Kansas-Nebraska Act and the spread of slavery. In 1838, addressing an audience at the Springfield Lyceum on the subject 'The Perpetuation of our Political Institutions', Lincoln stated that his generation was indebted to its 'hardy, brave and patriotic' ancestors for its 'fundamental blessings' (I. 108). Those blessings were political institutions more conducive to civil and religious liberty than any in former times, for the 'fathers' had toiled nobly to build 'a political edifice of liberty and equal rights' on the land they had won for themselves and their heirs. Though his own generation had merely inherited the blessings, having done nothing to earn them, its gratitude to the fathers and duty to posterity obliged it to preserve and transmit the political institutions established by the great men of the Revolutionary generation. In 1838 the principles of the Missouri Compromise meant that the spread of slavery seemed no threat, yet there is a sense of crisis, of imminent danger to the traditions of the Republic, in Lincoln's address. The threat comes, in his words, from 'the increasing disregard for law which pervades the country; the growing disposition to substitute the wild and furious passions, in lieu of the sober judgment of Courts; and the worse than savage mobs, for the executive ministers of justice' (I. 109). Lincoln denounces the 'mobocratic spirit' as vigorously as Poe had ridiculed it in his satiric tales, but his list of outrages has a special point, for together with looting of churches, plundering of stores, lynching of untried offenders, Lincoln attributes to the mobs the shooting of editors and the throwing of printing-presses into rivers. The allusion is obviously to the murder of the abolitionist editor Elijah Lovejoy by a pro-slavery mob at Alton, Illinois, on November 7 in the previous year. Twenty years later, Lincoln would recall this event as 'the most important single event that ever happened in the new world.'[6] That judgement was made with hindsight, of course, yet in 1838 it seemed to Lincoln that the furious passions, unrestrained by any respect for law, that had led to Lovejoy's death threatened the Republic because they threatened the reign of reason. To counter the danger Lincoln called on all Americans to 'swear by the blood of the Revolution, never to violate in the least particular, the laws of the country; and never to tolerate their violation by others'. Thus he made obedience to the rule of law the test of filial piety, for to violate the law is to 'trample on the blood of [one's] father, and to tear the charter of his own and his children's liberty'.[7] If it seems incongruous to invoke the spirit of revolution to endorse the rule of law, Lincoln explains at the end of his address that, though passion had helped in the great days of the Revolution, it must be replaced by reason now that the 'giant oaks' of the heroic generation have disappeared. In the diminished world of the post-Revolutionary generations, 'cold, calculating, unimpassioned reason' would have to be the defence and support of the Republic.

Four years after his Lyceum Address, Lincoln gave a temperance lecture to the Springfield Washingtonian Society. In his conclusion he equated political and moral freedom, arguing that the victory over drunkenness that he anticipated would be an apt culmination of the movement towards freedom begun in the Revolution. In an untypical flight of conventionally elevated rhetoric, Lincoln hails the 'fall of Fury! Reign of Reason' and the 'Happy day, when, all appetites controlled, all passions subdued, all matters subjected, *mind*, all conquering *mind*, shall live and move the monarch of the world' (I. 279). Significantly, the victory over uncontrolled passion will be complete when 'there shall be neither a *slave* nor a drunkard on the earth' (emphasis added). The hymn to reason and to freedom is followed by tribute to Washington, for the address was given on the anniversary of the hero's birthday. In the tribute, the causes of civil liberty and moral reformation are both supposed to have benefited by Washington's great work.

Lincoln invoked the spirit of Washington in his New Haven speech as part of his argument that '*the Republicans desire to place this great question of slavery on the very basis on which our fathers placed it, and no other*' (IV. 21–2). In a speech at the Cooper Institute, New York, a few days earlier, he had demonstrated at great length that 'our fathers' who framed the Constitution showed their belief that slavery should be restricted in their attitude to the Ordinance of 1787. That ordinance was passed unanimously by the first Congress in 1789: a Congress that contained sixteen of the thirty-nine 'fathers'. Of the twenty-three fathers of the nation who voted on slavery questions, twenty-one acknowledged by their votes that the Federal Government did have the right to interfere with slavery in Federal territory, while several of the remaining thirty-nine were known to have anti-slavery views. From this he had concluded that 'it was not we [Republicans], but you [pro-slavery Democrats], who discarded the old policy of the fathers'. In the New Haven speech, Lincoln does not rehearse all the evidence but he does reaffirm the principle that the Republicans are the true conservatives in their stand against the spread of slavery. Douglas's doctrine of 'popular sovereignty' is thus treated as breach of faith with the men who founded the Republic and who defined its principles. Reducing Douglas's 'gur-reat pur-rin-ciple' to the belief that '"if one man would enslave another, no third man should object!"', Lincoln treats that principle with the contempt he thinks it deserves. Although he accuses the pro-slavery men of dishonesty in their attempt to identify the Republican Party with Captain John Brown's violent and illegal action at Harper's Ferry, and although he accuses the South of unscrupulousness in its campaign against his party, he also warns his own supporters against doing anything 'through passion and ill temper'. The speech ends with a call to the performance of duty, even if that means facing menaces of the destruction of government and of imprisonment. 'Let us have faith that right makes might; and in that faith, let us, to the end, dare to do our duty, as we understand it.'

By the time that Lincoln made his speech at New Haven, feelings were running so high on the slavery issue that threats of secession if a Republican president were elected were already commonplace in the South. These threats were to be fulfilled when seven Southern states seceded from the Union between November 1860, when Lincoln was elected, and March 1861, when he was inaugurated. Yet up to the time of the Confederate attack on Fort Sumter on 12 April 1861, Lincoln's speeches continued to be conciliatory in manner. Even the famous 'House Divided' speech – often interpreted as a catalyst in the movement towards sectional conflict – offered a reasoned exposition of a moral case rather than an inflammatory appeal to emotions. It was, as Don E. Fehrenbacher says, a 'declaration of purpose' rather than an apocalyptic vision.[8] The tone was established in the opening words: 'If we could first know *where* we are, and *whither* we are tending, we could then better judge *what* to do, and *how* to do it' (II. 461). The emphases are Lincoln's; they fall on words that relate to a process of enquiry – of finding one's position and identifying a trend in political events – and they make any action depend on the formulation of a considered judgement. The structure of the sentence suggests the balance that its logic recommends. Impetuous action is ruled out by the very organization of the thought. Lincoln goes on to say that the policy initiated in the Kansas-Nebraska Act has caused the slavery agitation to increase rather than diminish. He adds: 'In *my* opinion, it will not cease, until a *crisis* shall have been reached, and passed.' He follows these statements with his most famous biblical quotation, 'A house divided against itself cannot stand', and continues with his own opinion: 'I believe this government cannot endure, permanently half *slave* and half *free*. I do not expect the Union to be *dissolved* – I do not expect the house to *fall* – but I *do* expect it will cease to be divided.' When, in the course of their debates, Douglas accused Lincoln of advocating war with the South in this very speech, Lincoln pointed out that he had not said that he was in favour of anything – in his words: 'I only said what I expected would take place. I made a prediction only' (II. 491). Lincoln had been a lawyer for over twenty years when he made his 'House Divided' speech, and showed a lawyer's concern with verbal exactitude. In a general comment on Lincoln's style, Jacques Barzun says that he expressed ideas with the care of a conveyancer, but Barzun also contrasts the characteristic brevity and terseness of Lincoln's formulations with the repetitiousness of much legal language.[9] In this particular case, the chief difference between Lincoln's language and that of any legal document is that, while preserving the sense of scrupulous definition, he dramatizes a process of thought through his syntax.

Most of the 'House Divided' speech is devoted to the elaboration of Lincoln's theory that there was a conspiracy to extend the area of slavery in the nation. Linking Douglas's bill with Chief Justice Taney's decision in the Dred Scott case and with two presidents' endorsements of that decision (President Pierce and President Buchanan), Lincoln argues that all four acted to undermine the Missouri Compromise. Some modern historians have dismissed the theory as an absurd bogey and have argued that Lincoln's purpose in making the speech was, in part, to forestall any alliance between the Douglas-Democrats and the Republicans in the 1860 election by so defining Republican aims as to exclude Douglas's 'popular sovereignty' doctrine. George B. Forgie has even argued that the 'House Divided' speech offered a melodramatic formulation of the nation's predicament, casting Douglas into the role of villain, making him the 'bad son' in a family drama whose theme was the defence of the fathers' institutions against the assault of the disaffected son.[10] Lincoln, we know, was a very ambitious man whose career was politics. An alliance between the Republican Party and the already famous and successful Douglas would, without doubt, have effectively kept Lincoln off the national stage in the years before the crucial election. Noting that Lincoln compared his own obscurity and failure with Douglas's reputation and political success in a private record made in December 1856 (II. 382), Forgie treats Lincoln's rivalry with Douglas as a psychodrama in which the latter was made the scapegoat in a ritual killing so that the good and true son could go on to accept the role of the new father of his people.

To convert public political and moral questions into private psychological drama can, plainly, be reductive. Since Douglas went on record in speech after speech to state that he did not consider the Negro worthy of the rights of a white man, that he did not care whether slavery was accepted or rejected by the settlers in the Territories, that the Negro was so inferior that he should be vouchsafed only such rights as were consistent with public safety, it is clear that a Republican-Democratic alliance under his leadership would have offered no effective opposition to the spread of slavery. There *was*, patently, a great public issue here; to see it in terms of Lincoln's own unconscious motivation is helpful only if we also see how his conscious concern with traditional pieties blended with his rational analysis of the political facts to give emotional power to his language. To recognize that Lincoln's force as a speaker was related to his adoption of the role of dutiful son and protective father of his people can only enrich our understanding, but we need not therefore accept the melodramatic scenario or the primitive plot.

When Lincoln presses home his charge of conspiracy in the 'House Divided' speech, he does so in an illustrative tale about four workmen who at different times and places have prepared framed timbers that are later found to fit together perfectly to make the frame of a building. 'In *such* a case, we find it impossible to not *believe*', Lincoln states, that the workmen were following a common plan from the beginning. The workmen's names are given as Stephen, Franklin, Roger and James (Douglas, Pierce, Taney, Buchanan). The use of the first names and the form of the fable operate here, as similar techniques would operate in the New Haven speech, to rob the charge of animus and bitterness and yet at the same time to bring it home to the audience. The colloquial style and the relaxed manner work much more effectively than denunciation could to carry conviction. Only at the end of the speech does Lincoln make use of military metaphors for the political struggle and talk of fighting the battle through to victory. The pro-slavery forces are labelled as 'the enemy' here and are said to have poured 'constant hot fire' on the Republicans in 1856. In calling on his friends to stand firm against a 'belligerent' foe, Lincoln is of course presenting the struggle in heroic terms, but it is important to note that even here his imagery permits only defensive action. The action Lincoln imagines is, moreover, always *moral* action, because the whole clash of interests and values is imagined on a moral stage.

To understand the way in which Lincoln imposed his moral vision of the slavery question on a Republican Party that was largely Negrophobe in the mid 1850s, we have to see the significance of his allusion to the Declaration of Independence as 'this Charter of Freedom' in his New Haven speech (IV. 16). To Lincoln it was the document in which not only the American ideal but also the hope of mankind was expressed. In his first great speech on the Kansas-Nebraska issue, made at Peoria in October 1854, Lincoln – as we have seen – had claimed that to resist the spread of slavery was to keep faith with the fathers of the nation. In that speech Douglas's doctrine of indifference was said to 'deprive our republican example of its just influence in the world' (II. 255). The institution of slavery seemed to Lincoln to undermine the principles of progress and to violate the American political system. 'Is there no danger to liberty itself', he asked, 'in discarding the earliest practice, and first precept of our ancient faith? In our greedy chase to make profit of the negro, let us beware, lest we "cancel and tear to pieces" even the white man's charter of freedom' (II. 276). The quotation, from *Macbeth*, Act III, Scene ii, is one of Lincoln's most effective. Contemplating the murders of Banquo and Fleance, Macbeth acknowledges that to kill them would be to 'Cancel and tear to pieces that great bond / That keeps me pale'. Commentators on the text differ on the interpretation of the 'bond', though there is a consensus on its sacred nature; whether the bond of human nature or the bond of man to his God, to destroy it must be sacrilegious. Further, the legal connotation of the 'bond' is inescapable; to murder is to cancel and tear to pieces the document that stands for the bond. If we return to Lincoln's 1838 Lyceum Address, we find already the image of the 'charter' of the children's liberty (in Basler's emendation of the newspaper text) linked to the idea of the sacred blood of the fathers of the nation. In the Peoria Address, Lincoln links the 'countenance' of the Kansas-Nebraska Act with the 'bloody hand' that – also in *Macbeth* – becomes the 'red witness of guilt'.

In the Peoria speech, the 'charter' is the 'white man's charter of freedom'. Throughout his campaign against the extension of slavery, Lincoln associated all slavery with tyranny and argued that the spread of the evil institution endangered the freedom of white citizens of the Republic as well as Negro slaves. Yet, before we decide that Lincoln was content to appeal to the self-interest of Negrophobe Northern champions of free soil in the Territories, we should notice how he answered Douglas's argument that the Declaration of Independence had claimed no more than the rights of British subjects and had claimed them only for the colonists living in America. Douglas asserted that the signers of the Declaration could only be morally vindicated if their words were taken to exclude the African: 'They were speaking of British subjects on this continent being equal to British subjects born and residing in Great Britain.' Replying to this interpretation in his speech in Springfield, 26 June 1857, Lincoln said: 'I had thought the Declaration contemplated the progressive improvement in the condition of all men everywhere' (II. 407). Conceding that the founding fathers had not at once placed the Negro on terms of equality with the white man (they had, after all, accepted the existence of slavery in states whose constitutions allowed it), Lincoln rejected the Taney-Douglas deduction that the authors of the Declaration did not intend to include Negroes. Clearly they could not have meant that all men were equal in all respects, but though they did not have the power to confer equality on the Negro immediately, 'the authors of that notable instrument intended to include *all* men'. In Lincoln's words: 'They meant simply to declare the *right*, so that the *enforcement* of it might follow as fast as circumstances should permit' (II. 406). The endeavour, as always in Lincoln's speeches, is interpretive; everything depends on the scrupulous reading of the relevant evidence. Yet the power of his eloquence can be felt in the measured phrases of the exposition: 'They meant to set up a standard maxim for free society, which should be familiar to all, and revered by all; constantly looked to, constantly labored for, and even though never perfectly attained, constantly approximated, and thereby constantly spreading and deepening its influence, and augmenting the happiness and value of life to all people of all colors everywhere.' Against the reverential attitude suggested here, he sets the effects of Douglas's interpretation; that reduces the Declaration to 'mere rubbish – old wadding left to rot on the battle-field after the victory is won'. By contrast, then, the moral struggle for the progressive improvement of all men becomes momentarily an heroic struggle once more, linked with the great deeds of the Revolutionary war. In this passage, Lincoln combines his military metaphor with words that connote organic life in the Declaration. In restricting its meaning, Douglas has made it nothing more than a memorial to 'the dead past' and has thus left it 'shorn of its vitality . . . without the *germ* or even the *suggestion* of the individual rights of man in it'.

In February 1861, on his way to Washington for his inauguration, Lincoln used the occasion of a brief speech at Independence Hall, Philadelphia, to define the 'great principle or idea . . . that kept this Confederacy so long together'. Rejecting Douglas's notion that it was merely independence from England, Lincoln argued that the American principle was the sentiment in the Declaration of Independence that gave liberty 'not alone to the people of this country, but hope to the world for all future time. It was that which gave promise that in due time the weights should be lifted from the shoulders of all men, and that *all* should have an equal chance' (IV. 240). Portentously, Lincoln added that he would rather be assassinated on the spot than give up the principle he had defined. In his first Message to Congress, 4 July 1861, he developed further some of the implications of his conception of the American 'idea' when he claimed that the war against the seceding states was 'essentially a People's contest'. The Union cause was, he said, the maintenance of 'that form, and substance of government, whose leading object is, to elevate the condition of men – to lift artificial weights from all shoulders – to clear the paths of laudable pursuit for all – to afford all, an unfettered start, and a fair chance, in the race of life' (IV. 438). Both these statements reveal that Lincoln conceived human life in terms of a struggle – with intractable circumstances and against recalcitrant forces. In the America of 1861 the most obviously 'fettered' human beings, those with the heaviest weights on their shoulders, were of course the Negro slaves, but the effect of Lincoln's language is to make the condition of the Negro stand for the condition of all men. Thus, though emancipation of the slaves was not at this stage Republican policy and though Lincoln was to resist attempts to make it Union policy until mid-1862, the essential American idea is so defined that it must lead inevitably to recognition of the black man's human dignity. Further, in making the liberation of the individual a means to the elevation of 'the condition of men', Lincoln's language insists that the individual and the common good are inseparable. Lincoln's submerged but implicit metaphor of the family of man (an extension of the national family) enables him to hold together ideas of individual and common enterprise that were pulling apart in nineteenth-century America.

In talking of 'the race of life' and a 'fair chance', Lincoln makes it clear that his devotion to the cause of freedom and equality went with a competitive view of life that hardly seems compatible with his familial metaphor. Not only have men to toil against an Emersonian Fate, they have also to compete with one another for rewards that will not be equally distributed. In his New Haven speech Lincoln was explicit on this point. Assuming that most men started poor in life, he argued that even the humblest should be given 'an equal *chance* to get rich with everybody else' (emphasis added). The best state of affairs was one in which each man was free to 'acquire property as fast as he can'. Though he repeatedly stated that 'capital is only the fruit of labor, and could never have existed if labor had not first existed', he did not infer from this that capital should be abolished, but rather that – as he said in his Message to Congress on 3 December 1861 – a just and generous political system would 'open the way for all' to improve their condition. When he had rejected the Southern claim that the industrial wage-labourer in the North was more exploited than the slave-labourer in the South, Lincoln had argued, in a speech given on 27 August 1856, that there was 'no such class' of labourers in the North as that invented by the apologists for slavery. The wage-labourers, he had said, were not bound 'always to remain laborers . . . The man who labored for another last year, this year labors for himself, and next year he will hire others to labor for him' (II. 364). Repeating this model in his 1861 Message to Congress, Lincoln imagined the 'prudent penniless beginner in the world' advancing through his own efforts. 'No men living are more worthy to be trusted', he went on, 'than those who toil up from poverty.' Replying to a committee from the New York Workingmen's Association on 21 March 1864, he stated that property was the fruit of labour and was in itself a 'positive good in the world'. In arguing that the strongest bond outside the family should be the human bond uniting all working people, he claimed that riches exerted a positive moral influence: 'That some should be rich shows that others may become rich, and hence is just encouragement to industry and enterprise.'

Lincoln had himself been a 'penniless beginner in the world', as his autobiograpical sketch, prepared for the guidance of his campaign biographer in 1860, made clear. Certainly he was 'prudent' in the decision he made in his early twenties to become a town-dweller and a lawyer. In doing so he renounced the life-style of his barely literate father, who had farmed in Kentucky, Indiana and Illinois without making any progress in the race of life. Lincoln's estrangement from his father – a fact of profound significance for a man whose political beliefs were founded on loyalty to the fathers of the nation – seems to have been the inevitable consequence of his determination to improve his own position in the world.[11] His impatience with those who lacked such a drive was revealed, within the microcosm of the family, in his response to his stepbrother's request for a loan in 1848. Instead of money, Lincoln gave John D. Johnstone a stiff admonition to break himself of the habit of uselessly wasting time. The evidence seems clear that, in D. W. Howe's succinct phrases: 'Lincoln manifested the Whig personality type of bourgeois compulsiveness in . . . his preoccupations with self-control, order, rationality, industriousness – and with money, too.'[12] But, as Howe also makes clear, Lincoln managed to transcend the limitations of his Whig political views, of his personal ambition and of his American nationalism. The evidence of that transcendence is to be found in his prose, for the greatness of the man is the greatness of his language.

The speeches Lincoln made on the Kansas-Nebraska Act and the containment of slavery between 1854 and 1860 are chiefly notable for their meticulous examination of evidence and their resolute and determined reasonableness. They did sound notes of profound emotion when the theme was the Declaration of Independence, as we noted when discussing the imagery of the 1854 Peoria speech and the 1857 Springfield speech, but their main impression is of emotional restraint. In the period from his election to the presidency to his death, Lincoln's addresses have a power of feeling and imagination that surpasses that of his middle period. Roy P. Basler, a leading authority on Lincoln's writings, finds 'a note of fathomless emotion, at once heroic and simple, sounded for the first time in his "Farewell Address"'.[13] Leaving Springfield, Illinois, where he had lived since 1837, Lincoln said farewell to his former life as well as to his friends on 11 February 1861: 'I now leave, not knowing when, or whether ever, I may return' (IV. 190). Looking towards the uncertain future, Lincoln stated that the task facing him was 'greater than that which rested upon Washington' and thus, for the first time, spoke of himself on terms of at least equality with the great leader of the heroic Revolutionary generation. In fact, in talking of himself as an old man whose children had been born, and one buried, in Springfield, Lincoln was stressing his role as a father, while in the allusion to Washington he was extending his own paternal role to the macrocosm of the nation and for the first time claiming the role of father of his people. The undoubted power of the Farewell Address depends on its compression, as a glance at the more loosely structured variant versions printed in *Harper's Weekly* and the *Illinois State Journal* after the address makes clear. Essential, too, to the rhetorical force of the address is the formal balance of phrase, suggesting a balance of alternative possibilities: 'Without the assistance of that Divine Being, who ever attended [Washington,] I cannot succeed. With that assistance I cannot fail.' The solemnity of mood is created by the liturgical rhythms of the prose – 'Trusting in Him, who can go with me, and remain with you and be every where for good' – but the power of the address depends on the content as much as on devices of parallelism, repetition, alliteration, assonance and rhyme.[14] In the Farewell Address, as in the more famous Gettysburg Address, Lincoln's stance is histrionic: he sees himself and his country as actors on the world stage adopting roles that will be judged by an audience that is posterity. This does not imply any insincerity, for the part he plays is his new self.

In the Gettysburg Address, delivered on 19 November 1863, Lincoln finds the meaning of history in the relationships of fathers and sons, yet the paternal-filial imagery that dominates the speech relates to another structural pattern in its imagery: that of birth, death, rebirth. The fathers who formed the new nation 'conceived' it in liberty and 'brought it forth' on the American continent. In the battle that tested whether any nation so conceived could long endure, young men 'gave their lives that that nation might live'. While acknowledging that his own words cannot 'dedicate . . . consecrate [or] . . . hallow' the ground where the dead lie, for only their deeds have the power to consecrate the soil, Lincoln looks to a 'new birth of freedom' in the nation to ensure that the young men 'shall not have died in vain' (VII. 19). The language of this address is the culmination of a process that has been found essential to all of Lincoln's political thought: the infusion of sacred meaning into secular concerns.[15] The union of 'the people', as conceived in the address, becomes a sacred and organic union, not merely a contractual one as it had been in the historical Declaration of

Independence. Part of that process depends on the attitude to the soil of America itself, for the earth is 'consecrated' by the sacrificial deaths, and those deaths ensure that 'government of the people, by the people, for the people, shall not perish from the earth'. Equally important is the choice of the word 'dedicated' in two phrases: the nation, when conceived, was 'dedicated to the proposition that all men are created equal'; the living must now be 'dedicated' to the cause of freedom for which the soldiers of the Republic have died. The word of course suggests self-transcendence in devotion to something beyond the individual self. Its dictionary meanings include a setting apart for sacred uses. But it derives from the Latin *dicare*, 'to proclaim,' and has to do with speech. Everyone knows that Lincoln was wrong when he said that 'the world will little note nor long remember what we say here', though he was right when he said that 'it can never forget what they did here'. We remember the deeds because of his words, and we remember his words because he was able to make of something as coldly logical as a 'proposition' something as sacred as the 'great bond' of his Peoria speech.

Notes

1 The text of the extract from Lincoln's speech at New Haven, Conn. on 6 March 1860 is taken from *The Collected Works of Abraham Lincoln*, ed. Roy P. Basler, 9 vols, New Brunswick, NJ: Rutgers University Press, 1953, IV. Parenthetic references to Lincoln's writings throughout the chapter are to this edition.

2 Jacques Barzun, *Lincoln the Literary Genius*, Evanston, Ill.: Schori Private Press, 1960, p. 48.

3 Chief Justice Taney's opinion is discussed at length in Harry V. Jaffa, *Crisis of the House Divided: An Interpretation of the Issues in the Lincoln-Douglas Debates*, Seattle and London: University of Washington Press, 1959, ch. 11 'The Legal Tendency toward Slavery Expansion'.

4 *Collected Works*, IV. 67.

5 See above, p. 9, and p. 10, notes 11–12. The thesis expounded in Rogin's *Fathers and Children* also forms a part of George B. Forgie's *Patricide in the House Divided: A Psychological Interpretation of Lincoln and His Age*, New York: Norton, 1979. The information in this paragraph is drawn from both these works.

6 In a letter to James Lemen, 2 March 1857, cited in Philip Van Doren Stern, *The Life and Writings of Abraham Lincoln*, New York: Modern Library, 1940, p. 236.

7 Roy P. Basler suggests this reading as more probable than that in the *Sangamo Journal*, 3 February 1838, which reads 'tear the character of his own and his children's liberty'. See, Basler, ed., *Collected Works*, I. 112.

8 Don E. Fehrenbacher, *Prelude to Greatness: Lincoln in the 1850's*, Stanford University Press, 1962, p. 75.
9 Barzun, p. 34.
10 Forgie, pp. 249, 261.
11 For the significance of Lincoln's rejection of his father's Jacksonian-Democratic faith, see David D. Anderson, *Abraham Lincoln*, Boston: Twayne, 1970, pp. 27–35.
12 Daniel Walker Howe, *The Political Culture of the American Whigs*, University of Chicago Press, 1979, p. 269.
13 *Roy P. Basler, 'Lincoln's Development as a Writer' in *Abraham Lincoln: His Speeches and Writings*, ed. Roy P. Basler, New York: World, 1946, p. 41.
14 See James Hurt, 'All the Living and the Dead: Lincoln's Imagery', *American Literature* 52: 3 (November 1980), 351–80. My analysis of the Farewell Address and the Gettysburg Address is indebted to Hurt's excellent article.
15 See Jaffa, pp. 226–9.

Index

Individual works (listed under authors) are indexed only if they are discussed at some length. Works used briefly to illustrate themes are not listed.